TRUTH AND BELIEF

STUDIES IN PHILOSOPHY AND RELIGION

Volume 14

AMERICAN UNIVERSITY PUBLICATIONS IN PHILOSOPHY

Volume 6

The titles published in these series are listed at the end of this volume.

TRUTH AND BELIEF

Interpretation and Critique of
the Analytical Theory of Religion

by

HEIMO E. M. HOFMEISTER

University of Heidelberg, Federal Republic of Germnany

KLUWER ACADEMIC PUBLISHERS

DORDRECHT / BOSTON / LONDON

Library of Congress Cataloging in Publication Data

Hofmeister, Heimo.
    [Wahrheit und Glaube. English]
    Truth and belief : interpretation and critique of the analytical
theory of religion / by Heimo E.M. Hofmeister.
        p.   cm. -- (Studies in philosophy and religion ; 14)
    Translation of: Wahrheit und Glaube.
    Includes bibliographical references and index.
    ISBN 0-7923-0976-6 (alk. paper)
    1. Religion--Philosophy--History--20th century. 2. Analysis
(Philosophy) 3. Philosophy and religion.   I. Title. II. Series:
Studies in philosophy and religion (Martinus Nijhoff Publishers) ;
v. 14.
BL51.H73513   1990
200'.1--dc20   90-47433

ISBN 0-7923-0976-6

Published by Kluwer Academic Publishers,
P.O. Box 17, 3300 AA Dordrecht, The Netherlands.

Kluwer Academic Publishers incorporates
the publishing programmes of
D. Reidel, Martinus Nijhoff, Dr W. Junk and MTP Press.

Sold and distributed in the U.S.A. and Canada
by Kluwer Academic Publishers,
101 Philip Drive, Norwell, MA 02061, U.S.A.

In all other countries, sold and distributed
by Kluwer Academic Publishers Group,
P.O. Box 322, 3300 AH Dordrecht, The Netherlands.

THIS VOLUME ALSO SERVES AS VOLUME 6
OF THE AMERICAN UNIVERSITY PUBLICATIONS IN PHILOSOPHY

BOOK INFORMATION

With kind permission of Oldenbourg Verlag, Wien/München/Salzburg.
Translated form the German *Wahrheit und Glaube*.

Printed on acid-free paper

Printed in the Netherlands

TABLE OF CONTENTS

6

SERIES EDITOR'S PREFACE

We are especially pleased to present Volume VI of American University Publications In Philosophy in as much as the author was a former colleague in the Department of Philosophy and Religion at The American University. Consequently, being afforded the opportunity now to publish his research is like welcoming him back to our community.

It also offers us the opportunity to introduce the author into the English speaking philosophical conversation. Although some of his essays have appeared in English language publications, including an essay on Kant in the very first volume in this series, we trust that this book may serve as a more thorough presentation of Professor Hofmeister's thought to an English speaking audience.

This volume, by a European author trained at The University of Vienna and now teaching at The University of Heidelberg, concentrates upon recent analytic philosophy of religion. Thereby the volume continues a focus of this series, since this inception, upon the dialogue between European and Anglo-Saxon philosophical reflection. Furthermore, it allows the author to introduce into the philosophical discussion the writings, insights and reflection of various European thinkers upon the interpretation of religious thought and language. In addition, the volume has the further interest of an author, trained more recently at The University of Vienna, commenting on the philosophy of religion of the Vienna Circle philosophers. For these many reasons we trust that this presentation will significantly enhance the dialogue and conversation which is contemporary Western philosophy.

Harold A. Durfee

FOREWORD

The task of the following considerations is the elucidation of the relationship of religion to thought. Every philosophical investigation with this task proceeds under the expectation that it will take into account religious self-understanding. Herein lies the special difficulty of a philosophical theory of religion. On the one hand, the philosopher of religion may not assume this self-understanding in order to avoid offering a religious theory (a theology) instead of the philosophical theory expected from him. On the other hand, he cannot by-pass religious self-understanding because this is the key to insight into the uniqueness of religious discourse. Without knowledge of this uniqueness, it is impossible to indicate the conditions under which religious statements lead to the question of truth. Even if religion cannot prescribe to philosophical investigation, whose methods the latter must apply to examine its object, it may in addition require that the standard by which it is measured be suited to grasp those special characteristics which mark it as different from other realms of life. Therefore, it may be required of the philosophical interpretation, that the question of the legitimacy and validity of religious self-understanding be treated from the very beginning as an open one, and not as one already decided. If this question is rashly decided in the negative, then all analysis of religious propositions is necessarily done along the guidelines of a method that in its foundation masks of the religious thematic. This results in the examination of religious statements only as expressions of human ideas and, in this respect, only in view of their being conditioned by other aspects of the reality of human life. The requisite arena for a philosophical theory of religion where it may be freely carried out with no other desire than that of the search for truth, is thus constituted in the requirement to purview the alternatives presented as those of two antagonists, the saint on one hand and the atheist on the other. The goal of this review is to observe to what extent these theories have attained their insight into the truth character of religious statements with or without the exercise of argumentative mediation. It follows that it is certainly not the business of philosophical reflection to ignore those theories that do not fulfill the requirements of philosophy from frequently the most contradictory motives. Rather its task is to expose, in its diversity, the concept of religion underlying these theories. It is this conception of diversity that is the object of variously stuctured considerations.

The confrontation of the philosophical understanding of religion with religious self-understanding contains in-itself the possibility of a critical reflection which serves both religious self-understanding and philosophy in their correlative inquiries. In the attempt to establish a philosophical theory of religion and consequently the necessity to grapple with the problem of what religion is per se, philosophy must also consider its obligation to be prepared to critically analyse its own self-understanding as it comes to grips with its object. *In concreto* this means that an investigation of the linguistic-analytical theory of religion is guided by a two-fold interest: first, this confrontation intends to exposite and develop the reflections of the philosophy of religion and thereby indirectly provide a possible corrective to religious self-understanding. Second, this examination will serve as a yardstick by which the validity of linguistic-analytical methods for treating philosophical problems as they confront the questions posed by the philosophy of religions are measured. This study will attempt to develop these two trains of thought, a detailed exposition of the philosophy of religion and an investigation of the efficiency of the linguistic-analytical methodology.

I am grateful for the many suggestions made in connection with this investigation in the course of conversations with members of the Department of Philosophy and Religion of the American University, Washington, D.C. and with members of the Philosophical Institute of the University of Vienna.

These considerations were first published in German by the publishing house Oldenburg Vienna-Munich-Salzburg. I am very happy that they can now be available in English and thus return to the language of their origin. Much of the interpretation that is offered here may not meet with much agreement. It is the attempt of a european and german-trained philosopher to treat a philosophy which has had its greatest echo in the english-speaking world. That it has in Wittgenstein and the Vienna circle renowned representatives who came from Vienna, like the author, may in addition to a similarity in thought also have affected a particular sensitivity to the weak points of these theories.

I would like to thank Ms. Jutta Schabert for help with the translation, along with Ms. Mary C. Nebelsick, who re-worked and completed the transcript. I would also like to thank Harold A. Durfee, the editor of the series "American University Publications in Philosophy" for his interest in the work.

Heimo Hofmeister.

PREFACE

This study will analyse thematically the current situation of the research of the philosophy of religion. The analytical philosophy of religion is a scientific theory of religion. It is a neoteric philosophical discipline, although its particular problems have occupied religious philosophical thought since time immemorial. Its very self-understanding as a scientific theory makes it obvious that it has arisen in the wake of the development of the scientific theory of the natural sciences. The development of natural science and the direction which Anglo-Saxon philosophy has taken since the thirties, demonstrate that scientific-theoretical considerations of religion have been considered inferior to those of natural science. Undoubtedly the inability of the concept of religion to be clearly and distinctly fixed combined with the lack of a clear-cut methodology has resulted in several aggrevating consequences (1). An attempt made by neo-positivism, in the wake of the Vienna Circle to usurp the concept of philosophy, led to the necessity that religious thinkers, especially in the Anglo-Saxon world, sought the justification for their cause within the thought of and dialogue with the problems of scientific theory (2). These modes of thought, which were originally limited to the Anglo-Saxon domain, due to its emphasis on language found an echo within the philosophy of continental Europe during a later phase. These concerns have been increasingly shaping the picture of religious-philosophical and theological discussion in recent years (3).

This study attempts to offer a history of the problems of the linguistic-analytical philosophy of religion from its positivistic beginnings to the stage it has reached today. Since it is not the historical development, but the systematic concern which stands in the foreground of this investigation, the individual models are not simply discussed, but the motives behind their origins are presented. Above all, the specific consequences of their standpoint are highlighted. This study is critically oriented to the extent that the present investigation lays out the history of problems inherent in the basic characteristics of the linguistic-analytical philosophy of religion. This investigation is concerned to show that, at this point, the attempt of the analytical philosophy of religion to deliver a scientific theory of religion has not been a complete success. This may be observed from the development of this philosophical discipline. The ascertainment of the probable reasons for this failure is also part of this investigation.

The current question, with which an analytical theory of religion has to deal, is the question of the truth of religious statements. Therefore, in the title of this study, we have highlighted this concept as the guiding thought for our investigation, relating it to the concept of belief. The juxtaposition of truth and belief implies the question of whether the linear concept of truth, as it is used in the analytical philosophy of religion, can ever come to terms with the delicate problems of religious statements, or if these are structured in such a way that their sense can only be measured in terms other than that of an analytical concept of truth.

In view of the very wide ranging arena of discussion within the linguistic-analytical philosophy of religion, a double restriction is set upon the attempt to treat this philosophy thematically. At first, we will limit ourselves to the discussion about statements of verification. This may be viewed as a disadvantage. It can, however, be justified because propositions of religious speech have the character of action not only when they are performative, but also when they are propositions of verification. The strong pragmatic element of the analytical philosophy of religion takes this into account and assumes as a premise that it is not sufficient for an understanding of religious texts to consider them in their relation to other texts, but that it is also necessary to consider them in the context of action. Religious statements are always related to a social situation in its entirety within which they are caught up merely through speech itself. The history of theological ethics has demonstrated the way religious statements can stabilize or change our behavior and can call forth action and omission. Due to the performative character of verification propositions a limitation to the investigation of performative religious propositions appears justified. A further aspect to be considered is the fact that the meaning of religious propositions of verification is by no means exhausted in the context of actions in which they were pronounced, unlike the case of performative propositions.

In this context, it should also be noted that I am speaking primarily of religious propositions and statements, and am expressly not making a distinction between statements of belief and theological statements. In neglecting this distinction, I am in agreement with the given texts. As a matter of fact these texts do not always deal with religious statements, but occasionally make statements of belief or theological statements. In the latter case, however, they determine attribution in a way deviating from my linguistic usage and they usually do not explain their choice of words. From their expositions, however, it is not evident whether it is solely a purely terminological distinction or not. Indeed, one can demonstrate a distinction between theological statements and belief-statements; however in this context this distinction plays only a subordinate role and may therefore be ignored

(4). In the concept "religious statement" as I use it, I perceive one concept subordinating two others. In this context, an insufficient explication of the distinction between theological statements and belief-statements is justified in that a theological statement albeit distancing itself critically from the statement of belief, it does not absolutely turn away from it. One is aware of it being a scientific form of a statement of belief. This is the case although a theological statement subordinates a literal statement of belief in that the former represents the latter's recognition in theory and is frequently its norm as well. My concept of religious language offers the fundamental possibility not only of taking statements representing exact theological analysis, in Scripture, in the Credo and in other official ecclesiastical documents into consideration but also such statements as are found in hymns, prayers etc.

The second limitation concerns critical confrontation with literature on this subject. This study is supported by a comprehensive compilation of the significant literature of the linguistic-analytical philosophy of religion. The scope of this list already makes it clear that detailed treatment of this literature and a special consideration of each of these studies is impossible. Therefore, in the text of this investigation, I have limited myself to a minimum of references to this literature. In order not to blur the central aspects of this investigation, I have only made use of those quotations which are indispensable for understanding, and those which were helpful pointers for the development of the analytical philosophy of religion.

On the basis of these restrictions, the following summary will serve to indicate the basic structure of the present investigation. In the first chapter, which serves as an introduction, I will seek to elucidate the genesis of the linguistic-analytical philosophy of religion. Here the decisive task is to show how the initial devaluation of religious statements in the philosophy of the Vienna Circle was overcome in a turn to the analysis of everyday language. The most important intention of the second chapter is to make the reader aware of the difficulties and the particularities of the religious use of language by dealing with the arguments put against the claim of meaning of religious statements, and by differentiating the religious statements from other kinds of statements. Chapters three, four and five are devoted to the analysis of the main directions of the analytical theory of religion. My interpretation of these theories will point out the dialectic of truth and belief implicit in religious statements, and make clear that the religious statement is not disposed to reflect tangible reality (5).

The exposition of this dialectic is necessary if the relations of religious theory, on one hand, and those of scientific and social realities, on the other hand, are to be adequately grasped. If the argument against the analytical theory of religion is merely that it has fallen victim in its orientation toward natural scientific or sociological analysis to the contemporary trend to interpret everything on the basis of science, then one is already impeded in comprehending the analytical theory of religion in its relationship to its own historical situation. This theory of religion is no doubt the consequence of a process of scientific interpretation, a process that takes as little notice of the boundaries of privacy as it does of the fundamental questions of the meaning of human existence. The danger of this development for the claim to meaning of religious statements consists in the separation of scientific theory from practice, that consequently allows religious thought and belief to be dominated by the force of technological circumstances. One does not escape the danger of such a development if one maintains that the application of linguistic analysis as limited to the realm of religious talk is an inadequate procedure. Rather the danger is only over if one interprets linguistic-analysis as a methodical approach whose intention it is to develop analytical theories of religion as models, so that they may be refered back to the historical situation of belief. The study of the linguistic-analytical philosophy of religion - and this is the interesting and perhaps also deviating point from other branches of analytic mastery - is, consciously or unconsciously, in a continuous battle with these problems. Linguistic analysis, understood as a method, is not an end-in-itself, but serves to elucidate definite material. However, the matter at hand differs not only according to each science. Rather in its scientific examination it comprises a particular way of referring back to the questioning subject and to the relationship between this subject and the object of analysis.

In the final two chapters, subject-object relations will be dealt with in their entirety. Whereas the third chapter is devoted to the non-cognitive understanding of religious statements, refuting their claims to truth but not their claims to meaning, the subsequent two chapters discuss theories that recognize the truth of religious statements. According to one theory, the concept of *intelligibility* gains central significance in its attempt to found religious propositions. This theory is aligned along a theory of coherence. In contrast those theories that are dealt with in the fifth chapter, are aligned along a theory of correspondence. Their basic conception is the idea of *eschatological verification*.

Heidelberg
Heimo Hofmeister

I. THE LINGUISTIC VETO

1. Philosophy as scientific theory

In a way far more radical than Immanuel Kant, who turned in his famous preamble to the *Critique of Pure Reason* to Galileo to steer philosophy away from mere "fumbling around" and unto the certain course of science, logical positivism sought to orient itself on the methodology of the natural sciences to instill new impulse to philosophy. This radicalization of the Kantian approach leveled, in the process, the difference between Kant's transcendental philosophy and the sciences of the modern age. The Copernican turn led Kant to the quest for the conditions of the possibility of experience. In comparison, this "new philosophy" which claims to be a scientific theory, is satisfied with the investigation of how predication occurs in propositions describing experience. Consequently, the question "whether there is something like a pure science of experience or whether, in the final analysis, not all empirical sciences possess a non-empirical foundation" (6) was, at least temporarily, stalled. Philosophy, like logic, was defined as a formal science. It must be added, however, that philosophy is distinguished from logic in that its investigations are directed towards the actual practice of a particular science (7). Such an understanding of philosophy can take into account, first, that the individual sciences develop, to a large extent, independently of philosophy and second, that even the clarification of the basic conceptuality of particular sciences occured to a great degree, in the framework of their process of investigation. In addition this was reflected in theology by the fact that the reference to divine revelation was treated not only as a prerequisite, but increasingly as the theme of theological reflection (8).

The "scientific philosophy" of logical positivism is characterized in its approach by a twofold renunciation.

1. In spite of its methodical orientation towards the natural sciences, it does not intend in its own research to compete with them.

2. Due to this tendency in research and method it considers the theme of the world as the totality of being to be inappropriate for research.

The acknowledgement of the natural sciences as a model as well as the assertion that philosphy is not entitled to a specific objective field, resulted in the opposition of philosophy to its own metaphysical tradition. In content, its main task was seen in the elaboration of the methods that form the basis of science. The conviction that in defining scientific statements, metaphysics has to restrict itself to abstracting the formal aspects from all content, necessitated a total disengagement from metaphysics. This stressed the uniqueness and singularity of its own approach. On account of the methodical inclusion of empirical states of affairs into philosophical reflection, the logical positivists claimed to achieve, on one hand, an escape from the muddy word-games of metaphysics and, on the other, a way to avoid their propositions from appearing, as in particular sciences, as statements of realistic scientific thought refering to a direct, physical or psychically given reality.

The way between Scylla and Charybdis was that of an understanding of philosophy as a theory of science reaching its limit not on the formal level, but feeling itself capable of laying down the conditions of scientific statements, even with reference to their content. This means that such theory feels capable of uncovering and determining the meaning of statements. An exact circumscription of the range of tasks of philosophy as a theory of scientific statements is also the clearest description of the way philosophy differs from science. Moritz Schlick's formulation captures this point in its pristine clarity:

In philosophy, propositions are clarified; in science, they are verified (9).

As will emerge later, in addition to an identification of philosophy with theories of science, this new definition also establishes the limitation of the latter to a theory of natural scientific statements. For the time being, it should be noted that philosophy interpreted as scientific logic, has the task of supplying the "logical analysis of the propositions and concepts of science", reducing itself in the process to "nothing other than the logical syntax of scientific language" (10).

The new logic developed by Alfred North Whitehead and Bertrand Russell in *Principia Mathematica* during the years 1910-1913, was decisive for this understanding of philosophy as a theory of science, as initiated, above all, by the Vienna Circle. On one hand, this new logic used symbols analogous to mathematics; on the other, in addition to the statements which until then were the only ones under investigation (i.e. those ascribing a predicate to a subject) it brought the relations of several sentence components to one another as well as to the function of the sentence as such into consideration. This exploded the traditional scheme of judgement: the subject-copula-predicate. In the Vienna Circle this new logic, originally developed for the structure of mathematics, became "the means for the theory of science" (11). Proceeding from the thesis that language forms the "body of perception" (12) and that the investigation of facts is reserved for individual sciences, linguistic analysis became the actual field of the logic of science. It follows that language is examined neither sociologically nor psychologically, but rather in respect to its suitability to be a representational system of a specific field.

If one disregards the problematic associated with the "linguistic turn" underlying this concept of science, it then becomes clear that the decision to found all on empirical science is an extremely important and, simultaneously, a questionable decision. As long as the orientation toward the empirical sciences did not introduce a linguistic veto and a banishment of those statements resulting from literary, aesthetic, metaphysical or religious insights, into the emotive realm, this orientation arose on the basis of the definition that an analysis of the meaning-content of linguistic signs and of the manner of their combination, must be limited to propositions in the formulation of which "scientific knowledge" can be represented. In the opinion of the early positivists, such scientific statements are exclusively those capable of empirical verification. It is true that the close connection with the principle of experience as sensual certainty was revised in the later development of positivism. Meaning was ascribed not only to analytical, but also to metaphysical statements, including religious statements, with the result that it was acknowledged as possible to construct a comprehensible metaphysical system. Yet the predicate 'scientific' was reserved only for those propositions and systems that permitted a recognizable reference to experience. This is well illustrated by an example then current within the Vienna Circle. This means that the proposition "There is a 300 m high mountain on the dark side of the moon" was assessed as scientific although this statement, at that time, could not be verified because the impossibility of its verification was merely empirically accidental and not logical. In a proposition such as "God created heaven and earth" a meaning, in this sense, could at best be ascribed to the individual words, not however to the proposition itself. Why? The reason is clear. It is not analytical and the empirical conditions under which this proposition is true or false cannot be stated.

In its definition of a scientific proposition logical positivism relies upon two criteria.

1. The proposition of contradiction that requires the logical correctness of statements with reference to their form.

2. The reference to experience should be propositionally demonstrable even with regard to content.

For the possibility of a theory of science, the following two questions are thus posed concerning these criteria:

1. How is one to conceive the relationship of form to content in a scientific statement? According to the positivists, the scientific theoretician is required to elaborate the conditions of the contents of scientific statements in order to arrive at the justification of the difference between the theory of science and metaphysics which they maintain.

2. How is the relationship of proposition to reality to be determined? It is the case that a theory of true scientific propositions cannot ultimately by-pass answering this question.

In answering these two questions, the decision that propositional verification implies empirical verification will be very significant.

a) The Hidden Dialectic of the Form and Content of Propositions

On account of the historical situation in which the modern theory of science originated, it is not surprising that, in logical positivism, mathematics assumed a privileged position alongside of natural science. In this connection, it is significant that mathematics, in contrast to natural science is not empirical science. Its propositions and statements, like those of logic, possess a merely formal character. The difference in the nature of the statements is found only in the informal, i.e. in the experience-related sciences. Whereas their analytic counterpart can be found, on account of its formal character, preferably in logic and mathematics. It is, however, not bound to a definite group of sciences.

To understand the context of the argumentation that led to a linguistic veto of religious statements, it must be kept in mind that logical positivism, at first, was guided by an ideal vision of a "universal language of science" (Carnap). This ideal vision, brought about repercussions not only for the assessment of religious statements and was reduced to a fundamental *aporia* with reference to the distinction between synthetic and analytic propositions. This was a result of the prohibition of dialectic thought, and a result of the requirement of the perspecuity of language and the propositions and expressions it applied. Although the propositional form of logic and mathematics is basic even to object-related synthetic statements and, although a unity of logic and language is postulated, the positivistic scientific theory took the normativity of two basic classes of statements that are independent of each other as a premise. This led necessarily to the question how general statements of conduct are possible. A question that could only find its answer in the determination of the relationship between the analytic and synthetic form of propositions.

Analytic statements are valid independently of experience and necessarily, according to Ludwig Wittgenstein's formulation, they are tautological in that logic merely sets up the rules to recast them. These statements make possible only a purely formal treatment of concepts without taking their contents into account. The *a priori* order of logic is, therefore, the same as conceived by both the Vienna Circle and Wittgenstein's "no order of the things a priori." "Everything we see could also be otherwise. Everything we can describe at all could also be otherwise" (13). The propositions of logic are not knowledge of reality, but rather the rules of the linguistic presentation of this reality under the aspect of logical syntax.

In contrast to analytic propositions, there are synthetic ones. The latter have assertorial content and say something about the existence or non-existence of a state-of-affairs; that is they are "substantial propositions... which (in common parlance) express a state of affairs..." (14). However, after Alfred Jules Ayer's analysis of the difference between synthetic and analytic propositions, they are no longer accounted generally as the only propositions having a meaning. Ayer expressly refuted this stance.

> When we say that analytic propositions are devoid of factual content, and consequently that they say nothing, we are not suggesting that they are senseless.... For, although they give us no information about any empirical situation, they do enlighten us by illustrating the way in which we use certain symbols (15).

Accordingly, synthetic propostions, in contrast to the analytic ones, must also be characterized as meaningful. However, the definition of the relationship between empirical sciences, whose propositions are synthetic and logic and mathematics, whose propositions are analytic, implies the difficulty:

> ...it is, in fact not possible at all to make philosophical statements about the *relationship* of the two scientific groups to each other, for such statements break out of the realm of those propositions that are allowable. They are not formal, but material. However, their content - the thematization of the *reference* of form and content - is not a scientifically permissible content, for a scientifically permissible content must, indeed have reference to real experience (16).

This circumstance makes the following apparent:

> The positivists are actually undertaking a dialectical reflection of the meaning of which it is to demonstrate the scientific theorist makes his science a medium for the expression of scientific propositions. However, the positivists do not accept this

reflection as meaningful, since they see meaning as a sense only within empirical science (17).

The negative effects of the neglect of the relation of form to content had to be admitted even by such representatives of mathematical logic as Gödel and Tarski, who concede a certain deficiency. It was on account of this deficiency that the attempt to establish an all-encompassing formal system as the quintessence of all possible contents had failed. It is true, mathematical logic has at its disposal an instrumentality whose effectiveness had proven itself in the empirical sciences. Yet the desire to grasp that which is given in experience in a formal-theoretical way, remained unfulfilled. This occured because formal-logical treatment turned out to be possible only if one already presupposed a preceding non-formal colloquial consensus, i.e. a preconceived definition of the relationship of form and content (18).

b) The Requirement of Verification and the Relationship of Proposition and Reality

The second point that was decisive for assessing logical positivism is its standpoint on the relationship of proposition and reality. If one considers that in the arguments concerning the sense-content and the significance-content of statements that have neither natural-scientific nor mathematical character, a role was accorded to the verification principle that made this principle the sole yardstick for the truth-claim of statements from the realms of art, metaphysics, theology and religion. This way one is able to measure the range of consequences following the failure to define the relationship of proposition and reality. It would be possible to justify the extraordinary position of this relationship only on the basis of a perspicacious clarification of this relationship. The verification principle is the center for reflection for the way in which this relationship must be viewed. The respective formulation determines the value of logical positivism per se and also those of directions of analytical philosophy developing from and freeing themselves from logical positivism. These groups were united in their recognition of the correctness of Wittgenstein's discovery that the significance of a propostion consisted in the method of its verification (19). However the dispute about what was to be understood by the method of verification led to the most varied interpretations. In this regard the validity of a clarification of the truth-claim of a statement that does not have natural-scientific character was called into question. Specifically, the clarification was attained by coupling it with positivism's principle of verification. This was already called into question by the fact that the ideal to trace all propositions to direct observation, steming from empirical science proved to be too lofty a goal. The methods of direct verification can neither be indicated for the universal propositions of empirical laws, nor for the basic concepts of their theories.

Following Ayer, one currently speaks of an extended and of a more precise version of the principle of verification (20). In contrast Schlick belonged to a group of early positivists who wanted to allot only a very narrowly confined scope to the principle of verification. The influence of Percy Bridgman's proposition "that things which cannot be measured have no meaning" (21) was of decisive significance for this group. Its formulation of the principle of verification as an empirical sense-criterion, according to which only those propositions refering to empirical facts are meaningful, took Bridgman's statement as its guiding principle. Above all, Ayer can be counted among the representatives of a modified and weaker understanding of the principle of verification. Accordingly a statement may be described as meaningful if it is "verifiable", in so far as any empirical observations can be described as relevant to answering its truth or falsity. As far as Ayer is concerned, he regards it as sufficient, for determining the meaning of a statement, to indicate "what it would be like to verify it" (22). According to this version, the meaning of a proposition with reference to its verification is no longer merely tied to a definite observation ascertaining the reality of a state-of-affairs that is perceptually intelligible. Indeed, all propositions are admissible provided that a possibility for verifying them can be proven.

> We inquire in every case what observations would lead us to answer the question, one way or the other; and, if none can be discovered, we must conclude that the sentence under consideration does not, as far as we are concerned, express a genuine question, however strongly its grammatical appearance may suggest that it does (23).

An example of the extended version of the principle of verification has already been given with the proposition concerning the 300 m high mountain on the dark side of the moon.

If, according to the original narrower version, the possibility of verification is understood in an empirical sense, then, in the sense of the extended principle, one talks of a logico-empirical criterion of verification. According to this criterion, not only are the propositions of empirical science verifiable, but the analytic propositions of logic and mathematics as well. To a limited extent, this modification affects metaphysical and religious statements. Here, religious statements can be acknowledged as meaningful as long as they possess a purely analytic character. An example of such a proposition is "God is love", which, according to the presuppositions of the extended principle of verification, may be ascribed a meaning, since to understand this proposition neither belief in God nor the possibility of empirically verifying it is presupposed. However, propositions such as "God loves humanity" or "God is revealed in the flesh" continue to be held as meaningless and incomprehensible because they cannot be added to the class of analytic statements. It is not possible to indicate the empirically determinable conditions of their reality. This is possible, according to Rudolf Carnap, for example for the proposition "Jupiter is growling at the place p at time t" (24). He qualifies this proposition as meaningful providing that the following definition is accepted: the proposition is proposed to be true if a thunderclap is heard at the place p at time t. However in this case the word "Jupiter" is given as little definition as the word "God" in the preceding propositions. Yet the proposition "Jupiter is growling at the place p at time t" acquires meaning through the indication of the methods verifying it. The difference from the preceding proposition "God loves man" does not merely lie in the fact that the word "Jupiter" in contrast to the word "God" is taken to be a proper name, but also in the fact that Jupiter as thunder is ascribable to the realm of experience and on account of this circumstance, a statement about Jupiter can be confirmed or refuted through experience. It will be demonstrated below, in the discussion of the conclusions to be drawn from Anthony G. N. Flew's parable, to what extent the proposition "God loves humanity" avoids all verification as a generally valid statement.

It was essential for the development of the analytical philosophy of religion that the modified version of the principle of verification was decisively influential. Not only did it influence the emotive theory of religion that undoubtedly is a non-metaphysical philosophy, but also those who defend the meaning of religious statements on the basis of eschatological verification, i.e. those who believe that it is possible to indicate the conditions that are necessary to verify a religious statement.

The thematization of the relationship between form and content in religious statements, dealt with in I/1, is highly significant in that this quest - unresolved both for the shortened and the extended version of the principle of verification - concerns the relationship of the proposition to reality which it describes. Indeed, we must not lose sight of the fact that, at this point, a "correspondence between two classes of phenomena is presupposed, namely one class of spoken or of written elements forming a word, and one class of objects (in the broadest sense) forming that which is attributed to the word" (25). The statements are not identical with the states-of-affairs they describe; nor can they be, as is clear from Victor Kraft's remark above that indicated that these statements are of varying modality.

However, the quest for the relationship of proposition to reality, treated by Kant as the central theme of the quest for the possibility of synthetic judgements within his transcendental logic, is of secondary importance. In this case the scepticism developed towards attempts to explain dialectically the epistemological process - a scepticism exercised by both the logical positivists and the circle of Wittgenstein followers. Without question, experience underlies scientific as well as everyday judgement. As a matter of fact, one would have to compare proposition and reality in order to ascertain their agreement; a possibility which, according to the premises of positivism, is not allowable. This possibility would fully require that the person making a judgement concerning the relationship of proposition to reality does so from a position of authority (26). Therefore, as the relationality that this is "produced by the presentation of something given from experience" (27), then any further reflection upon the relationship of proposition and reality is likewise declared to be meaningless. This applies also for reflection on the relationship of synthetic and analytic statements. The situation is quite analogous. In this case there is a suppressed presupposed dialectical relation. Here there is a turn away from the claim that religious statements have meaning. This included the claim that considerations of the relationship of propositions and reality are meaningless, and also the assertion that this relationship can only be empirically grasped.

2. The verification problem and religious language in Wittgenstein's early work

In this connection, Wittgenstein's argumentation is of special interest:

1. because he expressly takes a standpoint on the claim of meaning of religious statements and does not judge them only in conjunction with general metaphysical statements, and

2. because he does not limit himself, as late Carnap almost exclusively did, to pure semantics and syntax, i.e. to the investigation of formal languages. In contrast in his late philosophy Wittgenstein turns his attention to the analysis of everyday language and consequently to religious language.

Another point worth mentioning is that in his *Tractatus* Wittgenstein raises the relationship of language and reality to the focal point of discussion. The Vienna Circle, in contrast, had only considered this problem when the direct reference back to the things given, left no other way out. The difference between Wittgenstein and the Vienna Circle in this matter consists, above all, in the fact that the former does not initially exclude the question of the type of relation propostions have to reality, but rather ascertain that the discussion of this relation is meaningless as a consequence of reflection.

a) Concerning the Relationship between Propositional Reality and the Concept of the Mystical

To explain the agreement of a proposition with reality, Wittgenstein develops the picture theory of propositional meaning. In his *Tractatus* he states, "We makes to ourselves pictures of facts" (28). In the atomic proposition he sees the picture of an atomic fact, just as he comprehends rather complex sentences indirectly as pictures of facts, constructing them as truth-functions and dissolvable by means of transformation rules into complexes of atomic sentences. Since Wittgenstein also holds the view - why is of no interest to us here (29) - that the picture is a fact (30), there is an isomorphism of two facts in the relationship between picture and language, i.e. language is an isomorphic representation of reality.

Wittgenstein distinguished between facts and states-of-affairs. The latter are only what might be the case, whereas facts are something real. A true picture represents a fact, whereas a false picture represents a state of affairs i.e. a possible fact. According to Wittgenstein whether or not only a possible state of affairs is implied, can be observed from the external structure of the proposition.

> The proposition *shows* its sense. The proposition *shows* how things stand *if* it is true. And it *says*, that they do so stand. (31)

In contradiction to the opinion held by the Vienna Circle that propositions true in content are in agreement with empirical reality Wittgenstein believed that it is self-evident whether or not a proposition can represent an isomorphic picture. Consequently, in his opinion, whether a sentence may or may not be true is not dependent on the test of correspondence with its force of expression. It is sufficient to have proof that from its propositional structure it is certain that what it expresses depicts a fact. Therefore, for religious statements it is unnecessary to prove that that which is expressed is a fabrication. It should become obvious from their structure alone that they do not agree with reality.

The rejection of religious statements as meaningful propositions rested on two opinions Wittgenstein held as he wrote his *Tractatus*.

1) Language and logic form a unit. As has already been pointed out this was the general assumption of the Vienna Circle.

2) The isomorphy of proposition and fact is the criterion for the truth of a sentence.

Within the scope of the flawless construction of a proposition according to logic and grammar, Wittgenstein would otherwise easily have been able to accept religious propositions as being meaningful in contrast to sentences meaningless in form.

If one begins with the assumption, as Wittgenstein did, that there is "logic in the states of affairs with regard to content", one has to bring the limits of the world into alignment with those of logic and language.

> All propositions of our colloquial language are actually, just as they are logically completely in order. That simple thing which we ought to give here is not a model of the truth but the complete truth itself (32).

Everything that can be described in the logical form of descriptive language is conceivable. However, the logical form of reality reflected in the proposition is indescribable and inexpressible. Consequently, it cannot be thought either; it only shows itself. What *can* be shown *cannot* be said (33). What shows itself, is the correspondence between language and the facts representing the case. This correspondence cannot be conceived in a sentence, either empirically with regard to content or analytically. Wittgenstein calls it the inexpressible and the mystical.

> Man possesses the capacity of constructing languages, in which every sense can be expressed, without having an idea how and what each word means - just as one speaks without knowing how the single sounds are produced

> Colloquial language is a part of the human organism and is no less complicated than it. From it it is humanly impossible to gather immediately the logic of language. Language disguises the thought; so that from the external form of the clothes one cannot infer the form of the thought they clothe, because the external form of the clothes is constructed with quite another object than to let the form of the body be recognized (34).

Admittedly, the affiliation with mysticism characterizes something as being linguistically inexpressible. Sentences aiming to describe the mystical are nothing but meaningless linguistic structures. However, they refer to something that exists. As Wittgenstein points out, "There is indeed the inexpressible" (35). This is illustrated, for example, in the correspondence of language with the reality of the world. Wittgenstein himself states that "...not *how* the world is, is the mystical, but *that* it is" (36). According to Wittgenstein, the concept of the mystical implies not only the relationship between proposition and reality, but is a collective concept comprising everything that cannot be scientifically proven (37). The relationship above between sentence and reality cannot be expressed linguistically, and only demonstrates itself (38).

b) Rejecting the Claim of Truth for Religious Statements

The banishment of the linguisticly inexpressible out of the world, as Wittgenstein does, is essential for the definition of the mystical, in that it includes the object of religious statements as well; on the one hand, there is the expressible, the dimensions of facts, on the other, there is the mystical representing the existing meaning of the world, which as such is inconceivable.

> The sense of the world must lie outside the world. In the world everything is as it is and happens as it does happen. *In* it there is no value - and if there were, it would be of no value. If there is any value which is of value, it must lie outside all happening and being-so. For all happening and being-so is accidental. What makes it non-accidental cannot lie *in* the world, for otherwise this would again be accidental. It must lie outside the world (39).

Concerning our religious problematic we might alter Wittgenstein's sentence following this citation by saying, "And so it is impossible for there to be a proposition of religion". Such propostions can express nothing of what is higher. It is clear that religion cannot be put into words. (40)

It is not necessarily the separation of the expressible from the inexpressible that is characteristic of Wittgenstein's line of thought. Rather it is the undialectic way in which he carries out this separation, that is not simultaneously a connection with what has been separated. Only in this way does the positivistic paradox come into existence. This paradox separates "the expressible from the inexpressible in an undialectic way. It then 'changes over' from the expressible to the inexpressible in order, in an unauthorized way, to linguistically express this 'strictly-speaking' inexpresssible, after all" (41). The dialectical connection of separation and connection would, however, read:

> There is nothing inexpressible as such that does not have something in common with the expressible; and vice versa: there is nothing expressible as such that does not have a relation to the inexpressible (42).

Regarding the religious problematic this would mean: if reflection on the structures of incarnation is possible at all, it would be possible only as a dialectical mediation. Only in this way is it conceivable that the "Existence of God is principally and unquestionably a self-revelationary existence, insofar as the existence of God principally takes the form of historic revelation. This can be seen in the history of the people of Israel, in the history of Jesus of Nazareth, and finally in the opening of the genuine historic future through

Easter..." (43). Wittgenstein, however, curtails such deliberations with the assertion,

> *How* the world is, is completely indifferent for what is higher.
> God does not reveal himself *in* the world (44).

Wittgenstein's more sophisticated attitude toward the problems of religion when compared with that of the logical positivists, is demonstrated in that he ascribes an explanatory function to those so-called meaningless mystical propositions.

> My propositions are elucidatory in this way: he who understands me eventually recognizes them as senseless, when he climbed out through them, on them, over them. (He must so to speak throw away the ladder, after he has climbed up it.) He must surmount these propositions; and then he sees the world rightly (45).

This is not the place to discuss a sense claim of religious statements or a theology in the form of a teaching. As the well known final sentence of the *Tractatus* advocates,

> Whereof one cannot speak, thereof one must be silent (46).

From this last reflection it becomes immediately clear that all religious propositions are nonsensical, not because their assertatory object is absent, but because they relate to exactly that which Wittgenstein believed to demonstrate to be mystical. The object of religious worship as well as of religious and theological language is not a part of the world. Therefore, it cannot be made accessible to us in the form of an innerwordly describable factual phenomenon. God, the "most sublime" is understood to mean a limit of the world, not unlike the way Wittgenstein understood the concept of the subject. For Wittgenstein, God is the limit of the world, and nothing in the world permits the conclusion that the world is seen by Him. This can be said on the basis of 5.633.

It is difficult to establish to what extent Charlesworth's statement "that Wittgenstein himself did not consider that the idea of God is *literally* meaningless" (47) is correct. In my opinion, the *Tractatus* does not confirm this view. One can at best conclude that Wittgenstein attached value to religious propositions insofar as they have an explanatory function. One cannot deny that Wittgenstein categorically rejects any claim of meaning for religious and theological statements or any attempt to prove the existence of God. According to him, God does not reveal himself in the world. In other words, in the question of God we don't deal with an innerworldly object and, consequently, with anything that is descriptively expressible because, using Wittgensteins's language, "God is not a fact ."

In the entries in Wittgenstein's diary, written approximately at the same time as the *Tractatus*, we read that God does not reveal Himself because He is "the meaning of life" (48). To believe in Him means "to see that the facts of the world are not the end of the matter ... To believe in God means to see that life has a meaning" (49). According to Wittgenstein, only he who believes in God has understood the question of the meaning of life.

In devaluating metaphysics and the total sphere of religious and theological thought with the eradication of the possibility of even one statement of meaning about God, Wittgenstein is in agreement with both the representatives of the Vienna Circle and with logical positivism, represented in Anglo-Saxon philosophy. His expressed difference from these positions does not consist in the meaning, but in the value that Wittgenstein attached to these meaning-disqualified propositions. For traditional positivism religious statements are totally meaningless; whereas for Wittgenstein they form the ladder without which religous belief is impossible. Only by climbing its rungs is one lead to the insight that the world is a fact and the case cannot be the quintessence of meaning. What Wittgenstein denies is the existence of a transformation from the realm of thought to that of belief. On the other hand, he cannot avoid undialectically recognizing the value and also the influence of the inexpressible realm on the realm of facts, i.e. on the world in which our lives are lived. In this context, he writes in the conclusion to his *Tractatus*,

> We feel that even if *all possible* scientific questions be answered,
> the problems of life have still not been touched at all (50).

Wittgenstein also believed that by assigning "non-scientific problems" to the realm of feeling, the truth-claim underlying the religious statement is totally rejected.

3. The interpretation of religious statements as basic-propostitions and "tu quoque argument"

The definition of the relationship between proposition and reality has brought about insurmountable difficulties within its train for both positivism and Wittgenstein. From a variety of positions attempts have been made to by-pass these difficulties and to come to an optimal solution. It made no difference whether the agreement was reflected either explicitly, in the establishment of a criterion of meaning, or implicitly, in the framework of isomorphic thought. The result was the same.

> Propositions can represent the whole reality, but they cannot represent what they must have in common with reality in order to be able to represent it - the logical form. To be able to represent the logical form, we should have to be able to put ourselves with the propositions outside logic, that is to say outside the world (51).

As long as one accepts the premise of language as a pure propositional and descriptive logic, and as long as the original unity of language and reality is mystical, "and thus locatable first for the listener in reflective reproduction" (52), then the impossibility of a comparision between propositions and the structure of reality forces every scientific investigation to start from propositions that from a scientific standpoint are themselves insufficiently founded. Such propositions can be, for example, designated as propositions of observation, protocol, or basis. They have the characteristic in common that they surpass "what we can know for sure 'on the basis of direct experience'" (53). This is because the expressions used by such propositions to describe direct experiences or observations are not provable as they are already based on a theory that itself needs prior justification on the basis of another theory. Following from the vain efforts to isolate the empirical foundation of propositional truth in so-called protocol propositions of science, - as initial propositions, - and passing on to the unsuccessful attempts whose *a priori* presuppositions do go along with linguistic expression regarding the concept of facts (54), Karl Popper developed his theory of critical rationalism and his "trial and error" principle.

> Out of uninterpreted sense-experiences science cannot be distilled, no matter how idustriously we gather and sort them. Bold ideas, unjustified anticipations, and speculative thought, are our only means for interpreting nature: our only organ, our only instrument for grasping her. And we must hazard them to win our prize. Those among us who are unwilling to expose their ideas to the hazard of refutation do not take part in the scientific game (55).

In order to clarify the point of this quotation, it is necessary to refer to Popper's own example, "This table is white". The description of a table as white presupposes the concept of color, with the result that the qualification of the table as white already takes as its premise the theory that white is a color: or in the opposite case white is not a color but, for example, a general property of light (56).

William W. Bartley, a pupil of Popper, now claims that theology proceeds analogously to natural science in its efforts to establish the truth of its proposition. It takes - as does the latter - their starting point in the basic-proposition - in this case from so-called belief-propositions. According to Bartley, in grounding its procedure, theology takes advantage of Popper's insight into the necessary result of axioms which are not grounded on one hand, yet on the other, disputes that the requirement to expose their initial propositions to continual examination and refutation following from this insight should also be binding. Bartley thinks that he is able to produce evidence of such a methodical procedure that aims to escape theoretical justification in the works of both Karl Barth and Paul Tillich. The reproach made against Barth is that he is ready to expose all presumptions about the Word of God to criticism, on the condition that the latter - as the Word revealed in Christ, as the yardstick of criticism - must itself be spared any criticism (57). Bartley presumes to uncover a similar rationalism to Barth's in Tillich's symbolic interpretation of Christian doctrine and in his Protestant principle. The decisive passages from Tillich for this interpretation are as follows:

> 1. All speaking about divine matters which is not done in the state
> of ultimate concern (that is, in our terminology, "commitment")
> is meaningless ... that which is meant in an act of faith cannot be
> approached in any other way than through an act of faith (58).

> 2. There is not criterion by which faith can be judged outside the
> correlation of faith (59).

This reference to contemporary Protestant theology on the position of faith induces Bartley to diagnose a "retreat to commitment" (60), and warns:

> One gains the right to be irrational at the expense of loosing the
> right to criticize (61).

That Bartley's warning is justified cannot be disputed. The question must rather be, whether Popper's reflections concerning religious statements are valid, or whether the process of critical reflection on religious statements must proceed in a way other than that along the principle of "trial and error" prefered by Bartley. Success in regard to scientific statements cannot serve as an indicator for equal success in regard to religious statements. One must reckon in the application of the latter with the fact that testimonial character is ascribed to religious statements. This means that their effectiveness is not to be sought in prognostic relevance. The fact that even a religious statement must not be spared critical consideration, already conditions its innately necessary engagement, because the latter contains a risk factor in the form of a decision. This risk factor can only be required when such a decision is also intellectually responsible. If penetrating reflection and critical examination of a religious statement are by-passed as one indicates that scientific statements, too, rest upon presuppositions that are scientificly unprovable, then one must agree with Bartley's statement that this type of "*tu quoque* argument" only apparently provides an extra-rational engagement with a rational ground for an apology (62).

As Popper develops his theory of science he begins with the premise of the inadequacy of the Aristotelian doctrine of cognition and all subsequent doctrines based there upon. In his "application of critical rationalism concerning the critique of theology" (63), Bartley now overlooks that the justification of religious statements taken up by Thomistic theology, did not at all run parallel to other sciences. As a matter of fact, the model of theology as *scientia subalterna* had been developed in the wake of the Aristotelian concept of science. Yet because religious statements have no evident principles that are provable and on the basis of which statements could be expounded by means of logical laws and conclusions, a reductive concept of evidence was proposed for statements of revelation (64). This means that statements of revelation should be obvious to God and the saints. This is not to say that the formation of theological theories with this historical reprimand is withdrawn from critical examination. It is the validity of the unquestionable application of a method of demonstration that did not initially intend a criticism of religious and theological insights that is to be questioned.

Even if one wished to say that Bartley was right in using Popper's criteria for examining the truth-claim of religious statements, and even if one disregards the difference between these statements and those of natural science, this does not yet result in a deficient legitimation of religious statements. Indeed, according to Popper, basic-propositions must relate to "easily observable physical bodies" (65). Yet - and his theory depends on this - these propositions are acknowledged by a conclusion behind which no intersubjective examination can proceed.

> Basic statements are accepted as the result of a decision or agreement; and to that extent they are conventions. (66).

In this connection, however, it appears questionable whether Popper has been justifiably praised for succeeding where Kant had failed,- that is for bringing about the solution of the Kantian problem of rendering accordent both intellectualism and empiricism and explaining their useful components evading the errors of both these points of view (67).

One must admit that Popper tends to reject pure conventionalism that only knows unalterable propositions and for which both verification and falsification do not come into question. Yet neither the distinction between a "conventional moment", nor the integrated reality-content is sufficient for determining the truth of a basic-proposition, because the set of problems that arise in solving the truth-question rely on the fact that there is no method for separating these two (68). If, however, the language called upon to describe an experience "is a matter of convention, then there is, as Wolfhart Pannenberg critically demonstrated, "no longer any good reason to exclude, e.g. *at the outset*, the concept of God from the circle of admissible linguistic possibilities, "because for the Israelites the proposition that God saved them from their Egyptian persecutors when they crossed the Red Sea "might well have been the description of a direct experience-situation" (69). Exclusion of such statements, i.e. the proof of their falsity, might take place only in the form of a subsequent theory. In this connection, the dialectical relationship between basis-propositions and the theory based upon them, must also be considered. Basis propositions are a necessary condition for the theories based upon them, yet they are observed in their formulation from the viewpoint of the resulting theory.

With these reflections on Bartley's methodical approach and on the applicability of Popper's epistemology to theological statements, the reproach of retreating into an irrational belief-engagement has not yet been warded off. The passages cited, above all those from Tillich, are too clear in their language to be ignored. Pannenberg ruefully comments, in his thorough treatment of Bartley's work, that Tillich contents himself with the observation that one cannot pass judgement upon belief outside the relationship of belief "thus withdrawing, from the very beginning, not only the Christian standpoint of belief from any criticism which is not prepared to take over this standpoint itself," but "also for his part (Tillich) renounces the right to pass any kind of judgements on persons of a different faith, without...admittedly, being ready for such abstinence" (70).

Without wishing to offer an interpretation of Tillich's theology (71), and with exclusive reference to the textual passages quoted by Bartley, the question shall be posed as to whether the assertion of a "theological circle" is to be placed on a par with the rejection of any and every examination of religious statements once made and professed. The passages from Tillich, quoted by Bartley, do not appear to me to make such an equation obvious.

The observation that there are also limits to Popper's theory of verification must not expose it to the suspicion of a reference to the "*tu quoque* argument". This is because this theory has been developed for the purpose of explicating the pre-understanding present in the basis-proposition of the sciences. The reference to pre-understandings of a similar kind, for the religious statement as well, is consequently valid only because such a reference draws attention to conditions of recognition that are inexcludable. In the arena of the theological sciences such conditions are particularly conspicuous, because the object of the formulation of theory cannot be empirically grasped. The reproach of revelational positivism, like that directed against Barth, is only justified if, within this theology, one fails to make this attempt and also to critically examine its propositions. The same is true of Tillich's theology. Reproaches against him may be content with reference to particular statements. It must be possible to justify them on the basis of the total intention of his work. It will then be impossible to evade the fact that it is Tillich who regards the avoidance of every kind of absolutization, in particular, to be the essence of Christian doctrine.

> In the symbol of the cross, which is the most important Christian symbol, we probably find the most radical criticism of all such absolutizing is represented (72).

On the other hand, Bartley's attempt to apply Popper's criteria for the verification of a scientific theory of natural science to propositions that are not based on an act of perception, but on an act of belief, must be examined as to whether or not in the act of belief there is or is not a case of epistemological absolutization. In this context the following passage from Tillich's *Wesen und Wandel des Glaubens*, cited by Bartley in ellucidation of his theory, demonstrates the point.

> The assertion that something has sacred character is meaningful only for the asserting faith. As a theoretical judgement claiming general validity, it is a meaningless combination of words....The outside observer can only state that there is a correlation of faith between the one who has faith and the sacramental object of his faith. But he cannot deny or affirm the validity of this correlation of faith. He can only state it as a fact. If a Protestant observes a Catholic praying before a picture of the Virgin, he remains observer, unable to state whether the faith of the observed is the same act of faith. There is no criterion by which faith can be judged from outside the correlation of faith. (73)

The assertion that something has sacred character, in Bartley's opinion, is legitimate, according to the assertion's claim of validity. It is not clear from the quotation above that Tillich contradicts this opinion. In my opinion, he is merely asserting that an affirmation or a negation of the claim to validity is not possible from the position of the impartial observer. If this view is correct, then the demand for validity, without doubt, cannot remain restricted to certain forms of expressing faith like praying to the Virgin Mary. It must encompass the entire realm of faith - the symbolic realm described by Tillich - that serves to circumscribe that which is understood by the concept of God. Legitimation is necessary for the formation of theological theories because of the fact that it alone can avoid revelational positivism, i.e. the objectification of God. On the level of the formation of theories, it is ununderstandable why there is no possibility of talk of validity of the adoration of the Virgin Mary between the Catholic carrying out this act of faith and the Protestant observer, who does not see himself in a position to "participate" in this act. Tillich's argument was that the Protestant could not participate, and not that the Protestant could not talk of the legitimacy of such an act. If the adequacy of participation in an act of faith can be thought of by the believer as an issue for inquiry into his interpretaion of belief then, within this framework of the question of being human one must also pose the question whether and to what extent faith and the principle of knowledge presented here by Bartley is to be regarded as a component of this personal interpretation.

The passage from Tillich, quoted above, is hardly of value for Bartley's argument, because the difference between Catholics and Protestants dealt with by Tillich, is a theological disputation. Bartley, however, is not at all concerned with producing evidence to the effect that theology does not represent a system possessing its own inner logic. He wants to demonstrate that theology sets out from irrational and irrevisable premises. In spite of the arbitrariness of the approach this possibility admittedly does not exclude the fact that, the remaining propositions will follow by deduction. The issue of worshipping the Virgin Mary is, without a doubt, a theological problem. However, Bartley by-passed the question of whether an absolute explanation of religion is also a theological problem. Is it not a philosophical one instead or is an explanation of religion possible at all? Such a large scale theory has only once been attempted by Georg W.F. Hegel. However, the fact that Hegel failed in his attempt to claim that religion is irrational in origin is not a "rational" excuse.

Bartley's reservations about irrational decisionism's "*tu quoque* argument" are irrefutably legitimate. A theology that is completely in favor of such a decision, is without doubt, guilty of neglecting reason. Yet the question remains: must this necessarily be the case? Is not a belief grounded in self-reflective thought, even when its critique is not exercised from a standpoint external to faith, an alternative to the proposal of ethical argumentational offered by Bartley? For even this theology is unacceptable without questioning whether it corresponds, not only to the demands of critical reflection, but rather as it withstands reflective critique. Is it capable of mediating the decision as an individual or social process, with a self-critical eye? Consequently it can be understood as an answer to those questions for which religious statements give foundational answers. One will certainly not be able to withhold one's assent to Bartley's exortation to practise ethical argumentation. However his ethics and its plea for respect for humanity may already be regarded as an answer to an imminent religious problem; thus making the quest for the truth-character of religious statements superfluous. Something Bartley appears to believe: even though it is not exactly resolved.

4. Syntactics, semantics, and pragmatics

The criticism of the definition of the meaning of statements through empirical verification, as offered by A. Petzäll, Roman Ingarden, A.H. Weinberg, Hans Reichenbach, Otto Neurath, and even Popper, has not been echoless. Here the realization that it was not sufficient to preclude uncomfortable statements from a qualification of meaning by establishing limiting criteria of meaning prior to testing their type of claim to meaning was decisive. If only propositions of empirical science are recognized as meaningful, then the question concerning the meaning of religious statements is already prejudiced as a meaningless one. Another difficulty arose from the impossibility of establishing an absolute foundation for basic-propositions. It arose from the unclarified relation between proposition and reality.

Carnap shared this criticism in his treatise *Testability and Meaning* and attempted at first to replace the concept of verifiability with the concepts of testability, potential for confirmation, and observation. Later on, in his work *Logische Syntax der Sprache*, he sought to overcome the problems of verification by pushing the question of the relationship of language to reality as well as the problem of meaning into the background. He then turned to an investigation of the formal structure of language. His work is limited to the investigation of rules for forming and transforming expressions; to demonstrating how words and symbols form propositions, and to how a demonstrative proposition may be elucidated by means of other propositions. This type of syntactical investigation focuses on the speaking subject and on the situation in which this subject finds himself as he utters words and propositions.

Such an analysis of the formal structures of propositions, makes possible a statement on the presence or absence of direct, deductible relations of various propositions or classes of propositions to one another. It cannot be ignored, even when assessing theological propositional systems as a scientific theory. Unless one already accepts the fact that in theology systematization takes place somehow as proof of the fact "that that level of conceptualism and reflection has been reached which distinguishes theology from the proclamation" (74). However, the question of the actual process of forming theological theories is preceded by the question concerning the truth of the religious statement. This question cannot be answered in a purely syntactical way because a consideration of the purely formal structure of the expression of a proposition does not deliver insight into the truth or falsity of the proposition.

The knowledge of syntactical rules, the knowledge of the "mathematics of language" as Carnap once called it, is insufficient not only for understanding religious statements, but it is also inadequate for understanding the propositions of real, scientific language. The inadequacy of purely logico-syntactical investigations made it necessary to include the problem of meaning. This supplemented syntax with semantics, the teaching of the actual meaning of expressions used in a language. Carnap did justice to this in his book *Introduction to Semantics* (75).

Limiting oneself to an investigation of syntactical rules of the formation and transformation of propositions and of their formalization in symbols brought a further disadvantage in its train. By means of the empiricist criterion of meaning, it had still been maintainable that metaphysical as well as religious problems were meaningless pseudo-problems. However, the syntactical description of language alone does not satisfy this requirement. Rather, taken in itself, it is not even sufficient to declare as meaningless propositions such as "Caesar is a prime number" or "The absolute substance becomes apparent in the experience of the universe" (76). The syntactical method, therefore, needs to be supplemented by an investigation of the relations that exist between expressions and states-of-affairs described by language. The attempt to identify religious statements syntactically could not be undertaken at all; and the question whether religious statements already syntactically differ from statements in scientific language could, as a consequence, directly move on to the question whether religious statements are based on different semantics than other propositions. In this context, syntax was supplemented by the semantic so that, by acknowledging the necessity of a "syntactical consideration of language, this consideration withdrew in favor of 'an empirical interpretation' of worlds of language centered on themselves (77).

The situation regarding the definition of the meaning of religious statements changed. It had to be admitted that it is possible to think of linguistic systems within which religious as well as metaphysical statements - depending on the respective linguistic system - are to be regarded as meaningful. In this connection, it is to be noted that the failure of a scientific-theoretical investigation limited to syntax led to both the abandonment of the ideal of a unitary science and the replacement of the unitary language by a variety of possible languages among which scientific language is only one. However, the distinction between religious statements and those of natural science is not eliminated in that among the variety of possible languages, a preferential position is attained by that language according to which:

1. the demonstrability of what is accorded to a sign, i.e. its demonstration in experience given, is ultimately required for the meaning of a descriptive sign; and

2. demonstration by experience is required for statements about facts, and that means ultimately also its demonstration in given experience (78).

Thus the criterion of demonstration is not deduced from the conditions of the language itself, but is acknowledged as a condition of empirical language, that is regarded as a scientific language. Whether a proposition is considered to be meaningful, depends on the semantic and syntactical rules of a language. Therefore, according to Kraft, the proposition "The sky laughs", may be looked upon as devoid of meaning. If, however, "laughs" represents the expression of a condition of the soul, then the proposition may be regarded as meaningful, provided that "the qualification for evoking a mental condition is characterized" (79). This is unprofitable for the clarification of the truth-claim of religious statements on the basis of semantics, because this clarification, despite its acknowledgment of a variety of linguistic possibilities, recognizes the qualification of a statement to be true only in the case of statements that belong to an empirical system of language.

The syntactical investigation of language was supplemented not only by semantics, but also by pragmatics. According to Carnap pragmatics is a type of linguistic investigation that, "refers explicitly to the speaker of the language no matter whether other factors are drawn in or not" (80). According to this supplement, the specificity of the speaker - the use of words and propositions peculiar to him - is also included in the investigation. As will subsequently become clear, it was above all pragmatics that attempted to clarify the meaning of religious statements. Although it was generally acknowledged that these three views originally proposed by the American Charles W. Morris (81) belong together, the attempt had never been made to dialectically or transcendentally reflect on their relationship. Instead of elucidating the context of the condition of this relationship, one was content with the empirical consideration of linguistic patterns of behavior that took as their premise the essential insight that the meaning of words only becomes recognizable in their use. This is an insight that was later to form the basis for shattering the linguistic veto upon religious statements. However, this tendency to emphasize pragmatics, transfers the empirical patterns of linguistic behavior to the center. It cannot be unconditionally regarded as representative of the development of logical positivism. Hence, during his lifetime, inspite of the inclusion of semantic and pragmatic considerations, Carnap gave preference to the non-empirical view of language in his attempt to develop a pure - as distinct from an empirical - pragmatical science. On the other hand, the tendency towards empirical analysis received fruitful stimuli from late Wittgenstein. Wittgenstein revised his original notion of a scientific universal-language in favor of a notion of logical positivism - especially that of the Vienna Circle. In addition, it was he who ultimately made the analysis of religious statements a subject for serious discussion.

In logical positivism's late phase, as well as in Wittgenstein's late philosophy, the tendency is exhibited to thematize language as the real object of scientific investigation. They thereby limit the originally scientific-theoretical approach to a theory of scientific assertion. Language becomes the dimension of science, whereby the relationship to empiricism in different propositions will be reflected in varying degrees of strength, and indicating this relationship as the material criterion of truth. After the attempt to find an exact scientific language that reflected the world had been superseded by the notion of pluralistic language worlds and after everyday language in its various language games as conditioned by the situational content and the speaker's way of living had become the object of analysis, it was also natural that the question of truth would undergo a modification in its meaning. The analysis of those forms of speech that do not expressly refer to the representation of the given, came into the foreground. The confrontation of the analytical philosophy of religion with investigations of linguistic-analytical ethics was decisive (82). In analysing moral statements, it became evident to a strong degree, that in addition to apophantic propositions there are forms of speech such as orders, exortations, praise, blame and emotive declaration. Consequently, it was only natural to pose the following question: Which category do religious statements belong to?

The view of logical positivism that only the empirically given along with its logical propositional structure is of philosophical interest was refuted as it developed in this direction, leading to its absorbtion in the analytical philosophy of language. It must be strictly maintained that, historically speaking, the analytical philosophy of language can neither be regarded as a form of the logical positivism of the Vienna Circle nor of current American logical empiricism. Undoubtedly, it was a catch-all for logical positivists. Many of them saw a necessary connection between analysis and positivistic principles - a misunderstanding which was underscored by Ayer's work *Language, Truth and Logic*. Ayer clothed the main theses of the Vienna Circle on the language of analysis and intended to form a synthesis of the positivists with Moore and Wittgenstein (83). In order to determine the extent to which the historical difference between logical positivism and linguistic analysis is a real material difference, the study of an adequate evaluation of the meaning of religious statements on the basis of an analytical method can help.

Not without influence on beginnings of analytical philosophy and above all its philosophy of religion was Wittgenstein's *Philosophical Investigations*. As mentioned earlier Wittgenstein broke through the ban upon religious statements. In order to investigate their claim to meaning, Wittgenstein's late philosophy will be briefly treated. This will enable us to better understand his thought.

5. Philosophy as linguistic-analysis

I do not want to elucidate the question of why Wittgenstein turned to the philosophy of everyday language, nor will I question whether this turn represents progress in philosophy. I intend to point out only the essential difference between Wittgenstein's early writings and the philosophy of his later years. This difference consists in his "recognizing and abandoning, as metaphysical fabrication, the idea that states of affairs exist independent of language" (84). Thus, Wittgenstein revised his view that language depicts reality as such, and that language, if it is supposed to provide such a description, has to take into consideration its ontological structure. This change of thinking did not remain without consequences for his conception of the problem of truth. In his late work, Wittgenstein neglected reflecting upon the correspondence of reality and proposition and in reference to his own earlier method, he criticized the naive application of the contrast of proposition and reality. Stegmüller says it best when he comments:

> The world is not organized in such and such a way "in itself" and is described (whether true or false) according to this organization by means of language, rather the possibility of this organization only arises through the articulation of language: There are as many ways of describing the world as there are of separating the component parts (85).

Now Wittgenstein advocates the conviction that the meaning of a proposition cannot be fathomed directly or indirectly by means of verification, but can only be conceived in an analysis of the active use of words and sentences. Analysis gains an increasingly explanatory function by describing linguistic behavior in everyday communication. Such an analysis had already been hinted at in the *Tractatus*. Now it becomes the starting point for his so-called therapeutic philosophy. In this analysis, "the philosopher's treatment of a question is like the treatment of an illness" (86). The aim of therapy is to eliminate "problems that arise when language goes on holiday" (87), i.e. when language has not been used properly and consequently, "an simile that has been absorbed into the forms of our language produces a false appearance, and this disquites us" (88).

With regard to the question of the possibility of religious assertions, it was necessary within the scope of Wittgenstein's early philosophy, to pose the question of how meaning and truth could be attributed to propositions that do not represent a possible state of affairs; in other words, a state of affairs with empirical objectivity. Now the central problem is whether such propositions correspond to the system of rules governing language, as maintained by Wittgenstein; or whether, to the contrary, proof can be furnished that when one uses religious propositions one has misunderstood the function of language, and has succumbed to its temptation.

In his *Philosophical Investigations* Wittgenstein views language according to the situation content of its situation. His analysis is intended to disclose those rules peculiar to the use of language in context. According to him, they precede linguistic communication. Wittgenstein advocates the view that in different situations of life we use words in accordance with different systems of rules. He illustrates this with the analysis of time in Augustine's *Confessiones*: "*quid est ergo tempus*?" Augustine asks in his *Confessiones*. As is well known he answers his own question with the words, "*si nemo ex me quaerat scio, si quaerenti explicare velim, nescio*" (89). Wittgenstein sees the cause for Augustine's dilemma in the isolation of the word "time", which occurs in everyday usage in such phrases as "Do you have time?" "Take your time". The Church Father, according to Wittgenstein, has succumbed to a temptation of language originating in the grammatical form of the question. The question "What is time?" is formed by analogy to the question "What is that? Bread". And what bread is we learn - such is the argumentation - from the coherence of the language game. It is, therefore, a mistake to think there are such things as time, bread, a stone, etc. What there is, indeed, is only the different use of certain terms in a variety of situational contexts.

> When philosophers use such a word - "knowledge", "being", "object", "I", "proposition", "name" - and try to conceive the essence of the thing, one must always ask oneself: is the word ever actually used this way in the language-game which is its original home (90).

As a consequence of this analysis, Wittgenstein intends to guide words used external to the linguistic realm where they originally belong, back to their everyday usage. "The headache which Hegel gives the reader with his dialectic of the 'Here' and 'Now' in his *Phenomenology*", is for Wittgenstein precisely the same "headache which you get when, as you investigate the meanings of certain words, you may hit upon the idea of using these words, for once, in a completely different way from the way you have learned to use them" (91). In full accordance with Wittgenstein's theory, it can consequently be asked, who ever heard one person say to another, "This is a house", and received the answer, "No, this is a tree". For Wittgenstein, this dialectic is empty comparable to the turning of a wheel with no connection to any productive mechanism (92).

It is true that the word "God" is not explicitly mentioned in the earlier quotation from Wittgenstein. However, there can be no doubt that Wittgenstein would count it among the examples enumerated there. In a modified and radicalized way, we may even apply Wittgenstein's question of how the word "God" is used in its original language-game. This question is radicalized in that Wittgenstein sees in it the possibility of inquiry not only into the actual and correct use of the word, but into its proper home. The question of whether or not the use of this word is the consequence of the temptation brought about by a linguistic picture, i.e. a metaphorical semblance (93), is the issue at hand.

> The word 'God' is amongst the earliest learnt - pictures,
> cathechisms, etc. But not the same consequences as with pictures
> of aunts. I wasn't shown that which the picture pictured (94).

Wittgenstein leaves the question as to the proper home unanswered. He does not object, as Carnap did, to further use of the term "God". However, he refuses to inquire if there is a god. His main concern is to show that this word does not comply with the rules for using such a term as "aunt".

> "Being shown all these things, did you understand what this word
> meant?" I'd say: "Yes and no. I did learn what it didn't mean. I
> made myself understand. I could answer questions, understand
> questions when they were put in different ways - and in that sense
> could be said to understand" (95).

However, the question must remain open as to how far the "understanding" Wittgenstein is discussing here, can be understood in the sense of analogous problems according to which various predicates are ascribed to God. Admittedly, these predicates cannot be applied to God in the same sense in which they are used in - what Wittgenstein calls - everyday language games. Nor can they be considered to be anthromorphisms and equivocations with regard to contents. On the contrary, the assumption may be correct that Wittgenstein sympathized to a certain extent with an interpretation of the *analogia entis*, that says that these predicates, while failing to predicate God, in fact stride towards God, who cannot be defined (96).

It is a striking feature of the analytical philosophy of religion that a lot of attention was paid to the problems of the *analogia entis*, and how it tried to revitalize a discussion which today, as a matter of fact, is no less important and significant than before. Nevertheless, within the scope of traditional philosophical thought, it has been taken from its central position and relegated to a position on the margin of the philosophy of religion.

a) Wittgenstein's Annulment of the Linguistic Veto

In his *Lectures and Conversations on Aesthetics, Psychology and Religious Belief*, from which the above quotations were taken, Wittgenstein expressly discusses the problem of religious language. However, here too it is striking, as it was in his *Philosophical Investigations*, that he was not concerned with providing a new basis for philosophy, let alone for a philosophy of religion. He left such efforts to his followers. In these lectures, Wittgenstein offers insight into his personal attitude towards religious questions. On the whole he contents himself with general remarks. For instance, he points out that in a religious conversation an expression like "I believe that this or that will happen" is used in a different way, than it could be used in science. Likewise, religious expression differs not only with regard to its object but:

> ...entirely different connections would make them into religious beliefs, and these can easily be imagined transitions where we wouldn't know for our life whether to call them religious beliefs or scientific beliefs (97).

When asked about the meaning of concrete religious content, Wittgenstein lacks a systematic focus because he does not propose that language is a basic philosophical principle. This was attempted only later by his followers. Rather he tries to achieve an immediacy inaccessible to philosophy (98). When asked if he believed in the Resurrection, he answered "No", but he would not contradict such a possibility either (99). In his opinion, this is a question that does not have an answer. To begin with, it would be necessary to state how the question is to be understood at all. From the very beginning, there is no criterion whatsoever by which it can be decided whether the person believing in the Resurrection and the person denying it really mean the same thing (100).

According to Wittgenstein, answering this question would require an implicit definition of the use of the word 'resurrection', both in the question and in the answer. In both forms of speech, this word would have to be used in exactly the same way. No indication can be found that Wittgenstein might have meant his answer to be dialectial. Nor is there any indication that he assumed that an answer in support of the belief in the resurrection has the character of a private language. He thinks that the language to which such an answer can be ascribed, connects only it *own* and private *notion* of the word 'resurrection'.

In his *Philosophical Investigations*, Wittgenstein adamantly rejects the notion of a private language. For him any possibility to regard religious language as private language is out of the question. Consequently, the ambivalence of the answer to the question concerning belief in the Resurrection cannot begin with the fact that, first the person putting the question speaks a language understandable only to himself, and that second the interlocutor does not at all know what the conversation is about and is, therefore, unable to take a position on the matter. This ambivalence rests on the possible difference of notions ascribed to a word; in this case, the word 'resurrection'. In connection with talk of death, Wittgenstein discusses the different notions attached to a word, asking how it is possible to have different notions of death. He contrasts notions of death with the use of the word 'death', which he considers a "public instrument which has a whole technique (of usage)" (101). We may see also a reference in § 272 of the *Philosophical Investigations* that when discussing this problem, the essential thing for Wittgenstein seems not to be to discover whether every person has his own notion among the multitude of existent notions, but to investigate how it is possible at all to understand the idea of another person. Wittgenstein defines understanding as "the mastering of a technique". With regard to the presentation of religious states of affairs, Wittgenstein sees the problem in the fact that "my normal technique of language leaves me" and I do not know whether I shall say that I understand religious propositions or that I do not understand them (102).

Left in the lurch by normal language technique, Wittgenstein is faced with the problem concerning the claim validity of religious propositions. He pays attention to this problem only insofar as a discrepancy between the word and the notion intended by it or between the sentence and the state of affairs expressed in it becomes obvious. The discrepancy normally veiled by the smooth functioning of our technique of language, that becomes obvious in religious propositions, does not cause Wittgenstein to make comprehensive reflections on the relationship between language and reality, at least not within the scope of religious language. Rather, he contents himself with the requirement to clarify those rules that guarantee alignment.

For Wittgenstein, language has an inter-subjective character. If the ideas underlying religious language have a private character, then they have nothing in common with language. Therefore, their linguistic formulation presupposes a "reference to the technique of the word" (103). Consequently, for Wittgenstein, the truth of religious propositions is proven when this connection with the technique of word-usage can be demonstrated. In his

Philosophical Investigations Wittgenstein distinguishes surface-grammar from deep grammer in the use of a word. At the same time, he stresses that deep-grammar cannot be included in logical syntax. In this grammar it is immanent to the connection between the state-of-affairs and the word immanent to it that is under discussion. It contains the criteria for defining sense and nonsense, the truth and falisity of a proposition, in that it "tells what kind of object anything is" (104). That Wittgenstein does not exclude religious sentences, as might be expected, can be seen from the aphoristic comment at the end of this paragraph: "Theology as grammar".

With this remark, that assigns theology the task of elaborating a system of rules that constitute the meaning of religious propositions, the "linguistic veto" (105) of logical positivism against the investigation of religious propositions was annulled.

It may be of interest for Wittgenstein's late philosophy to note a further remark that according to G.E.M. Anscombe, Wittgenstein himself made upon the relationship of his investigations to the problems of religious propositions.

> Its (the 'Philosophical Investigations') advantage is that if you believe, say, Spinoza or Kant, this interferes with what you believe in religion; but if you believe me, nothing of the sort (106).

It is in accord with his modified view of language in his late philosophy that a proposition like "God created heaven and earth" can be proper. In the context of the language game among believers, this assertion is certainly meaningful and true. If, however, it were propounded with a geophysical theory, it would not be really wrong but, at any rate, meaningless. That kind of valuation was not yet possible for Wittgenstein in his *Tractatus* because he acknowledges only a language of elementary propositions. Since these elementary propositions, as pictures of states-of-affairs, had to agree with the latter in their logical form, there could be only one meaningful proposition. Different sentences concerning the same state-of-affairs, which are supposed to be true, were conceivable only insofar as they showed the same logical structure, even though differently clothed. In contrast to the *Philosophical Investigations*, the *Tractatus* does not acknowledge, for instance, the distinction between a logic of scientific statements and a logic of religious statements.

If a language of precision, assumed to be isomorphic in its logical form within the structures of the describable world, is renounced in favor of the validity of language games controlled by a technical procedure according to given rules, then a higher valuation of the plurality of world-views devalues the contemporary scientific world-view. As a consequence of this reevaluation, it is possible to question a universal concept of truth.

Wittgenstein's statement on religion cited previously demonstrates the difference between his early and late conceptions of language. In the first instance, the correspondence of a state-of-affairs with a proposition was insured by the "ideas implied in the sense of the sentence". Here Wittgenstein continues to conceive meaning as a mental act constituting the sense and significance of words and independent of psychic experience. In the second case, Wittgenstien sees the meaning of words and sentences demonstrated by their usage.

> Every sign by itself seems dead. What gives it life? In use it is alive (107).

A word gains meaning by being used in a certain way in a language game. "The meaning of a word is its use in the language" (108). It would, therefore, be wrong to presuppose that there is a definite basic meaning of such a word as 'bread'. What there really is, is the use of this word in a variety of meanings. This use comprises the fact that bread can be spoken of both in scientific and in religious language games.

> During supper Jesus took bread, and having said the blessing he broke it and gave it to the disciples with the words: "Take this and eat; this is my body" (109).

Outside a particular language game, it does not make sense to talk of bread and wine representing the body and blood of a certain person. Sentences about the chemical composition of wine and bread do not belong to the constitutive parts of the religious language game. According to Wittgenstein, the religious language game of equating bread with the body of Christ would not actually be untrue but senseless and inappropriate within a language of chemistry game. Similarly, the language game of analysing bread in order to determine its basic components; water, protein, fats, carbohydrates, minerals, as well as the language game describing the disintegration of bread's micromolecules by enzymes resulting in the formation of carbon dioxide, would be out of place within the scope of the religious language game. Consequently it would not make sense in the context of the situation.

b) Linguistic Pragmatism and the Religious Language Game

The identification of meaning and use not only entails the determination of both the word and the sentence with reference to pragmatism. It requires a greater variety of meaning than a mere reference to semantics. It leads at the same time to doubt concerning the doctrine of the descriptive function of language and to a distinction between the sentence-radical and the sentence-mode. This was to become the basis for the emotive theory of religion. According to Wittgenstein, the sentence-radical the gains a different meaning depending on the way in which the sentence-mode, i.e. the interlocking of the use of the sentence with the situation in which the sentence is used, finds its expression be it an interrogative, an imperative, an indicative, a subjunctive, an optative, a conditional, or any other mood.

Reflecting the influence of pragmatism, Wittgenstein begins with the presupposition that the use of sentences and words in practical speech is known with regard to the definition of their meaning. Because Wittgenstein investigates the use of language in its pragmatic context, trying to obtain the meaning of words and sentences by analysing this text, we ought to be conscious that, where pragmatic meaning is to be conceived, linguistic usage must not be fixed. The model regarding language as an instrument, which Wittgenstein presents at the beginning of his *Philosophical Investigations*, is only partly valid, even for his own understanding of language. For Wittgenstein, language is in the end not only the "'given' instrument in the already linguistically constituted world" (110), but also the "inner dialectic of the problem itself" that led him to the "exposition of the transcendental dimension of the language problematic" (111). It likewise led Wittgenstein to view language as an action (ἐνέργεια), as an instance of mediation , although he did nothing to categorize the "λόγος of the ἐνέργεια of language ...on the basis of this ἐνέργεια itself" (112), in order to be able to represent the philosophy of language as a logic which must look after itself (113) in its own unique dimension, as outlined in the *Tractatus*.

In order to understand linguistic usage, Wittgenstein presupposes rules included within the language game. These rules constitute the deep-grammar of language, and determine the structure of the situational world pertaining to the respective language game (114). This conception results from a view of analytic philosophy, that the understanding of a language system or, in Wittgenstein's opinion, the understanding of a pragmatically oriented language game is possible only in accordance with the respective *a priori* characteristic structure of the form of life.

Essence is expressed by grammar (115).

As mentioned earlier, theology was defined by Wittgenstein as grammar. It is noteworthy that, for Wittgenstein, it is one thing to know a rule, and another to obey it. A person who knows the rule and can cite it, need not necessarily obey it. This means that the theologian who explicitly knows the respective rules of religious speech and conduct does not necessarily need to compose examples of religious propositions and actions. Vice versa, a person who does not know these rules, may apply them by making religious statements and by performing religious actions.

Wittgenstein's evaluation of the importance of the rules for understanding the sense of a language game is contradictory in many aspects (116). As is well known, Wittgenstein has often been criticized for regarding the learning of language and consequently the application of religious propositions as well as the mastery of any rule-bound conduct as "training".

When I follow a rule, I do not choose. I obey the rule blindly (117).

On the other hand, only two paragraphs before this quotation, Wittgenstein states in his answer to the question, "How am I able to obey a rule?" that this question, unless it is a question "about causes", is to be characterized as a question "about the justification for my following the rule in the way I do" (118).

On the one hand, in his conflict-ridden conception of rules, Wittgenstein presupposes that being taught rules is prerequisite to participating in the situation of the language game. He justifies the notable success that training may claim. On the other hand, Wittgenstein also knows that, since the knowledge and mastery of rules do not warrant smooth communication in the language game, their relevance in linguistic communication is only limited. The reference to responsibility in the selection and the adoption of rules as one reaches "bedrock" and "one's spade ...is turned" and justifications are exhausted (119), is to clarify this, while at the same time clearing Wittgenstein of the self induced suspicion of being a behaviourist.

Are you not really a behaviorist in disguise? Aren't you at the bottom really saying that everything except human behavior is a fiction?" (120)

Wittgenstein was unable to give a direct answer to this question. The conception of the language game will make this clearer. Even the Wittgenstein of the *Philosophical Investigations* cannot avoid the separation of the expressible and the inexpressible. Without doubt, the inexpressible includes the reason for participating in this or that particular language game, as well as the readiness to accept and obey certain rules.

It becomes apparent that Wittgenstein's concept of a rule is determined by two divergent considerations. First there is the thesis as to the impossibility of a private language (121). Wittgenstein is firmly convinced that the correct use of a word can be developed only in the intercommunicative context of a language community. According to him it is not possible to speak of the correct use of a word unless it is the word of a community. He thinks that criteria concerning the correct use of language imply that the standards governing it can be checked as to their application. Second, this conception rests on the attempt - and this is the motive for maintaining that the choice and the appropriation of rules are unfounded - to prevent fixing a criterion for sense that might be supposed to lie outside the language. He asserts, on the contrary, that

(a) the understanding of sense is possible only within the self-understood process of a language game and that

(b) philosophical and theological problems occur only where the language game no longer functions.

In order to escape the infinite regression that "any understanding which has always been conveyed linguistically, rests on existing understanding (pre-understanding)" (122). Wittgenstein discontinues such high flying reflections on the understanding of the sense of a language game in favor of a reference to the immediacy of language. He confines himself to observing the correctness of rules, the following of which constitutes the sense of a statement, and the knowledge of which is prerequisite to deciding on its truth, with a dependent relationship to public speech and to a traditional form of life or institution. He considers this dependence to be sufficient for justifying the use of rules, and does not look for it in the science that rises above the actual statement. The science in question is theology when a religious statement is concerned. Thus, theology is merely grammar that has to behave as if the unity of word and thing were insured. Theology must be satisfied with indicating only those rules of deep grammar that safeguard this unity.

The compensation for the disinclination to justify the occurrence of various rule systems by an over-emphasis of the community character of language is presented as an alternative to the restriction of the truth of statements, due to an unreflected junction of language with the language of the natural sciences. The fact that different language games are effective with rules contrary to each other and corresponding to different forms of life is considered by Wittgenstein to be possible only because the idea of the uniform character of language underlying the multiplicity of the use of languages is illegitimate. That is why Wittgenstein refuses to give a definition of the language game. In this sense he writes that the concept "'game' is a concept with blurred edges"; which begs the question, "But is a blurred concept a concept at all" (123)? Instead of giving a definition, Wittgenstein tries to explain what he means with the term language game by referential examples, in other words by means of language games themselves:

> Giving orders, and obeying them -
> Describing the appearance of an object, or giving its measurements -

Constructing an object from a description (a drawing) -
Reporting an event -
Speculating about an event -
Forming and testing a hypothesis -
Presenting the results of an experiment in tables and diagrams -
Making up a story; and reading it -
Play-acting -
Singing catcher -
Guessing riddles -
Making a joke; telling it -
Solving a problem in practical arithmetic -
Translating from one language into another -
Asking, thanking, cursing, greeting, praying (124).

The insights, which these examples are supposed to establish do not rest on philosophical or metaphysical considerations, but on purely grammatical ones.

Our investigation is therefore a grammatical one. Such an investigation sheds light on our problem by clearing misunderstandings away. Mis-understandings concerning the use of words, caused, among other things, by certain analogies between the forms of expression in different regions of our language (125).

Wittgenstein characterizes a language game as the "whole, consisting of language and the actions into which it is woven" (126). Exemplifying this by means of his own language game is, for Wittgenstein, "not an indirect means of explaining. - in default of a better one" (127). Rather it is already an explanation and, in fact, the only possible one. Essential to this view is the modified assumption already known to us from the *Tractatus*.

...every sentence in our language 'is in order as it is'. That is to say, we are not striving after an ideal, as if our ordinary vague sentences had not yet got a quite unexceptionable sense, and a perfect language awaited construction by us. - On the other hand it seems clear that where there is sense there must be perfect order. - So there must be perfect order even in the vaguest sentence (128).

In this conception of a language-game, "the whole process of using the words" (129) masks the tension which lie in the relationships between a thing and a word, between language and states-of-affairs. Indeed, the understanding of the general rules governing a language game guarantees the understanding of empirical behavioral facts that follows from this rule.

However, does the knowledge of rules governing a language game also guarantee the understanding of propositions in a religious context and the corresponding conduct resulting from it? The question is whether such a language game, if the attempt of an external specification of its rules does not reveal their meaning, could not more accurately be interpreted as a "dialectical unity encompassing the use of language, the way of life, and the understanding of the world, i.e. as a unit that does not exclude the contradiction between its constitutive moments (130).

Without knowing the rules of the game determining, for instance, the religious conceptions of a monk, the meaningful conduct of such a monk would neither be perceptable nor understandable (131). The question is whether the knowledge of the rules according to which the monk lives will also enable us to understand his motives for choosing this religious form of life. As we have already seen, Wittgenstein himself does not attach any importance to that question. For him, the truth-criterion for a language game is the reference to its practical function.

A religious language game, however, does not at all function this way, because they imply permanent inquiry into its own presuppositions and into meaning. What can be said of theology that represents exact reflections on religious propositions may be said to apply also to philosophy and to the philosophy of religion. These philosophies "have never been solely contemplative (or descriptive) science. Since their beginnings, they have been in everlasting and absolute revolution" (132) and, because of their critique of the corresponding form of life they have been corrective and regulative agents. A study of the history of the occidental Christian religion might clarify how, under the influence of theology and philosophy, religion is characterized by the cooperation and the opposition of language games. This has brought about the dispute between the variety of forms for understanding religion. Next to the prophetic and the mystic types of piety, there is also the rational and the philosophical understanding of religion. Next to Jakob Böhme's experience of all senses and Meister Eckhart's *unio mystica*, there are the questions of Thomas Aquinus about the relationship of *lumen naturale* to *lumen gloriae*. Whereas Hegel holds the idea of an analogy "*participata similitudo*", presupposing the thought of resemblance, Friedrich W. J. Schelling disavows this connection for the sake of the transcendence of God. In its history, the Christian occidental religion has been concerned with self-investigation into its principles and into its forms of life, and thus reformatory correction is a component of its reality.

If this is true, then the linguistic pragmatism of Wittgenstein and his followers, which claims to derive the sense of language through the use of language cannot be considered a philosophic method. It is itself "the most general way of characterizing what can be called the beginning of philosophizing whatsoever, i.e. the recognition of every immediate linguistic sense in theory and practice, in universal impartiality" (133).

II. ON THE PROBLEM OF THE USE OF RELIGIOUS LANGUAGE

1. Rationalist criticism of the religious proposition

Wittgenstein's proposal to investigate religious statements with regard to the structure of depth grammar, paved the way for philosophical considerations of religion within analytic philosophy. However, this cannot to be equated with the demonstration of the meaning of a religious statement. Such proof remained a task to be accomplished. In the same way as linguistic analysis failed to silence positivism, the positivistic arguments against the claims of the meaning and truth of religious statements were also rejected, with the withdrawal of the ban on these statements.

In linguistic analysis, Flew's gardener parable (134) represents the modified version of rejecting the religious statement's claim of meaning, with a violence matched only by early positivism. The question may remain unanswered as to whether Flew's criticism of religious language aims to sharpen our attention of use terms that do not simply denote something already existent and can be shown as such, for instance, this book, this fountain pen; or as to whether it is his primary concern to bring the meaninglessness of his belief to the attention of the believer, who is expressing himself by using religious statements. The philosophical and historical significance expressed in this parable lies in its having set in motion the meta-religious discussion. This critique, which is neither new nor evidences intellectual thoroughness, is presented in a way so true-to-life that it forces the philosophizing individual not oriented in a positivistic way, as well as the believer, to comment on its arguments.

The parable that Flew uses stems from John Wisdom. In his essay "Gods" (135), Wisdom introduced this parable into the discussion in order to demonstrate the specific usage of the word "God" in our language, and to illustrate that the question of the existence of God is not a question of the existence of an empirical subject. Flew, whose version of the parable became the standard one, altered the allegory, presenting in it - with literary embellishment - the well-known reproach of the immunizing strategy (conventional twist) (136) against the metaphysical differentiation which religious statements have undergone. The alleged intention of this differentiation was to protect metaphysical statements against the objections of the empirical sciences. The argument supporting this reproach is a statement traceable to Carnap i.e. that in the religious proposition, a statement that originally had been understood to be empirical has been emptied of its meaning in the same way, as in Flew's parable, that the assumption of an imaginary gardener has been modified so that it died "the death by a thousand qualifications" (137).

The criterion for the possibility of judging religious statements replaced, within meta-religious analysis, the requirement of verification. This came about after this requirement and simultaneously with it the attempt to associate the question of the sense or the meaninglessness of propositions with the requirement of their empirical verification had been rejected as untenable. Accordingly an empirical verification, as commented upon by Popper, was "just as destructive of science as ... of metaphysics" (138).

> This criterium excludes from the realm of meaning all scientific
> theories,...for these are no more reducible to observation reports
> than the so-called metaphysical pseudo-propositions (139).

In agreement with Popper's alternative requirement for falsification of scientific statements, that assumes that these statements can be maintained to be true not only when they explain the existent phenomena, but also when the conditions can be indicated under which they are not true. Flew puts forward the following question concerning religious propositions:

> What would have to occur or to have occurred to constitute for
> you a disproof of the love of, or of the existence of God (140)?

With the falsification requirement taken over from Popper, Flew thinks he has found a criterion that is absolutely necessary to indicate a truth value of a statement for which religious propositions are inadequate. Yet the expressed reference to the criteria suggested by Popper for checking scientific statements is missing. Even a superficial reading of Flew's text shows that those criteria against which a religious statement is measured in an open or revealed way, are identical with those criteria developed by Popper, or are at least very similar to them (141). The empirical applicability of the conclusions required from a proposition are valid for Popper, along with the logical comparison of these conclusions with one another in order to prove the non-contradictory inner nature of these deductions. For Popper, these investigations are valid whether or not the logical form of the theory or the comparison with other theories for the purpose of pointing out scientific progress as the main criterion for all scientific statement, (i.e. for a statement claiming truth) are of a tautological character (142). According to the criticism of the induction principle, that maintains that a general proposition can never be verified through observation alone, the requirement of empirical demonstration for at least deductive statements means that it must be possible to indicate at least those cases in which the sense of an assertion cannot be proven to be true (143). Popper has made the negative corroboration of a statement and of the theory implied in this statement, the condition for checking its truth-value in order to avoid the difficulty that, with the exclusion of metaphysical statements, all scientific statements would also be eliminated.

> Admittedly, if we do not know how to test a theory, we may be doubtful whether there is anything at all of the kind (or level) described by it, and if we positively know that it cannot be tested, then our doubts will grow; we may suspect that it is a mere myth or a fairy-tale. *But if a theory is testable, then it implies that events of a certain kind cannot happen; and so it asserts something about reality* (144).

For the empirical sciences, Popper proposed recognizing only those statements as scientific and true that do not deduce statements based on observable aspects contradicting other observation-statements. One calls a theory empirical if possibilities can be named for falsifying it, i.e. when the class of possible falsifications is not empty. In this connection it is not the logical impossibility of the verifiable contents of incompatible situations that declares a statement to be true. It can merely negate its empirical existence. The observation, for instance, "all ravens are black" excludes the existence of white ravens. The intersubjective and testable observation that a family of white ravens lives in the New York Zoo is sufficient to disprove the previous statement. On the other hand, the religious statement "all men are loved by God", as it is understood by the believer, is not refuted by the statement that "in New York, a child is dying from an inoperable pharyngitic cancer" (145). Popper sees the religious statement affirmable in such a way that the class of falsification possibilities remains empty for it and that therefore, this statement cannot be falsified.

While Popper sees the criterion between scientific and metaphysical propositions in the applicability of the principle of falsification, Flew concludes the insufficient meaningfulness and insufficient truthfulness of religious propositions form the insufficient applicability of his principle. In this connection, he takes as his premise the grammatical similarity of religious statements to empirical ones.

A statement like "God created heaven and earth" has, at first glance, as Flew correctly remarks, the look of a "vast cosmological assertion" (146). The former statement is, however, distinguished from the latter by the fact that it cannot be understood by means of reference to situations that are incompatible with it. Following Flew, Crombie states:

> In the case of "God created the world", if I am to know what this means, I must have some idea of the incompatible situations, and if I am to be able in this way to envisage them, they must be situations which can be constructed by rearranging familiar elements, and in that case what the assertion we are considering rules out must be something which logically might be the case (147).

While Flew sees the meaninglessness of such a statement confirmed by its rule-infringement, Crombie tries conversely, by making use of this very rule-infringement in regard to religious statements, to establish their reference to reality. Thus he chooses a middle course between the possibilities proposed by Flew and Popper for understanding a religious proposition.

If one follows Popper and not Flew, then the possibility of falsification is only a characteristic of differentiation between the empirico-scientific and the so-called metaphysical propositions (148). By delimiting metaphysical propositions in this way, they are not yet categorized as non-understandable and irrational, as long as they refer to problematic situations and suggest solutions to cope with them. This means that the impossibility of falsifying a theory must not be valued as a blemish, especially if motivations for scientific research initiated from it which according to Popper applied to some theories held by the Pre-Socratics (149).

If Popper and with him Hans Albert consider it possible to develop "metaphysical ideas" into theories which are refutable in principle and competitive with previous scientific theories, then it must after all be doubtful that a similar procedure may be possible for the religious proposition as well. As a matter of fact, Popper and Albert maintain that a metaphysical theory can be changed into a scientific one only under the condition that the metaphysical theory does not *claim a priori* validity. In this context, metaphysics would be assigned "some type of heuristic function for the scientific formation of a theory" (150). This would be comparable to utopia for political thinking (151). In the opinion of Popper, "scientific research, seen psychologically, is probably not at all possible without a belief that it is not worth discussing scientifically, i.e. without a 'metaphysical' belief in some highly obscure theoretical ideas" (152). It cannot be denied that metaphysical and religious considerations simply cannot be excluded from the history of the formation of scientific theories. It is, however, a different question whether the religious presuppositions that stimulated the natural sciences fully exhaust themselves in their function as a stimulus for scientific progress, or whether they are not distinguished from other similar stimuli in a specific way. The effort to grant religious statements a meaning must not lead to the fact that the difference is blurred between differing metaphysical ideas (e.g. Utopias) as they are seen by Albert and Popper and the eschatological hope typical of the religious statement and expressed by the Word of Promise. Utopias are meant to be forced "to undergo revisions through testing on the resistance to reality" (153), whereas the problem of the "sameness of the Utopia or the steady insecurity regarding this sameness" (154) does not apply to religious ideas and statements of belief. As a matter of fact, even religious thought knows the danger of ideological misrepresentation in an apocalyptic dream. The believer, the individual, who makes religious statements, maintains that he possesses true conviction, - in contrast to Utopian insecurity when he knows himself to be free from apocalyptic dreams (155). Whether this acting out of belief takes place rightly or wrongly in view of history is a question that must not elude investigation. Therefore, it is not possible either to pass judgement before such an investigation, nor to allow religious statements and statements of the empirical sciences to be equated. An explanatory strategy, that consists in confronting and comparing non-scientific statements with statments of a scientific nature would, by leveling this difference, eventually bring about a mere *petitio principii*, if as a result of investigation, religious statements appear to be non-scientific.

To maintain that a statement is true against every human perception and insight, as believers do regarding some of their statements, is opposed to critical thought and the sciences. In addition to the right to maintain such a claim to validity, it must be discovered what kind of interest is decisive for such an assertion. Flew accepts as proven that the motive for denying the direct or indirect applicability of religious statements in empirical theories, as well as the negation of a possible fasification of such statements, is to protect these empirical theories from competition with scientific ones. In order to reject such a reproach of an "immunization strategy" belief as the foundation of religious statements must not "be presented as unfounded knowledge. One would, on the contrary, have to admit that belief is the best founded thing because it alone has that in which all doubt is conquered" (156). This evidence would have to be demonstrated. The difference between religious and scientific statements would then have to be sought in the fact that scientific statements, also start from "belief": but this belief's goal is to replace "belief" with knowledge ("trial and error"). In contrast religious statements do not look for subsequent substantiation by scientific research. However, Flew's suspicion of immunization presupposes that religious belief is not the end, but the beginning or the search for truth. This undeniably applies - even if religious statements are used as hypotheses of scientific research - only when a primary explanatory interest in scientific procedures can be proven in the case of such religious statements (157).

It seems to me justified to interpret the fact that a religious statement does not compete with a scientific statement, with a theory that in principle may be confuted, as a deficiency that has to be removed, even "in the light of the principle of critical examination" (158). However this is justifiable only if one, as above, presupposes that religious and scientific statements are supported by similar interests (159). If similar interests cannot be demonstrated, then the following question remains: What kind of meaning and what kind of truth can be attributed to a religious statement, if it cannot be measured by the standards of the "logic of research" ?

The "immunization strategy" reproach originates from the undeniable fact that the arena of authority of religious statements became more and more limited. Even theology could no longer be looked upon as a universal science that could answer every question. We cannot deny that the field of belief is reduced as the field of knowledge increases. It would be rash to see this shift of focal points only negatively. The ousting of religous statements from the realm of scientific research might clarify the intention of these statements. In this context, an approach of science to those realms accessible to scientific considerations and methods provides not only the corresponding explanation for natural procedures but may also provide religious thinking with new insights into what the subject of religion really is and what may be considered to be a religious statement.

> The notion of atmospheric electricity, for example, was introduced to account in a scientific way for lightning and thunder, and to that extent displaced Zeus as the thundermaker, but it was never intended to take over Zeus' role as the "divine father" as well. Rather the two roles have been separated, so that thunderstorms are no longer regarded in the old way, as a topic for theology (160).

This quote from Stephen Toulmin indicates that he does not yet see a justification for the supposition that the concept of God has become totally unsuitable. As natural scientific research progresses, the concept of God has become superfluous as an explanatory and relevant component of natural procedures. This fits in with the picture that immunization strategy gives. Yet Stephen Toulmin classifies such a supposition as being just as barely divorced from mythology as the statements of cosmology during the Middle Ages.

> If we do think ourselves myth-free, when we are not, that is (I am suggesting) largely because the material from which we construct

our myths is taken from the sciences themselves. The situation is the one we meet in those trickiest of crime which the detective himself turns out to have done the deed: he is the last man we suspect. ... And why, after all, should not the purposes of myth be served as effectively by picturing the world in terms of mythical machines as by invoking mythical personages? Still, in the main, it is because our contemporary myths are scientific ones that we fail to acknowledge them as being myths at all. The old picture of the world has been swept away; Poseidon and Wotan have suffered death by ridicule; and people not unnaturally look to the scientist for a substitute.

Therein lies the misunderstanding, for only in part were the ancient myths half-baked science, and only in part was their role an explanatory one. So far as this was so, we can reasonably look on the natural sciences as their descendants; but only so far. The other non-scientific motives behind them remain, and the sciences are not obliged to cater for these (161).

The reproach that Popper in his scientific teaching, "like the positivists eventually wanted to give exclusive validity to the concept of experience and empirical testability corresponding to the experimental method" (162), is repeated - by expressly referring to Flew's interpretation of Popper's falsification demand - within the analytical philosophy of religion. Hick has shaken the basic validity of Flew's requirement with his statement that matter-of-factly, ignores the difference between the respective possibilities of validity for mathematical and religious statements.

It must be rash to assume...that verification and falsification must always be related in ...symmetrical fashion. They do not necessarily stand to one another as do the two sides of a coin, so that once the coin is spun it must fall on one side or the other. There are cases in which verification and falsification each correspond to a side on a different coin, so that one can fail to verify without this failure constituting falsification (163).

The emotive school of the analytical philosophy of religion recognized Flew's arguments to a large extent and methodically left the limits set by the falsification principle as well as the well accepted verification principle. In its extended form the verification principle does not insist on the possibility of direct revertion verifying the contents in sensual data, but it demands the indication of rules for using words and sentences used in order to check their agreement with the function assigned to them in the statement in which they are employed. We are to judge, in this respect, Flew's ungenerous but not unjustified question on the adequacy of the word "gardener" in the statement:

"Some gardener must tend this plot" (164), that one must understand in a religious sense. The same semantic difficulty arises in the question on the common character of and on the differences between human and divine love, when it is said of God that he loves us like a father. Undoubtedly, the predicate "love", when referring to a person, does not have the same meaning when it refers to God. Flew states:

> ...We see a child dying of inoperable cancer of the throat. His earthly father is driven frantic in his efforts to help, but his Heavenly father reveals no obvious sign of concern....God's love is "not a merely human love" or it is "an inscrutable love" perhaps -- and we realize that such sufferings are quite compatible with the truth of the assertion that "God loves us as a father (but, of course,...)". We are reassured again. But...perhaps we ask: what is this assurance of God's (appropriately qualified) love worth, what is this apparent guarantee really a guarantee against (165)?

Here Flew is trying to put the claim of the meaning and truth of the religious statement in question from two sides. The first side is from the stance of an analogical conception: i.e. when one thinks that one predicates something of God, one only predicates something known to us about humanity. In its historical form, the conception of analogy has managed seeing the guarantee of the possibility of the meaningful predication of God in relationship to creation. Here Flew finds the starting point for making his second objection: Christian monotheism - and that's what he is referring to - has, in contrast to the dualistic conceptions of religion as they are found, for instance in Manichaeism, given up the possibility of explaining the development of evil without any relationship to God. The creator *ex nihilo*, as the Lord of heaven and earth, does not find Himself, in His power and freedom, in relationship to other gods who might have been able to set a limit to His creative work.

With reference to religious statements, the way in which Flew presents his objections indicates a modified linguistic-analytical approach - comparable to early neopositivists (166). The reference to the theistic antinomy of the absolute goodness of the Creator of the world, and to the reality of evil in the world, is already based on the inquiry into a genuine logic typical of religious propositions. Here sceptical reflection is no longer founded on a mere identification of prevailing sense with empirical data, in order to submit religious statements to the same procedure of refutation used for sentences like "Caesar is a prime number" (Carnap) and "the naked child is dressed in a wonderful nightgown" (Schlick).

While the inquiry into the origin of evil has only secondary significance for the analytical discussion of the criteria of a religious proposition, the question concerning the possibility of an analogous predication of God and men forms a focus in the linguistic-analytical discussion. As a matter of fact, with Flew it already became clear that the discussion about the sense of religious statements must not start with the conception of analogy, because it is already preceded by the belief in God as the creator of heaven and earth. Yet, it was still not certain if a change in the direction of the procedure, would achieve a similar result meaning that the quest for the truth claim of religious propositions, in its turn, can be explained only by religious propositions whose truth claims are in question. Only one thing was definite: Given the idea of creation, if I determine the love attributed to God is analogous to the love of man, neither the presupposition in the light of which this determination is carried out is justified, nor is its result. This is the case because the attempt to analogously predicate the Creator and the creature does not prove the analogous relationship between them but implies it. According to Dorothy Emmet, this means that:

> (the) appropriateness of the analogy depends on the reality of the relation which it exemplifies. The existence of the relation cannot be established by analogical argument; but if there are independent grounds for asserting it, it can be described analogically (167).

The cognitive tendencies of the analytical philosophy of religion that recognize a proposition like that of God as the creator of the world as a religious statement and want to clarify its truth content by meta-theoretical questioning, cannot evade the problem of analogy. Their attempt to substantiate religious propositions without a recourse to belief but not without disregarding the peculiar character of these proposition, again and again stumbles upon the problems connected with the inquiry into the relationship between language and reality. A linguistic-analytical investigation, for which the significant intention of the word "God" and its reference to a state-of-affairs intended by it is under discussion, cannot ignore the fact that the relationship between religious language and everyday language is the condition for the possibility of understanding religious propositions. Otherwise it is only guided by the logical syntax of religious propositions, is not attempting to reveal the deep-grammatical structures and connections. Therefore, according to McPherson, the following question must be asked:

> Now what do such beliefs mean? How are we to understand them? Or is it wrong to try to "understand" them? Are they absurd or non-sensical? If they are not, then, why not? If they are,

then how exactly is it that they are absurd or nonsensical? Is it because they do not make "literal" sense? But do they then have some "deeper meaning" which is not their literal meaning; do they make sense on a different "level" from that of literal meaning? And, if so, what is this level, and how is it different from the level of literal meaning (168)?

2. The three main trends in the analytical philosophy of religion

The various trends within the analytical philosophy of religion outlined here, can only be clearly separated from one another *in abstracto*. In reality, they are often combined, in addition the motifs turning up in the various groupings are often used in arguments for or against the other. Therefore, it is possible to note specific tendencies in the analytical philosophy of religion that are sometimes absorbed by other tendencies or even, having been discovered to be irrelevant in their original form are called to our attention in a new guise and with a new name. It is in this succession of shifts in position that the analytical philosophy of religion reveals itself in a respective refinement of the instrument of reasoning supporting a position.

Despite their differences and occasional contradictions these three attempts agree that the claim of meaning of the religious proposition cannot be proven by verifying or falsifying statements relating to sensual-empirical data. Opinions are divided concerning the understanding of the claim to meaning of such propositions being cognitive and verifiable, or non-cognitive. No matter how individual attempts to rehabilitate the religious question are made according to propositional analysis, this must not be looked upon as a restoration of metaphysics and its methods as opposed by early positivism.

From its positivistic predecessors, the metareligious theory has adopted the conception that language as language is the measure by which a statement can be considered to be meaningful. If it had to be recognized that the desired result was not achieved by reverting to empirical experience in refuting the independent role and the substantivation of philosophical concepts imputed to metaphysics, then the tendency would grow toward making language an absolute datum. This would dispense with a direct relation to the subject matter of religious statements by taking the religious statement as a datum that has to be analyzed and elucidated in its meaningfulness. However, this turn from a critique of metaphysics to a critique of religious language does not imply a dissociation from empirical experience and an abandonment of the verification principle. Although testing the truth character no longer expressly depends on the possibility of tracing the religious statement back to sensual data, the requirement for a possible relationship to reality indirectly remains. This is more or less obvious depending on the metareligious diversity as truth transcends the mere meaning of a sentence in its grammatical and logical aspects.

3. Neutrality in method and religious interest

There is a methodical limit for the attempt to give a nonpositivistic foundation for the religious statement. Irrespective of the admittedly non-empirical content of the propositions under examination, and in accordance with an understanding of the philosophy of religion as an anylysis of religious language, this limit determines:

1) that the explanation and justification of such propositions have to be made without appealing to non-empirical, metaphysical principles and should, if possible, have a reference to directly available facts;

2) a strict neutrality of the method applied should be maintained toward the subject under examination. Applied to the sphere of religious propositions, this means that it cannot be the task of meta-religious reflection to put forward reasons for or against a decision of faith.

> The analytic method does not commit the one using it to any specific stand on questions such as the ultimate nature of reality or the limits of knowledge ... and, indeed, some of its contemporary employers profess their complete freedom from all epistemological and metaphysical beliefs... While as a technique it is neutral to them all, what it is allowed to reveal is frequently determined by the stands taken on these matters by the individual philosopher using it (170).

Whereas the possibility of carrying out the first point can be examined only in a treatise on the analytical theory of religion, which follows in chapters III - V, the requirement of neutrality is a separate problem. Therefore, this will now be discussed without taking a set position on the truth-claim of religious statements.

In maintaining the claim of methodical neutrality, the analytic philosophy of religion protests *a limine* against being mistaken for a religious doctrine. It trys to secure a scientific status as the scientific theory of religion.

> This method implies the notion that it is *not* the task of philosophy of religion to defend a specific form of the Christian faith, or for that matter, of any religious conviction.

(1) Philosophy of religion is not a branch of theology, nor a preparation for systematic theology.

(2) Its task is not to broaden a faith which tends to be too much absorbed in itself, by means of a consideration of the "truths" of science, art and philosophy.

The conception of philosophy as analysis of languages implies the interpretation of philosophy of religion as analysis of religious language. This means that philosophy of religion is simply a branch of philosophy in general (171).

The securing of this status is bought at the expense of the restriction of philosophy to analysis. Such a reduction of the philosophical problems to linguistic analysis advances the view that philosophy itself does not work out its own propositions but serves only to clarify the insights of rigorous thought.

For the philosophy of religion, the most important questions are: First, to what extent does the requirement of neutrality want only to prevent reflection whose validity has not been proven and thus to prejudice a definite answer to the claim of meaning of religious propositions to be included in the process of knowledge? Second, to what extent does the requirement of neutrality imply simultaneously a suspension of the question of truth in religion, no matter whether it seems possible to answer this question or not? Here it must be taken into account that the realization that the content of religious conviction does not concern objects of knowledge, but objects of faith, does not necessarily exclude the question of truth as irrelevant. Even from this position it leaves the possibility of searching for an answer open.

Such a starting point lies, for instance, in Kant's attempt to restrict knowledge in order to make room for faith. This attempt has met with the approval of the analytical philosophy of religion at least in so far as this philosophy sees, in the attempt, the rejection of a metaphysical justification of statements of faith. However, it goes its own way instead of following Kant as he objects to leaving the justification of the claim of the validity of religious propositions to the proofs of God's existence and to the deduction of His attributes, and attempts to reveal the transcendental-logical problems of the concepts of believe and of what is believed. This is all the more surprising because it is particularly the transcendental problems which the analytical philosophy of religion confronts in its concern for the different structures of faith and knowledge and the type of intentionality in statements of faith etc. The reason for this is not to be sought in Kant's neglect of reflection on language, but rather in the fact that the analytical philosophy of religion treats language as a *de facto* existent system of meaning. It is content with making sure that this system of meaning is used consistently and without contradictions. Analytical philosophy sees the requirement for neutrality as best fulfilled in the following manner: by being impartial to meaning within religious language and by restricting its interest to the guarantee that the language of faith becomes aware of the specific status of its semantics. It is essential to such a program of neutrality that the inquiry into what is really the subject of analysis should be disregarded. Meta-religious theory is deluded that its discourse is detached and isolated from what is being discussed. It does not realize that even a descriptive procedure of analysis already establishes a relation to the state-of-affairs under discussion. The erroneous estimation of their own procedure subjects a neutral analysis to an unintentional dependence upon empiricism. This analysis has set up its program by refraining from any kind of judgement and by examining only meanings and kinds of meaning in religious language without being at all affected by the substance of what their sentences state. It is a matter of fact that elucidating the structure of a religious proposition, as well as clarifying the meaning of religious terms and their interrelations, implies that they are delimited from other kinds of sentence and word (e.g. moralistic, aesthetic and scientific). However, this delimitation process runs contrary to the concern of meta-religious reflection because such an attempt necessitates the working out of categories that would go beyond the mere descriptive program of analysis. Therefore, linguistic analysis is forced to trust the empirically existent practice of language when defining what is to be considered as a religious proposition and when selecting the words and sentences that are to be examined for religious semantic content (172).

In one further respect, the opinion that analysis is a "technique", reflecting a neutral procedure, is problematic. For example analysis cannot account for the dilemma that religious language does not mean the same thing to different thinkers. The prerequisites of a neutral analysis would require this. This can only be explained if the thesis of neutrality is abandoned and if one is ready to acknowledge the presence of a normative element as a cause for the divergence of interpretations.

> One who holds that all talk of the transcendent is nonsensical finds analysis revealing only attitudes or feelings at the heart of religious assertions, while another whose positions in this area are less constrictive might find analysis helpful in isolating and characterizing the knowledge-content which believers insist is present in at least some of their uses of religious assertions (173).

Thus analysis unintentionally assumes a position of critique that enables it on the basis of actual experience to prejudge prescriptively not only what has or does not have to be or not to be considered a religious proposition and what constitutes religious meaning.

If the aim of philosophy is taken to be clarification through the method of linguistic analysis, then it would seem that the aim and method of philosophy of religion would be the clarification of religious language through an analysis of the language used in a religious context - that is, language in so far as it is related to the religious act of worship (174).

Despite the *a priori* non-qualified empirical origin of the concept of religion underlying its analysis, this shortcoming need not jeopardize the undertaking of the analytical philosophy of religion as a whole. It must be admitted that the analytical philosophy of religion considers it indispensable as it verifies the truth of a religious proposition, to take into account the historical experiences of a language community and therefore the life pattern of the proposition in question. The alternative to analytical and empirical deduction would be to claim a validity superior to the empirical concept. It would not be realized in a concept of religion based on pure reason because that would entail the risk of falsely "rationalizing" the reality of religion (175). It could be realized in a concept giving unity to the otherwise rhapsodically accumulated material of meta-religious analysis by means of a transcendental principle. The characteristic abstention of the analytical procedure from re-examining the specific method in principle, precludes the possibility of even thinking, let alone unfolding, an interaction of empirical and *a priori* religious concepts in the definition of what can be called a religious proposition. That is why no use is made of the insight implicitly gained by renouncing the neutrality thesis which maintains that religious language is not to be taken as mere talk about something, but as a movement involving a decision of the believer. Many analytical philosophers tend to equate the logic of religious speech, including the decision it expresses, with the logic of theoretical statements. They look for the justification of the religious proposition in the non-dialectical separation of engagement and statement.

The neglect of the Kantian transcendental problematic of religion, the neglect of the inquiry into the conditions of possibility and right, as well as the concentration upon describing and analyzing religious propositions as empirical phenomena cannot justify the refusal to accept the analytical philosophy of religion as philosophy or to see it as a rigorous investigation of religion. It is philosophy 1) because it does not indulge in its own empirical research but is dependent on the material of the study of religion, and 2) because its work is directed towards comprehending the genuine structures and rules of the religious proposition. This is never done by a science or history of religion. Finally, the inquiry made by analytical philosophers into the claim of meaning for religious propositions and their justification goes far beyond mere description and analysis of a concrete state-of-affairs. Above all, this inquiry comes into the foreground where the thesis of neutrality is abandoned. Hence, already in its initial questioning, the analytical philosophy of religion, partly without any reflection, extends the methods of description and analysis in a way that would be unthinkable in an empirical science. Moreover, although allegedly dispensing with a transcendental deduction of categories, analytical philosophy tacitly employs such categories as they occur e.g. when a judgement is made on what a religious proposition is. Likewise, from the moment meta-religious reflection renounces the thesis of neutrality and begins to analyze such propositions in which the believer gives account for his belief, analysis no longer puts forward the question "*quid facti*", but puts forward the transcendentally orientated question "*quid iuris*". Here it should be taken into account that the believer's language usually does not give the reasons that determine his stance. Very often, these reasons can only be deduced indirectly from his utterances and behavior (176).

If one starts from the assumption that reasoned reflection has its place in theology (177), and that it is in theology that the believer gives account of his religious conceptions and actions, then theology receives the task of pointing out to religious consciousness a learning process resulting in the possibility that consciousness becomes aware of its religious contents. For the analysis of religious language, it must be taken into account that such a learning process must be orientated by the historical development of religious consciousness. It occurs only as the formation of consciousness develops in rational discourse that includes the history and origin of the contents of belief.

Moreover, we should keep in mind that theology, too, is linked to religion. Theology's task consists in transforming the content of religious propositions into scientific ones - meaning that any attempt at meta-religious analysis is confronted with the situation of a dialectical conversation necessitating an inquiry into the entire tradition and history of anyone using the words "religion" or "God" in order to discover their religious meaning (178). This complicates the situation of the linguistic analist. It is hard to see how he should be able to adequately comprehend religious thought as expressed in religious language as well as the history of religious thought, without having had some kind of religious experience. The simplest form of this experience requires one to know "what it means to call a particular assertion or utterance part of a religious belief as distinct from a moral code or a scientific theory" (179).

The difficulty of determining the meaning of religious statements in this case is similar to that encountered with moral statements (180). The description and the objective analysis of their propositions also contains the requirement of adopting the original standpoint of these propositions. For this reason, the distinction made between theoretical description and attitudinal meaning in the emotive theory of religion is extremely problematic. For example, whoever identifies himself as a Christian in conversation with an atheist, presumes a standpoint on reality. No matter whether one plays the role of the Christian or of the atheist in this dialog, one elicits, by maintaining the truth of statements, an action forcing the dialog partner to take a presupposed linguistic representation as real provided that one's utterances are not taken as merely verbal ones, but are given a well-founded basis for the assumption that one is its advocate. The fact that the arguments under discussion must be taken as a process in the course of which one partner may always expect the other to review his previous position and adopt a new stance, does not by any means alter the necessity to acknowledge as a reality the final result of the discussion, however opposed this may be to the conviction of either dialog partner. Here, the point is not to convince the partner of a theoretical truth, but simply to convince him in such a way that the state-of-affairs which he admits to be true are reflected in his actions. For instance, the fool in Hare's parable does not only theoretically consent to the general proposition that his superiors will not make an attempt on his life, but that the acknowledgement of truth is reflected in his actions in such a way that these actions are no longer prompted by the fear of his superior (181).

The similarity with ethics becomes evident in the fact that religious knowledge as belief represents not only theoretical understanding, but also implies an interest in the concrete content of belief. Therewith arises a set of questions similar to that of Socrates' proposition concerning virtue as a kind of knowledge. In the same way as the word "knowing" in Socrates' sentence, the word "believing" in our case is not to be understood as a merely theoretical intention. In addition belief must not "remain ... the last (and then empty) word, either as an achievement of theoretical cognition or as a 'positivism' distancing itself from reason transgressed, but by thinking, belief must materialize itself in a 'knowledge' which at the same time, ... is the rational practice of fundamental action" (182).

4. The uniqueness of the religious use of language

The preceding reflections on the thesis of neutrality should facilitate an understanding of the essential elements of the position of the analytical philosophy of religion concerning religious statements. It has already been demonstrated that the linguistic philosophy of religion attempts above all to discuss the problem of religious truth as an inquiry into propositional truth. Thus, the elucidation of a concept of religion is replaced by "what appears to be a more promising task" in an attempt "to characterize the nature of religious language -- how it is used, how it functions and what kind of meaning it may be said to have" (183). Quite in line with Wittgenstein's objections to essentialism, this philosophy of religion turns to analysis, to discover through research into the structural and semantic system of religious language an answer to the question of the role that language plays in organizing the world of experience shared by those speaking this language.

> By examining religious language we may gain some insights into the manyfold complex of human experience which we call religion (184).

Thus, as a first step in following the path of late Wittgenstein, we have taken into account how he meta-linguisticly overcomes neopositivism by recognizing religion as a separate semantic realm of linguistic sense. Yet the extent to which religious statements may also have a claim to truth has not been decided.

For the analytical philosopher, the only established fact is that it is not difficult to discover "that religious language is not meaningful in a straight-forwardly scientific or logical sense" (185). As a matter of fact, the study of the wide variety of the usage of religious language may be regarded as a more fruitful and promising undertaking than the quandry-filled efforts of logical positivism. Because of its procedure of classification and description, it involves the danger of obscuring the quest for truth or falsity.

> For many of the items in a list of religious uses of language must cover non-cognitive modes of expression which are not properly characterizable as either true or false; and this circumstance can (although it need not) direct attention away from the more central question of the cognitive claims of religion. The problem which they raise is not of course the (logically) simple question as to whether such claims are true; this is not a question which comes within the province of philosophy. The problem is rather precisely what these claims are, what kind of truth (if any) is professed, what kind of fact (if any) alleged (186).

A naturalism becomes perceptible within the analytical philosophy of religion that maintains that language has to be analyzed as something given. It is similar to that criticized by E. Gellner concerning epistemological theory. The criticism of the descriptive program as is shared by some analysts who are able to think only in terms of the "third-person viewpoint" (187), intends to re-instate the "first-person viewpoint" in its right; within the framework of the analytical understanding of language. It correctly puts in question a possible theory of epistemology in which the "first-person viewpoint" does not take precedence over the "third-person viewpoint". This is a reflection that must influence the analytical philosophy of religion if it regards itself as a theory of religion (188). Hick's reservations against the methods of description and classification method, as recommended by Binkley and others and his request for a "more adequate account" of religious statements acknowledge Ernest Gellner's criticism of analytical philosophy even for the analysis of religious propositions. They try to break through the *circulus vitiosus* between linguistic philosophy and logical positivism advocated by Gellner.

> Linguistic philosophy is only possible as the second stage of a process of which Logical Positivism was the first: if all transcendental theories are first eliminated by Logical Positivism, Linguistic Philosophy can then overcome Positivism. But it would not prevail if the transcendental theories were still in the running. Positivism is like the paper in the children's game that can wrap the stone but can be cut by the scissors, that could not affect the stone though it can cut the paper. It is parasitic on Positivism which it also destroys.
>
> Thus Logical Positivism is invoked as a tacit premiss when necessary (189).

The task of defining the religious statement is more important than the quest for the character of truth in religious propositions. Whether all of them have to be added to the group of non-cognitive propositions, or whether some of them may be rightly designated as cognitive propositions, is preceded by the task of defining the religious statement. Regarding the formal characteristics implied in such a definition there is full agreement. It is acknowledged from the beginning that such statements are religious ones that directly or indirectly claim to define God.

> ... all theological statements are, by definition, about God, ... however they are worded, we may say that God is the subject of them all (statements about grace, for example, are not about a commodity which is dispensed from heaven, but about what God does to men) ... theological statements are to be interpreted as if their subject was a particular individual, and yet differ in logical character from all other statements about particular individuals (190).

As mentioned, next to this characteristic attributed to the subject-concept (God) in religious statements it is possible to highlight as a further characteristic "that nothing which happens is allowed to necessitate the withdrawal of theological statements; they are allowed to overrule all factual objections" (191). In this connection it must be noted that position three mentioned initially will be analysed in detail (V), although to designate facts of experience objecting to the truth-claim. It does this in full recognition of the diverse rules for interpreting empirical and religious statements.

a) Anomaly of the Subject

To what extent religious propositions differ from all other propositions in regard to their subjects, has already become evident in the discussion of believing and unbelieving researchers on the understanding of the concept "gardener" in Flew's parable. Admittedly, a comparative analysis of meaning allows a delimitation of the concept 'subject' in religious statements from others that are taken from the vernacular or from scientific language. Yet in the end it reveals only an anomaly characteristic of all religious statements.

Therefore, the proposition "God loves men" is syntactically formed in the same way as the proposition "Tom loves Mary". But the question "Who is God?" can never be answered with the indication "That is God", as in the case of the second proposition, "That is Tom" (192).

The best answer to the first question is, "He created us". An apparently improper answer is given to an apparently proper question. Therefore, I.M. Crombie characterizes the concept God, which takes the place of the subject in the religious proposition, as an "proper-improper" concept.

> It resembles a proper name like "Tom" in that we are told that
> statements about God are direct statements about God and not
> oblique statements about something else, and yet it differs from
> ordinary proper names in that its use is not based fundamentally,
> as theirs is, on acquaintance with the being it denotes. It is not
> easy to see how such a symbol could have a valid use (193).

At first glance it looks as if the God-concept would have to share its improper-properness with other concepts such as the wife of Oberon in the fairy-tale figure Titania, or the point in geometrical concepts. In the first case, however, the problem becomes more acute because Titania's way of being, in contrast to God's, is fiction. In the second case, according to Vaihinger; it is impossible to maintain the claim that the non-three-dimensional point constituting space is scientific fiction. However, in the indication of the possible transformability of this geometric concept there looms, if not a philosophical solution, nonetheless, a way out in a delimiting criterion of religious concepts.

> ... we tolerate the expression "point", although in a sense there
> could not be such a thing as a point (nothing could conform to the

definition), because we know clearly enough how talk about points is useful in talk about spatial relationships. If then one appeals to statements about points (admittedly respectable) in support of statements about God, one will be told that statements about points are valuable because one knows how to translate them into statements about sets of volumes; into what are statements about God to be translated? Here of course the religious man must reply that they are not to be translated, and so the point of the comparison is lost (194).

According to analytical philosophy, there is one more argument against an equation of 1) propositions in which God functions as the subject, and 2) propositions like those concerning Titania or the point: The self-understanding of religion opposes such an equation. This reasoning cannot fail to have its effect as one analyzes propositions whose understanding of religion is primarily empirically gained.

But the religious man will of course insist that this comparison in no way illuminates the nature of theological statements (195).

Nor can, in the sense of the before-mentioned arguments, the religious proposition "God loves men" be assigned to the following type of sentence: "The average person falls in love at least once between the ages of 18 and 27". Although, even here, the reference of the subject of this sentence cannot be directly indicated, the average person cannot clearly be named as clearly as, in the previous example, Tom could be indicated. However a far-reaching reduction does permit clarification of what is meant by the "average person". Therefore, the attempt to conceive of God as the subject of the religious statement or as a universal concept (God as "man"), and to clarify this by individual concepts is unpromising from the very beginning. This attempt would fail for the same reasons decisive for the failure to define universal concepts on the basis of individual ones. The assumption that it is possible to ascend from individuality to universality overlooks the "formation of a general concept by definition already presupposes something general in the defining concepts" (196). This has been demonstrated by Kraft among others.

The characteristic essence of statements on God may be described by assessing that they are more likely improper than improper-proper statements. This ascertainment is meant to express a difference between God as the subject of the proposition and other subjects. On the one hand, statements about God cannot be reduced to other subjects. On the other hand, they do not have a distinct object, as in the case of the sentence "Tom loves Mary". The difficulty lies in the attempt to indicate where the difference lies between "God" as the subject of the sentence and "Tom" or the "average man" as the subject of the sentence. It is, as Crombie formulates, "in some ways like a logical difference, and yet it is not a logical difference" (197). It cannot be adequately described either as a logical difference, or as a physical one.

In religious linguistic usage this difference is frequently characterized as metaphysical. God is designated as transcendental essence. Here it should be observed that the attributes "meta-physical" and "transcendental" are mere labels for an existing problem as long as their semantic contents are inexplicit. In this situation, descriptive analysis encounters a difficulty which, in view of the specific methods of such analysis, seems to be almost insurmountable. If analysis keeps to the path outlined by Wittgenstein, then what is meant by transcendental essence can be clarified by means of examples only by pointing out the rules used for this word combination.

> One gives examples, wanting them to be understood in a certain way. - But with this expression I do not intend to say: he should see, in these examples, the common chord which - for some reason - I could not pronounce. But: he should now *use* these examples in a certain way. Here, exemplifying is not an *indirect* means of explanation - for want of something better, for even any general explanation can be misunderstood (198).

Replacing the traditional quest for essences in this way does not overcome the difficulty of explaining the metaphysical difference, because the problem consists only for propositions in which the concept "God" occurs, directly or indirectly as the subject of the proposition. However, it is exactly for the function of the subject of the word "God" in the proposition that there are no further examples that clarify the issue.

> The religious man may claim that the difference is a metaphysical difference, that the point is that God is a transcendent being; but the critic will reply that he could only understand the meaning of these phrases - "metaphysical difference" and "transcendent being" - in the light of an example, and that the example offered is of no use to him because he cannot understand what statements about God are supposed to be about (199).

b) Anomalies of the Predicate

Whereas the first characteristic of the religious proposition refers to the grammatical subject of such a proposition, the second characteristic refers to the predicate. Also in reference to the particularity of the predicate, Flew's argumentation should be recalled (200). Concerning the predicate, similar characteristics may be indicated. They were first discovered with reference to the subject. Thus, predicates in the religious proposition are not formulated according to the usual norms of the vernacular, although familiar words from everyday language are used e.g. "...loves us", "...created St. Paul's" etc. Accordingly, propositions such as "God loves us" and "God created heaven and earth" can be equated structurally with "Tom loves Mary" and "Wren created St. Paul's". As a matter of fact the words "Tom", "loves", "Wren", "created" in these propostitions are not used as signs. A positive content is already conceived that allows the proof of grammatical relations between the configurations. In contrast semantic reference to the religious statement seems to be limited to the operative, i.e. to their use as empty signs. The rules of usage, as is well known, cannot be formulated on the same linguistic level. They have to be presented in a particular meta-language that presupposes an additional meta-language so that its own rules of usage, in turn, may be laid down. However, the consequence of this is that the reference to the operative rules as semantic constituents is only conditionally justified, because these rules cannot ultimately be formalized. This does not question the fundamental difference between everyday or scientific language and religious language. It merely mentions that the interpretation of the word as an unequivocal sign suppresses the problem of mediating by labeling. In addition what is designated to such propositions because this interpretation already presupposes them in the sense of a postulated unity of reality and language is also suppressed.

Within the discussion of the religious statement the issue of unity of reality and language is now raised in a particular way. The supra-sign character of language is highlighted, because in the language of belief it is difficult to designate something as given (for instance, Tom or Mary, or their respective behavior towards each other) for which the linguistic label could be assigned. Even the requirement of "incompatible situations" for grasping the truth of the religious proposition does not originate exclusively from the presupposition of the possible reduction of words to signs or to such convertible or inconvertible structures. The formulation "familiar elements" reveals this in the following quotation.

> But in the case of "God created the world", if I am to know what this means, I must have some idea of the incompatible situations and if I am to be able in this way to envisage them, they must be situations which can be constructed by rearranging familiar elements and in that case what the assertion we are considering rules out must be something which logically might be the case (201).

The presupposed familiarity with the elements of the proposition confirms the presence of a definite experience preceding the operative use of the words as elements of a proposition. The particularity of a religious proposition, according to Crombie, becomes evident not in the fact that it places itself outside the realm of experience, but rather in a definite interpretation of this experience. It seeks to assess the fundamental possibility of experience as well.

> "God created the world" is not meant to prejudge the deliberations of astronomers; the theist does not pretend to know how the world began; he only claims to know that, however it began, God created it. In other words, says the critic, the theist says what he says, not because he has discovered that there are in fact no situations incompatible with his assertions, but because, in his opinion, there could be none (202).

In the framework of this transcendental perspective, it is not a matter of metaphor in the case of the statement "God created heaven and earth" or of assertions such as "God said x and there was x", "By the word of the Lord are the heavens made". Here the original event "of the creation as an utterance of God calling into existence the basic form ... of every subsequent utterance, and of our human way of speaking" is seen only as an echo of that very first utterance through which the universe came about (203). From this difference, characterized above as a metaphysical, there now emerges the question concerning the possibility of indicating incompatible situations in another light. We have to deal with the possibility of the scientific refutation of religious statements in a different way from the proposition, "the cat is on the mat". For a scientific statement, no matter whether it is formulated as an affirmation or a denial of a state-of-affairs it refers to an empirical field that corresponds epistemologically to its statements. For example, astronomical statements correspond epistemologically to the field of astronomy. However, the statement of the believer in our example does not aim at an epistemological accomplishment, as for instance in the sense of astronomy or any other science for that matter. It discusses "the constitution of the world .. itself in which, among many other possibilities" (204) even propositions of astronomy are to be found including the proposition that the cat is on the mat.

Thus, a religious statement differs fundamentally from both scientific statements and vernacular assertions. Indeed it differs with respect both to the particularity of its subject and to that of its predicate. If God is qualified as loving, creating, knowing, it becomes evident on every occasion that a meaning different from the proposition "Wren made St. Paul's" must be ascribed to the subject and to the predicate of this proposition. These anomalies, which so far have only been formally demonstrated do not constitute ultimately a discovery in the field of linguistic-analytic philosophy (205), having found their most pregnant formulation in the proposition of St. Thomas: *"Impossibile est aliquid praedicari de Deo et creaturis univoce"* (206). They offer, in reference to their substantial reflection (i.e. here with the genuineness of the use of religious language) the topics for discussing the problem of the proofs of God's existence. This depends on whether one starts from the subject of the proposition, or in the case of *analogia entis* from the predicate. However, a precondition of this thematic alignment is the acknowledgement that religious statements are not prejudged as non-cognitive.

5. *"Believing that" and "believing in"*

The religious statement differs decisively from other statements. Irrespective of the anomalies of its subject and predicate, it does not trace the truth of its content back to knowledge but to belief. Therefore the question arises whether these statements may be attributed to the character of rationality, reasoning and justification by general principles by virtue of the uniqueness that distinguishes religious propositions of the kind "I believe God created heaven and earth" from sentences such as "I know the cat lies on the mat". The alternative to this possibility would be to place religious propositions into the class of non-cognitive propositions and designate them as being direct because there is no further rationality behind them.

If at the outset we posit a formal similarity between the sentences "Tom loves Mary" and "the cat is on the mat", with the sentence "God created heaven and earth", then we should now distinguish the latter from those so-called belief-sentences such as, "I believe that the cat is on the mat". The first two sentences are formally so different from each other that the first one is preceded by "I know" and the other is preceded by "I believe". A simple, phenomenological-descriptive stock-taking of the usage of the word 'believe' shows that the point linguistically formulated and expressed in indirect speech lies exactly in the situation "that the truth of what is believed, meant or said remains in suspense and yet the proposition on believing what is believed can be true" (207). When the believer says, "I believe God created heaven and earth", he is not talking of intentional pseudo-state-of-affairs but in his opinion of an objective condition. The expression "I believe" designates here a *way of comprehension* different from the one "I know". However in the believer's opinion this is not a way of comprehension inferior to knowledge but is at least equivalent if not superior to knowledge.

At least in the sense of the Christian concept of belief, something is not regarded as being true, but the believer is quite sure of his belief and of what he believes. The strenuously acquired convictions of believers like Job, Paul, Augustine, Luther, or Pascal may be described as absolute trust. It is not an anticipatory acknowledgement of an event that is more or less probable, nor a cognitive act having a lower degree of evidence than knowledge. Therefore, belief as Christian belief simply cannot be understood as a form of theoretical perception that refers to pre-scientific or scientific evidence. It does not refer to something that, like a state-of-affairs, may be regarded to be true. However, because it is as Charles Hartshorne expressed it, the belief in "the Source of states-of-affairs", "but not one of them" (208). It is like a belief in a person, in this case, God.

From the point of view of religion, the theological formation of theory must preserve its independence of the particular scientific realm of perception - be it of the scientific or historic kind. It does not take its object from this realm, but refers to the presence of the reality of God asserted by the believer to exist in this realm (209). That the believer in his statements presupposes a specific reality, which may not be verified sensually. It is undeniable that his propositions have the character of an assertion that refers to this reality. Regarding the question of verifying the assertive character of the believer's proposition, it is possible to see these propositions in a close relationship to philosophical propositions. Like philosophical propositions, they assert concrete statements about the totality of reality. With such an attempt to surpass concrete experience and the assertion of a divine reality, the believer does not yet unconditionally withdraw his propositions from the possibility of being checked and examined. On the contrary by surpassing experience he looks for the ground and cause of what may be experienced. However, a proposition that aims to name the ground and cause of what may be experienced cannot harden itself against the claim of truth for the sake of the assertive aim of this proposition. This is the case even in view of the circumstance that a verification cannot be concluded considering that the process of human experience is still going on.

Because hypotheses and pre-decisions about reality as a whole enter into all tangible experience and into every non-religious statement, one may expect preliminary evidence for the truth or falsity of the religious statement when its pre-decisions and hypotheses are compared in its place. In such an argumentation, religious statements share with scientific propositions the fact that they must be verifiable and open to comparison with regard to their function within the systematic framework. Here, the close relationship of theological and philosophical propositions concerning reality becomes evident. Religious statements even in view of asserting their transcensive rather than discensive foundation, must be measurable in terms of those criteria which are also decisive for the truth of philosophical statements.

Therefore the attempt to interpret the expression "I believe" in the religious proposition as "wishful thinking", as H. H. Price did in his essay "Faith and Belief" fails to understand the proposition as it is spoken and understood by the believer. The concept as well as the assertion that theistic discoveries "seem too good to be true" can no longer be regarded as the result of an analysis of the *logic* of religious language, its basic characteristics and fundamental laws. They must be regarded as the result of a belief-concept that "has been honed into shape" by critical thinking. Therefore, Price is obliged to replace "believing", understood as wishful thinking, by "feeling" in order to make a further step toward the description of what constitutes religious experience.

> Surely when a person is actually in the faith attitude, he would never say he believed that God loves him. It is rather that he *feels* God's love for him or feels the loving welcome he receives, like the Prodigal Son in the parable. It does not seem to be a matter of believing at all (210).

This, one might almost say, insignificant exchange of words, whose aim was to preserve the purity of the religious proposition and to protect it from being equated with belief-propositions, took place at the cost of the question of truth.

> Faith, ... is not a propositional attitude at all. It is more like an attitude of loving adherence to a person or at least to a Being with whom one may have personal relations. It is as if (in the old feudal manner) one had given one's allegiance to someone and accepted him - voluntarily and gladly - as one's lord.
> If this is what the attitude of faith is like or what it feels like to be in it, does believing "that" have much to do with it? Is it a propositional attitude at all? If you find yourself addressing someone and giving your allegiance to him, it is a little late in the day to ask the question "Does he exist?" and look for evidence to support the hypothesis that he does. Such a question does not even occur to your mind. So if we use the word "belief" we have to describe the man who has faith ("a believer") as one who believes *in* God, and distinguish between believing "in" and believing "that" (211).

Admittedly we should agree with Price when he states that God and his Word is the starting point of belief and of theological reflection. Indeed, it seems inappropriate to question the existence of someone to whom one pledges one's faith. However, decisive in the justification of this question is not the starting point, but whether it is possible to let a theory of the belief in God start so that theology, described as the talk of God is equated with "speaking God's Word, the Word that can come only from Him" (212). However, it is impossible to prove this equation. Religious statements cannot undergo their final verification here and now. A statement like the proposition, "It is a little strange to seek for someone who has been with you all the time" (213) is not a statement of a theology speaking the Word of God, but of a theology that speaks of God. Such a discovery, as Schelling cites in his criticism of the ontological proof of the existence of God, is not an artificial deception but quite a natural one. Someone who can assert, "I am with you everyday" does exist. Only God as subject of this proposition is not identical with my "I" as the hearer and therefore not determined as "I" (214). Arising from this discrepancy is the problem of verifiable religious statements. Yet one must agree with Price and Schelling that God, understood as the content of belief, cannot be conceived of as an object but only as "I". However, there are two possibilities as one recognizes this impossibility. Either one confronts the question of truth with regard to religious questions or backs off from it. An understanding of belief excluding Price's "propositional attitude" on the question of truth cannot be fully carried out. This is true even for Price's analysis of the belief-concept. In the element of uncertainty the claim of belief concerning verification turns up again and again. Even God's very existence may become a matter of believing "that".

> Again, even though we have actually been in the faith attitude sometimes, our faith may still be a very weak and vacillating one. (Hence it is proper to pray to God to make it firmer.) We may easily lapse out of the faith attitude even when we have occasionally been in it. In those periods of lapse -- and they may be long -- we have to fall back, as it were, on believing "that", and even God's very existence may become a matter of believing "that". When we were actually in the faith attitude the question "Does he exist?" did not even arise. We may remember that it did not, and how it seemed to us then that we were somehow in his presence. Or perhaps we do not remember this, because there is something in us which makes us wish to forget it (215).

It is because of Price's differentiation of belief and knowledge that he is obliged to refer to Sigmund Freud's concept of active forgetting. This is the case because he hopes to answer the question why the justification of the believer's statements of belief is not permanently significant for the believer. Why does he not seek corroboration in the reality he experiences? The tension between belief and knowledge is revealed as one reflects on ones belief-situation. Therefore even for Price it seems to arrive at a very insufficient solution in reference to the process of the empiricist formation of theories.

> ... it is worth while to notice that the empiricist
> notion of "try it and see for yourself" is by no
> means absent from religious literature. "O taste and
> see how gracious the Lord is " is an example (216).

The courage to risk as well as the courage to decide are undoubtly elements of belief. However, the reference to courage as an answer to the quest for the truth of religious statements is a recognition of empiricist limitation and a replacement of theory by a theoretical pragmatism. The extent to which this step is possible and meaningful will have to be examined. However, it cannot be denied that this pragmatic turn is the determining motif of Price's differentiation of belief and knowledge as he differentiates "believing that" amd "believing in" in his analysis.

The discussion of the logical relationship between "believing that" and "believing in" is not new. Augustine had already pointed out the difference between "believing something" and "believing in". He elucidated the difference by indicating that demons believed that Jesus existed but did not believe in him. Accordingly, whoever believes in God, believes Him, as a matter of fact. However, not everyone necessarily believes in Him who believes Him. From a theological point of view, the orientation of belief on a definite person is highlighted as the fundamental and novel characteristic of the New Testament. As regards syntax, the focus on a person of the belief-concept is reflected in the development of the prepositional combination "believing in" ("believing that") accentuates for the theological discussion that belief (here Christian belief) is understood fundamentally not as a consideration of the truth of a state-of-affairs but as a personal belief in a person.

Whereas the expression "believing in Jesus" is frequently found in the New Testament, the expression "believing in God" occurs rarely. Although it is precisely this expression that forms the first central affirmation of the Credo (217).

In the analytic philosophy of religion it is insignificant if this analysis refers to the expression "believing in God", or to "believing in Jesus" as one seeks the sense of the formulation "believing in". This is true provided that under Jesus one adheres to the religious evidence that he is the figure of Christ, the one coming from God in the sense of the Gospel and not the isolated person as such. If this aspect of analysis is not taken into account and the name "Jesus" is treated analogously to the name "Tom", then the proposition of belief in

Jesus loses its specifically religious dimension and is of no further interest for a philosophical consideration of religion. In order to pre-empt such a misunderstanding, the analysis starts for the most part from the expression "believing in God".

The problem lying in this formulation is the quest for the mode of being which is appropriate to this person in reference. This inquiry remains open despite the emphasis on the personal reference. However, this means that the belief in God as Creator, Preserver, Redeemer etc. is based on a reflective "believing that" which is inseparable from the belief that he exists. Both the belief-concept of the Old Testament and that of the New Testament encourage the critical reflection for such minute examination. If one starts from the meaning and the use of the Hebrew word (root: אמן) or from the Greek word πιστεύειν ,then one is struck by the relationship with the former word to the term אמת = truth. It is "true" what has proven itself and what has shown its fidelity. In this connection it must be noted that in Hebrew the word "truth" does not belong "in relationship to human concerns" and is "not the correctness of propositions, but the being and behavior of individual persons" (218). This means that the expression "believing in God" already implies the certainty of His existence. The understanding of the relationship between believing 'in' and believing 'that' is significant to the extent that it stamps the God-concept on every founded belief. If one separates the two moments or if one sees them in their logical connection to each other, then the difficulty arises that the concept of belief is either 1) emptied of content so that in the end nothing is left to believe; or 2) the object of my belief is considered only as an object and not in its subjective character. Crombie's position is an example of the latter possibility.

> The distinction between *believing that* and *believing in* is, of course, valid; but it does not help us, for *believing in* is logically subsequent to *believing that*. I cannot believe in Dr. Jones if I do not believe that there is such a person (219).

As a criticism of this position we can take Malcolm's remark which in fact is not leveled at Crombie, but at Alston. He remarks that a difference between the moments "believe that " and "believe in" cannot be asserted for the concept of religious belief because the reasons for the belief that He exists and for the belief in Him must be thought of as the same with reference to God. As in Crombie's example of Dr. Jones they cannot be different from each other.

> What is unrealistic about this assumption? [nämlich die Unterscheidung von "glauben, daß" und "glauben an"]? First of all, I must confess that the supposed *belief that God exists* strikes me

as a problematic concept, whereas *belief in God* is not problematic. ... Belief in God is partly, but only partly, analogous to belief in one's friend or in one's doctor. Belief in another human being primarily connotes trust or faith in him. ... You believe in your doctor: that is, you trust his skill or his humane interest in his patients. ...When you believe in a person what it is that you trust him to do (or to say or to think) would depend, of course, on the particular circumstances of the case. ...

A man could properly be said to believe in God whose chief attitude toward God was *fear*. ("A sword is sent upon you, and who may turn it back?") But if you were enormously afraid of another human being you could not be said to believe in him. At least you would not believe in him *in so far* as you were afraid of him: whereas the fear of God is one form of belief in him.

Belief in God encompasses not only trust, but also awe, dread, dismay, resentment and perhaps even hatred. Belief in God will involve some affective state or attitude, having God as its object, and those attitudes could vary from reverential love to rebellious rejection.

Now one is inclined to say that if a person believes in God surely he believes that God exists. It is far from clear what this is supposed to mean. Of course, if "believing that God exists" is understood to mean the same as "believing in God" (and this is not an entirely unnatural use of language) then there is no problem. But the inclination we are discussing is to hold that you could believe *that* God exists without believing *in* God. As I understand it, we are supposed to think that one could believe that God exists but at the same time have no affective attitude toward God. The belief that he exists would come first and the affective attitude might or might not come later. The belief that he exists would not logically imply any affective attitude toward him, but an effective attitude toward him would logically imply the belief that he exists.

If we are assuming a Jewish or Christian conception of God I do not see how one can make the above separation. If one conceived of God as the almighty creator of the world and judge of mankind how could one believe that he exists, but not be touched *at all* by awe or dismay or fear? I am discussing logic, not psychology. Would a belief that he exists, if it were completely non-affective, really be a belief that he exists? Would it be anything at all? What is the "form of life" into which it would enter? What difference would it make whether anyone did or did not have this belief? So many philosophers who discuss these matters assume that the first and great question is to decide whether God exists: ... I think on the contrary, that a "belief that God exists", if it was logically independent of any and all ways of regarding him, would be of no interest, not even to God (220).

In summary, the difficulty of understanding what belief is lies in the fact analysis attempts to pre-classify or post-classify "believing that" which is contained in the concept "believing in". This depends on the respective theological or linguistic-philosophical viewpoint. The post-classification refers to the fact that intuition underlies the understanding of religious proposition. This intuition cannot be directly derived from an interpretation of such statements. In contrast, the pre-classification starts from the premise that the same sense and truth criteria must be applied for the understanding of religious statements as in the investigation of the sense-claim of propositions. These criteria are not taken from the realm of religion and belief. This second position is correct in so far as religious statements in formal generality are also subject to those conditions of understanding which must be fulfilled with respect to any other text. Yet the possibility of a specific intuition for religious statements is not yet called into question by such an assertion. The question is what is understood here by the premise of an intuition. "Is this premise given along with human existence as such? Is there a preceding reference to the truth of divine revelation in every human being because the human as such is moved by the God-question" (221)? If the answer to this question is positive, then there is no reason for a pre-classification or a post-classification of "believing that". If, however, the answer implies that human existence experiences the state of being moved by the God-question only through its belief in God, then indeed post-classification would be correctly maintained. At the same time, however, the sense of such a post-classification would become questionable. According to it religion would be asserted to be an "esoteric language game"(222), from which spectators remain in principle excluded. The history of the proof of the existence of God and its failure to convert a single atheist, produces persuasive evidence for the inconclusiveness of pre-classification (223).

III. BELIEF WITHOUT TRUTH

The emotive theory of religion presupposes the epistemological positivist stance which advocates that only facts and sensual data can be cognitive sources (224). According to this theory religious propositions are expressions of emotive insight. They do not meet the requirement obligatory for cognitive propositions concerning the objectivity and intersubjectivity of their cognitive content. The query of whether a proposition meets these requirements or whether it is to be understood as a conviction based upon the speaker's feeling, is decided upon the basis of the applicability of the empirical sense-criterion. This is done by means of verification or falsification. It is true that emotive propositions, like cognitive ones, may describe facts and make statements, but the correctness of their descriptions and statements cannot be substantiated by observation and sensual perception (225). Since the majority of religious statements are not meant to demonstrate perceptually verifiable observations or to demonstrate the establishment of facts, the emotive theory rejects the possibility that they could be true. Their sense must be looked for beyond theoretical and scientific thought and speech and therefore beyond causal explanations and conclusions.

The uniqueness of many religious statements is that their outward form resembles that of a statement of verification. Also, without further explanation, it is not possible to maintain that the sense of religious statements lies in decisions, value judgements and recommendations as it is in the case of practical propositions. In the opinion of the emotivists, these must be included in the class of non-cognitive propositions. In addition to the influence of the basic theses underlying positivist epistemology held by the Vienna Circle and early Wittgenstein, the theory of Wittgenstein's *Philosophical Investigations* left its imprint on this theory of religion. Yet this theory gained importance only when the attempt was made to undertake an analysis of religious propositions for which there is no doubt that one can demonstrate them to be devoid of all truth and meaning. Yet it should be the purpose of this analysis to claim some kind of sense for religious propositions. That attempt met with some success concerning the understanding of sense and its determination. However, the emotive interpreters of religious statements agree that religious propositions can neither be true nor false. Truth can be accorded only to propositions concerning an empirical object.

Empirical knowledge was elevated to the sole criterion of truth or falsity. This gave new direction to the discussion of the relationship between belief and truth. This prejudiced them against such statements, for the knowledge derived from sensual data came to be the final arbiter in resolving the question of the claim of validity for religious statements.

Even David Hume in the dialogue between Philo and Cleanthes abstained from a verdict upon the truth or falsity of either point of view, allowing each character an equal footing for putting forward arguments in support of his view. Concidering this and keeping in mind that since then Kant's rigorous reasoning has pointed out that the conflict between belief and knowledge is an absolutely necessary antinomy of reason, it is even more striking that the emotivist is not responding to the opinion implicitly contained in Hume's dialogical experiment and openly expounded by Kant that the truth or falsity of thesis and antithesis cannot be decided on the basis of speculative reason.

Using Kant's terminology, we can maintain that having made theoretical reason the arbitrer over faith and knowledge and having acknowledged theoretical reason as the source of cognition, the emotive theory of religion forces one to reject the truth-claim of statements of faith. This is the case because, according to the emotivist theory of religion, both thesis and antithesis cannot possibly be true. Despite its unmistakable pragmatic character, the emotive theory of religion cannot leave this decision concerning thesis and antithesis to practical reason. Nor can it modify this decision by the notion of linguistic pluralism found in Wittgenstein's later works. For the emotivist religion can neither be based upon exact knowledge nor upon a belief that is valid in a different way and for different reasons than theoretical knowledge. Religion is to be based on a belief that is an expression of a mental disposition. This disposition cannot be further substantiated and must be called emotion according to its origin (226).

1. Founding the emotive turn in meaning according to Wittgenstein.

Both the Proposition 4.022 in Wittgenstein's *Tractatus* and the remarks following § 22 in the *Philosophical Investigations* refer to the multiplicity of possible turns in meaning of a proposition (227). Wittgenstein points out that the speaker makes statements and comments that form the content of the sentence. The latter assigns, within the conversational situation a definite function to the presentation of this content that is not exhausted in mere presentation. Whereas the state-of-affairs as represented for instance in the proposition "God created heaven and earth", is usually designated as the descriptive content of this proposition. The function of such a presentation within the linguisitic behavioral context is called the propositional mood. It is Wittgenstein's concern to show that the meaning of a sentence remains inaccessible without the semantic or the modal component because the descriptive content must remain incomprehensible when taken as the mere radical of a sentence, i.e. its presentation of content. This is inaccessible regardless of its role in the language game. The sentence "it is raining", he explains, becomes "a means of communication only" when one has differentiated its modal function (statement, order, question) (228). Neither Wittgenstein nor the philosophy of ordinary language, which continued this line of thought, hold the view that in a language-game the applicable possibilities of the use of a sentence's radical in the above-mentioned moods, has been sufficiently considered. Therefore one attempted to stipulate that a religious statement has its own emotive mood. In some cases, this led them to argue that a sentence with emotive meaning does not assert a verifiable statement. Therefore they held that it had no descriptive content whatsoever (229).

By emphasizing moods, Wittgenstein's line of thought greatly differed from that of the early positivists, who continued to believe in the possibility of equating the meaning of a sentence with its descriptive content and of the verification of its truth by comparing perceptual data. For Wittgenstein, the distinction between descriptive content and mood was the first step towards including practical behavior in reflection on truth. The decisive factor here is that contrary to those who continued to espouse Wittgenstein's notion of an emotive theory of religion, Wittgenstein does not yield to the temptation to take the modal context of a religious statement as merely an emotive component separable from varifiable content. For the emotivist it had psychological, but not verifiable meaning.

Fully in accordance with the results of John L. Austin's later research (230), Wittgenstein regards the mood of the sentence as being constitutive for the descriptive part of the sentence. Yet he refrains from discussing thoroughly their interlocking relationship. He contents himself with stating that their interdependence is demonstrable. In this sense, Wittgenstein speaks of the similarity between sentences and arrows. Sentences are like arrows insofar as their sense has direction, in contrast to the merely static meaning of a name. The direction is given to a sentence by its modal character. Therefore, for example, if the radical of a sentence is indicative, this already presupposes a direction. This sense, however, cannot be given to a sentence by using it in the indicative "because what is asserted by a sentence in the indicative to be true, is the directed sense of the radical of the sentence" (231).

Especially in his later works, Wittgenstein distinguishes not only between the meaning of a word and the sense of a sentence, but also between the sense and the meaning of a sentence. The sense of a sentence can either be true or false. According to Wittgenstein's terminology, a sentence becomes meaningful only when the state-of-affairs it expresses corresponds to an analogous state in reality (232). According to early Wittgenstein, religious propositions had neither meaning nor sense. However, according to the late works of Wittgenstein, it seems impossible, without committing oneself to Wittgenstein's understanding of reality, to answer the question if Wittgenstein was prepared to grant them meaning in addition to his recognition of their sense. For the emotivist, the situation is clear. One denies meaning to religious propositions while attempting to plea for their sense. Following Flew's parable one concludes that the semantic rules by which, for example, a sentence like "God created heaven and earth" may be understood, cannot be the same as those applied to the verifiable and empirically ascertainable sentence "it rains". The emotivist believes that both sentences have something in common. They indicate a descriptive state-of-affairs which can be understood only by including the modal function fulfilled by the language radical in the communicative situation. However, the emotivist begins with the assumption that the modal sense of a sentence can be understood even when its descriptive contents is disregarded. By attaching little significance to the verifiable statement of a religious sentence, the sentence stating that God is the creator of the world is no longer meant to be a statement on the origin of the world. It is, within the non-descriptive sense-function, merely a stance or a commitment of the speaker to the subject under discussion. The sentence takes on the declarative function of professing a definite way of life with regard to a disposition concerning life such as an optimistic world-view.

2. The reduction theory of the religious statement

This attempt to understand the religious proposition as emotive and to reduce its sense to the *function* of a statement runs parallel to the attempt to understand moral propositions. The reduction to descriptive content is applicable even to the treatment of religious propositions which are verifiable by their form unlike so-called ontic propositions. As such they are propositions expressing how things should be. In the discussion of meta-ethical linguisitic usage, the concept *attitude* is similar to the concept "blik" of religious propositions and finds its expression in the non-descriptive function of language, that has the linguistic form "I approve of *x*" (233). The concept 'attitude' stipulates a characteristic of the speaker. Having an attitude is not correlative to giving a description, but to the expression of an evaluation or an engagement. For instance, the function of a sentence in which a society is predicated as capitalist shows disapproval when asserted by a Marxist. Conversely, the same statement has a different sense if spoken by an economic theorist, who does not use this sentence explicitly in the sense of an evaluation, but as a scientific description of an economic social structure (234). The differentiation of attitudes can immediately be recognized even in a clear-cut religious sentence like that of grace said at the table. Here its own religious sense can get lost in the situation in which the prayer is said, - either when it is said demonstratively for an indifferent public, or when the sentences of a prayer are intended to be provocations or are felt as such (235).

According to metareligious linguisitic usage and following Hare's parable (236), the specifically emotive religious tendency is designated as "blik". This is the formation of an analogy for which the motives can be named. The 'attitude' concept of metaethical theory rests primarily on the assertion that "ethical propositions express *attitudes* of the speaker and so tend to call forth similar attitudes in his hearers" (237). In this connection, the characterization of the sense-content of a proposition by the designation "blik" is meant to elucidate a method for linguistic validation. This validation is not supposed to be meaningful in a cognitive or descriptive sense but is supposed to be practical. It is supposed to be an expression of a *decision* for a certain disposition in life. This means it is a decision which, in the religious realm, is characterized as *decision for belief.*

If what the emotivists are really doing is designating the emotive sense as independent, then it is presented in the communication of a religious proposition apparently in the indicative mood as in the majority of religious propositions. However, in its expressiveness, it need not be assumed to be verifiable. According to such an explanatory strategy, the clarification that reveals the sense of a religious proposition is not burdened with the requirement to state the conditions of truth. It is true that the demonstration of the difference between the descriptive content of a proposition and the mood, as well as the categorization of the sense of a religious proposition as "blik" cannot yet be recognized as proof for the correctness of separating the emotive component from the descriptive one. This cannot be done because the reasons for excluding the problem of truth may not be given as an answer to the question "*quid facti?*" concerning the actual existence of the difference between mood and content or the possibility to prove a plurality of sense. But only by answering the question "*quid iuris?*" concerning the rightfulness of a component to become independent.

These circumstances come to light when we cast a glance at the emotive understanding of language. Accordingly the subject speaking is in a relationship of distance to the object addressed. The objectification of language caused by this distance allows language to analyse a sentence into its different components, thus distinguishing different tendencies of sense. However, it makes it impossible for language to see, in such an objectified language, the linguistic constituents in their mutual relationship and interdepedence. This separation means that in judging religious language and religious conduct the decision for belief is different from its reasoning and justification. They are opposed to each other as stances that cannot be substantiated as language performance that is cognitive and descriptive in character. This is so because "blik" and attitude, as linguistic expressions of the subject, do not offer rational justification on the basis of their descriptive and verifiable content.

The emotive theory of religion appears to have yielded to the very temptation Wittgenstein rejected as he opposed the view that sentences consisted of a "neutral core" receiving their sense only from an additional modal component (238). However, the numerous renowned advocates of the emotive theory think differently. According to them the neutral core is without any verifiable sense of its own.

In order to understand this and its consequences, it is necessary to realize that, for the emotive theory of religion, the descriptive content of meaning in a religious statement is exclusively the professed attitude of the speaker. Thus, the statement of a sentence is indifferent to truth and falsity. Even if possible reasons were produced for its support and consideration, they would not be accepted as arguments for or against the truth of a state-of-affairs demonstrated in such a statement. If in a conversation in which all persons concerned share the same emotive view 'A' says, "God created heaven and earth", and 'B' denies this statement, then there is no disagreement between the two interlocutors on the truth value of the descriptive content of a statement, concerning the declaration of 'A'. If 'A' tries to produce reasons for his argument, then he does not question 'B's' basis for its content. This is because the latter, according to the emotive understanding of the religious statement said only that he could not approve of 'A's' optimistic philosophy of life (239).

Seen this way, an attempt to justify an indicative religious proposition cannot really originate from the state-of-affairs described by it because the state-of-affairs, due to its assigned function as a mere means for expressing the attitudinal makeup of the subject, stands in an external relationship to the subject.

Such a classification of religious propositions in the indicative does not explain the reason for their use in contrast to sentences in interrogative or imperative moods. Therefore, if we do not want to return to the characterization of senselessness of early neopositivism, then it is necessary to attribute a function to these sentences which makes their further use in the indicative appear meaningful.

Many advocates of the emotive theory try to make a virtue of a necessity when they refer to the fact that religious statements, like moral ones, cannot be included in either a class of factual statements or in a class of general empirical statements. Neither can they be evaluated as logical and mathematical statements. These common negative facets are considered to be sufficient to maintain the interdependence of theological and moral statements or to declare the two to be identical. It is true that a standardization cannot explain the reason for the use of religious propositions in the indicative mood, but they consider it an alternative to returning to the thesis of senselessness. The attempt was made in this context to avoid the problem that religious statements, due to their verifiable character, are not like moral statements "primarily declarations of adherence to a policy of action, declarations of commitment to a way of life" (240). This attempt was initiated with the statement, "The primary use of religious assertions is to announce allegiance to a set of moral principles" (241) (5,a), and supported by a secular interpretation of the gospel. According to this interpretation, Hare's conception of "blik" is in complete agreement with the Holy Scriptures as the "way of life" (5,b).

3. Existential participation

The way the emotivists received Flew's criticism, forced them to maintain the existence of a non-cognitive realm of sense whose content was no longer subject to the requirement and application of verification and falsification criteria. They wished to maintain that the religious statement has a claim of sense. The first step for establishing such a realm was sketched out by Wittgenstein's theory of the different linguistic patterns of sense. The second step was the separation according to sense of the performance of descriptive language from the function of expression. The function of expression became independent. This resulted in the denial of rationality for the belief and stance of the believer and of a specific religious nature. The development of the emotive theory was encouraged by K. Barth's criticism of the knowledge of God. They saw this to be in full accordance with their conception, in that it could be interpreted as a form of expression for a certain view of life (242). Thus, theological authorization was given to the attempt to characterize belief exclusively as an immanent attitude that does not result from a situational analysis of a decision founded by general religious rationality.

Such a definition has unambiguous results. In the question of the truth-value, the religious proposition is denied any commitment to its verifiable sense. Because knowledge equated with rationalism and belief is identified with immanent behavior, the so-called attitudinal disposition of the speaker, lacks the common ground of religious reason. A foundation is lacking on which what is expressed in belief could be anchored and proven to be binding.

Even though this is the case, the emotive theory of religion continues to attempt to dissolve the tension between belief and knowledge into mere appearance. It continues to assert that the two domains have nothing in common. It is difficult to say whether the reason for attempting to differentiate between belief and knowledge should be sought in distrust of belief or of thought. This difficulty arises because thought is not considered to be able to prepare the ground on which an acceptance of belief could have effected the transition from a direct state to a reflected stance with its own inherent sense. This omission is primarily due to the opinion that the meaning of words and sentences can be seen only from their use. This is true even where the disjunction between belief and knowledge is not supposed to be complete. In this light Hare formulated the following statement in complete accordance with the pragmatic-behaviorist theory of meaning:

> If believing something is a kind of thinking, we can only find out
> what a man believes by studying his actions (243).

This pragmatic orientation demonstrates a strength of the emotive theory of religion. This theory is able to differentiate between scientific and emotive statements not only negatively as to the applicability of verification or falsification criteria, but also positively in the recognition of existential participation as a specific feature of the interpretation of religious statements (244). This implies that it is absolutely necessary for the hearer to imagine himself in the life situation of the speaker when he wishes to comprehend the horizon of sense (245) in which a statement is made. In this way, the attempt is made to comprehend even those elements of sense important for the statement that are neither expressly pronounced, nor consciously or subconsciously intended (246).

Thus, the emotive theory begins its search for the sense of religious statements at the point where Bartley saw the greatest hinderance (247). It begins in the recognition that they are valid. Bartley stated that the implied participation in the religious-language game is the exclusive reason for understanding the sense of such statements. However, the participation in a certain form of life, as a presupposition for understanding a language game (248), remains problematic for the emotive theory. This is so because it begins with the linear conception of language. Accordingly, it cannot be appreciated how a person can come to understand a language unless he is already determined to follow a certain form of life" (249). Even if Bartley intended this, one could not accept his criticism of the possibility to understand religious statements as a criticism of their claims of sense and truth but as a criticism of the linguistic model on which his own theory as well as the emotive theory are based. The turn to pragmatism does not facilitate but rather aggravates the transmission of tradition, so important for understanding the sense of religious statements. The element of "the revival and the adaptation of the past to the present form of life (250) is absent.

The difficulty of comprehending theological tradition is strikingly reflected in a statement made by Gill. He sees the universal remedy *for solving* theological problems in the "examination of the 'forms of life' of religious experience and expression" (251).

> Coming at theology in this way would cause the theologian to feel that many of the great debates and problems of historical theology are really pseudo-problems which arose because of an insensitive use and inadequate understanding of language. Theologians, like philosophers, have been misled by the grammatical similarity between religious statements and scientific or literary statements. To be sure, many of the former do function like the latter in certain ways, but there are also basic logical differences which have very often been overlooked. One cannot help but wonder how much the early church councils could have been enlightened by the insights of the language analyst in their task of forging the main Christian doctrines. Such issues as the nature of Christ and the nature of God might well be greatly clarified by paying closer attention to what is really being said and how it is being said. Likewise, the medieval theologians could have saved themselves a lot of time and the Christian church a lot of confusion if they had understood that the nature of logic language is such that it is irrelevant to questions of existence in general and God's existence in particular (252).

This criticism is justified insofar as in the course of the historic development of theological systems and their interpretation of religious statements, the attempt has over and over again been made to use language for verifying independent systematic lines of thought. Yet this criticism overstates the issue when it overlooks the fact that language is misused only where theological predecisions have been made. In this sense, it would be surprising if Gill's criticism of Plato's "mania for definition", or that of John Calvin, Spinoza, Hegel, Karl Jaspers and Martin Heidegger (253) is not itself based on a prejudice. It postulates that theological and religious statements must be understood as figureheads of meaning that become obvious in the game (254).

It cannot be determined whether the pragmatist definition of meaning, relating meaning to a definite kind of activity, is the cause or the result of an exclusive view of language as an instrument of representation and description. This no longer leaves any possibility to see anything else in religious language but the descriptive representation of a "certain metaphysical attitude towards the world" (255). Undoubtedly, behind this reduction to the descriptive function there is Wittgenstein's proposition, "*We* again restore the words from their metaphysical use to their everyday use" (256).

4. "Blik" and the decision for belief

Hare's theory of religious statements proceeds from the fact that because their sense is viewed on an existing decision on a principle it is possible to arrive at their sense. This decision is expressed in the "blik" which describes the existential concern manifest in the decision. This concern indicates the difference between a theoretical discovery and a practical statement. In this context, Hare characterizes the difference between the characters of Flew's parable and his own by hinting at the lack of emotion of Flew's characters.

> The explorers do not *mind* about their garden; they discuss it with interest, but not with concern. But my lunatic, poor fellow, minds about dons; ... It is because I mind very much about what goes on in the garden in which I find myself, that I am unable to share the explorer's detachment (257).

In trying to understand the personal state-of-being expressed in a "blik", the specific feature of religious statements, Hare goes beyond Tillich's position which requires that this necessary state-of-being should be a condition for participating in the religious language-game. Hare does this as he reduces "blik" as a state-of-being in theological terms to the experience of rebirth. As a matter of fact, Hare does not distinguish between the state-of-being concerning a state-of-affairs with the state-of-affairs itself. Instead he considers it to be the reason for such emotional engagement. However, only with reference to such a distinction is the question of the *correct* "blik" meaningful. This question, which was raised by Hare himself, will have to be dealt with later. As a matter of fact, the question implies that the content of the "blik" may be handled and reconsidered for every way of thought. It does not matter whether the issue of seeing all those in a position of authority as potential murderers, or that of an individual who is carried away by a religious conviction is being considered. Nor does it matter whether we move inside or outside this "blik".

Hare's view that religious propositions cannot claim to have verifiable character rests on a return to Hume's characterization of the distinction between reason and feeling. Hume characterized reason as cold and indifferent to commitment, contesting that reasoning could ensue from action. The impulse for action, Hare maintains, can be initiated only by desire and inclination (258). If one founded decision-making on reason, then reason would have to be in possession of all information necessary for making a decision. Hare agrees with Hume that, if this is not possible, then we cannot rely on our thought in our everyday decisions. Such thought is suited to verifiable statements, observable descriptions and sensory perceptions. We have to retire to our "blik" in the last instance.

> When I am driving my car, it sometimes occurs to me to wonder whether my movements of the steering wheel will always continue to be followed by corresponding alterations in the direction of the car. I have never had a steering failure, though I have had skids, which must be similar. Moreover I know enough about how the steering of my car is made, to know the sort of thing that would have to go wrong for the steering to fail - steel joints would have to part, or steel rods break, or something - but how do I know that this won't happen? The truth is, I don't know; I just have a *blik* about steel and its properties, so that normally I trust the steering of my car; but I find it not at all difficult to imagine what it would be like to lose this *blik* and acquire the opposite one (259).

Without question reason's task of describing and establishing facts compares with the task of belief to motivate practical behavior. This has to be done in order to pave the way for the process of taking the view which has the task of making decisions and was noted in Hare's "blik" concept. Hare's interpretation of "blik", which intends to characterize an immediate state-of-being, must be critiqued by pointing out that, if such a belief is regarded as being the authority for making decisions, then the question of why someone has made such a decision can never be answered in any other way than that a person actually made such a decision. It must be mentioned, however, that this answer is contradictory. The attempt is made to motivate direct behavior and to rationally prove its correctness. But whoever tries to prove the direct state-of-being concerned through a process of justification, extracts from it the character of immediacy.

On yet another point, the "blik" theory runs into difficulties. Hare refers to the circumstance that we no longer believe in God as in Atlas. According to the concept of "blik", this cannot be understood as the consequence of progress in religious thought. Accordingly, the everyday concept of God could not be seen to be the result of discourse on the content of a "blik", but it would have to be regarded as its accident. However, in order to avoid considering belief external to an historical process and be able to conceive of belief as a result of a history of thought and action, belief cannot be looked upon as merely a direct state-of-being.

Nevertheless, even if we disregard these contradictions, we should point out a characteristic of Hare's "blik" theory. This characteristic should not be ignored when the "blik" concept is applied to the clarification of religious statements. The confrontation of the believer with the madman who fears for his life already shows that the "blik" is not initially part of a particular process of taking a religious point of view under whose presuppositions religious propositions are asserted. For Hare this is the final presupposition for every possible consideration of one's existence and even of the whole world. If one understands the concepts "religion" and "belief" in a way that one can speak of the believer as one who does not believe in anything and also regards the contrast between belief and unbelief as an inner-religious problem, then the "blik" may not be applied as the designation of a *definite way* of comprehending the so-called last presuppositions. However, it is possible to grasp the "blik" generally as a basic presupposition of action and of every kind of world-view. However, it is just on this point that Hare's "blik" theory remains unclear. On the one hand, he understands the "blik" only as a basic presupposition. On the other hand, however, he already identifies it with a definite world-view.

> But it is nevertheless true to say that, as Hume saw, without a *blik* there can be no explanation, for it is by our *bliks* that we decide what is and what is not an explanation. Suppose we believed that everything that happened, happened by pure chance. This would not of course be an assertion; for it is compatible with anything happening or not happening, and so, incidentally, is its contradictory. But if we had this belief, we should not be able to explain or predict or plan anything. Thus, although we should not be *asserting* anything different from those of a more moral belief, there would be a great difference between us; and this is the sort of difference that there is between those who really believe in God and those who really disbelieve in him (260).

Hare contents himself with the discovery of the "fact" that, behind all attempts to explain reality, there are decisions which are neither accessible to justification, nor to rational control. As a matter of fact he does not consider these to be irremedial. In any case, however, he thinks that they cannot be influenced by either rationality or criticism. The question of how the decision for a definite "blik" comes about, is neither raised nor answered. In this sense, there may be a rational dialogue only within a realm of decisions in which definite basic presuppositions are already accepted. Varifying the correctness of the decision within the domain of the unknown, would be possible only *post factum*. Owing to the multiplicity of world-views, irrationality must be conceded to one's own supreme "primary decision" because, otherwise, the contradiction would arise that one's own personal "blik" would be given rational preference.

With the rejection of the possibility to eidetically penetrate the "blik", a generally binding rational standard can no longer be specified. The reference is lost according to which a "blik" could be recognised to be correct. Therefore, it is necessary to suspend judgement on the respective decisions of belief held by persons of differing perspectives. The suspension of the question of truth by an attitude of tolerance, stipulating that individuals can achieve salvation in their own way, must actually be considered to express resignation rather than liberalism. Such liberalism refuses to recognize anything unproven as authoritative as it tends to recognize as significant only the affirmative result of an investigation. Where the notion of justification cannot be maintained to the end, it attempts to replace justification by critical reason. Accordingly, all statements resulting from a "blik" must be reviewed. Like Kant's critique, their truth content is to be examined as an attempt to secure the legitimacy of belief *and* knowledge.

As a matter-of-fact, following R. B. Braithwaite and Paul Van Buren, if one rejects the claim of meaning as well as the merely psychological and pedagogical interpretation of the religious statement, then it is basically unimportant how one uses the fool's privilege. How I speak of God and of the world is of no relevance because these sentences are not connected with assertions that have even the slightest trace of truth. It can be seen from Hare's last quotation that his understanding of "blik" differs slightly from the understanding of the two previously mentioned authors. However, the "blik" as a constitutive factor for explanations and actions and as an absolute presupposition for every explanatory attempt is not only beyond the explanation, but must be regarded as something that cannot be substantiated. For the materialization of the "blik" concept, which is typical of linguistic-analytical reflection, prohibits the understanding of the "blik" as the basis of all thought and speech. This allows one to develop principles and categories that form a platform from which the uniqueness of stance taking indigenous to the religious statement can be seen as worthy of affirmation or rejection.

In this sense, it is obvious that it is Hume and his followers and not Kant who developed the "blik" concept.

> ...differences between *bliks* about the world cannot be settled by observation of what happens in the world. That was why, having performed the interesting experiment of doubting the ordinary man's *blik* about the world, and showing that no proof would be given to make us adopt one *blik* rather than another, he turned to backgammon to take his mind off the problem (261).

If the decision for a definite "blik" is not grounded in the fact that its contents have been substantiated, then the essential prerequisite of the "blik" is its form. This leaves the contents untouched. Yet it is because the contents are of coincidental character, in contrast to the presupposed form, that it should be possible to examine asserted contents made by the "blik" in regard to its correctness. However, the question is neglected of how one can understand the fact that the contents of the "blik"'s interpretation of the world are so multifaceted and frequently contradictory. This is so even though for the emotivist it is undoubtedly the case that the formulation of a "blik" with its contents has practical consequences. The "blik" is regarded definitely as a designing process borne by a definite expectation for which it cannot be insignificant whether or not everything happens by mere coincidence. This is the case even in the consideration of the possibility of a scientific explanation. Every theory of causal relationship presupposes certain expectations. Hare is confronted with the problem of the practical consequences that result from religious expectations, depicted by his reference to the various attitudes among the Sikhs and Moslems having the same origin in the Punjab (262). This reference might have been the impulse for a new attempt to conceive the "blik" along a unique line of thought that could review the substantiation of its contents, and overcome the claim of sufficiency of a mere authentication, such as that of the sentence, "World history is the Last Judgement". According to Hare this sentence as well commits itself to a certain "blik" which, because it remains unproven, cannot legitimize such a conclusion. The thought that the correctness of a religious "blik" can be seen from the consequences which a religious act or its omission entails is not possible. The validation made on the basis of empirical expectation, would imply a step backwards, according to the emotive substantiation of the religious proposition (263). According to this theory, what should have been avoided, would happen: the attempt is made to measure the sense of religious propositions by the positivistic criterion of truth.

The sentence "God created heaven and earth" does not claim to be a scientific empiricist statement of belief. As such, it is a religious statement. Without a doubt Hare has correctly recognized the uniqueness of this sentence when, at the end of his essay "Religion and Morals", he more or less explains it by pointing out:

> Christians believe that God created the world out of chaos, or out of nothing, in the sense of no *thing*. What I am now going to say I say very tentatively. It is possible that this is our way of expressing the truth that without belief in a divine order - a belief expressed in other terms by means of worshipping assent to principles of discriminating between fact and illusion - there could be no belief in matters of fact or in real objects? Certainly it is salutary to recognize that *even* our belief in so-called hard facts rests in the end on a faith, a commitment, which is not in or to facts, but in that without which there would not be any facts (264).

Appropriately as the unique religious sense of the sentence "God created heaven and earth" may be interpreted, and although none of the emotivists have come to discuss the matter, besides the legitimacy of religious convictions, the legitimacy of their contents. This is the case even though this problem had already recognized before the noted revision of the "blik".

> Man has not changed biologically since primitive times, it is his religion that has changed and it can easily change again (265).

5. The religious attitude and its justification

The criticism of the methodical solipsism of present-day philosophy has had a substantial influence on the development of analytic conceptuality. It stresses that language normally refers to objects, and that it does not serve the self-reflection of the subject, that is anonymously present in the every-day use of language. The emotivists tended to over-emphasize the function of representation and were strongly dependent on the early period of positivism. In order to evade solipsism they required that neither reflective investigation nor the justification of one's own stance could be labeled a direct subjective conviction. Language remained limited to its exclusively descriptive representative function. This lack of readiness to include one's own stance meant that the belief manifested in representation could be described only as a fact attributable to an empirical reality. As such it is explainable only as the result of causally conceivable processes. The horror of a self-interrogation and the recognition of causal language blocked the possibility for the emotivists to answer the question of the correct "blik", even as it turned up again and again in the meta-religious "blik" theory. One should note that the emotivist critique of the concretization of the belief attitude and its basis is expressed by means of causal language. The emotivists thought that they could save the unexplainable character of the decision for belief by listing actual causes, and merely negating all possible cognitive explanations. One can correctly conclude that a question which cannot be answered cannot be recognized as legitimate. This would be in keeping with Wittgenstein's conviction that questions are only asked when answers can be given. It is therefore astonishing that Hare, nevertheless, raises the question of the correct "blik".

> It is important to realize that we have a sane one, and not no *blik*
> at all; for there must be two sides to any argument - if he has a
> wrong *blik*, then those who are right ... must have a right one ...
> but nevertheless it is very important to have the right *blik* (266).

We do not deny that his requirement does not primarily intend to refer to cognitivity. However, the question of the correct "blik" must not be seen to be independent of the background of Wittgenstein's thought. Wittgenstein tried to conceive of thinking as language. Therefore, he rejects the appeal to practical reason as an authority for practical notions that are thought to be theoretical guidelines for the self-realization of the believer. In contrast to Braithwaite, the consequence for Hare and those emotivists who do not want to equate the sense and function of religious propositions with moral ones, is that they address the "blik" as an indication of a decision. They understand its reality as a structure of thought, speech and action common to the life and language of a community. However, the requirement for the correct "blik" dissolves for the understanding of language as reality on whose ground the decision for belief is carried out cannot be recognized. Consequently, there is no longer the possibility of speaking of the decision for belief in a different way than one would when one speaks of objects that are describable and explainable by language. If one tries to interpret the decision for belief in the sense of the common structural agreement between thought, speech and action, then language cannot speak of itself in the same way as it speaks of objects (267). One can correctly say that the "blik" does not belong to those objects which can be described and explained by language. This is the case following Hare, the creator of the "blik" theory, because the "blik" is regarded as the acting and explanatory constitutive for those objects on which an opinion is formed. This means that the "blik" constitutes the stance on the basis of which a judgement is passed. If this reflective possibility goes unrecognized and in addition the general validity of the "blik" concept characterizing the concept of "blik" as stemming from a cognitively and scientifically explainable notion of causal reason is excluded, then the classification of the "blik" as a psychological fact provides a solution.

However, it must be investigated whether or not it is the case that the "blik" concept is being negotiated under its value. At any rate, it must be borne in mind that according to the emotivists there is no other possibility to understand the question of the "why" of an attitude of belief or of a perspective on life. It is to be understood as a fact seeking question for a fact which has a different fact, the effect, as a consequence. At the same time, the emotivists are unable to grasp the "blik" as a result of a rational consideration within an historical situation. They cannot see that this result is direct and at the same time conveyed and explained through the experiential history of the believer.

According to the emotivist understanding of the "blik" - if I plead that I have decided in favor of this or that course of action *because* this or that "blik" determines one's decision, then this explanation of one's behavior can only be regarded as tautological. This "because" does not imply a reason, but only indicates the psychological fact which then finds expression in one's action. The indifference towards the substance of the statement is partly due to the causal understanding of language which admits only a linear interpretation of its contents. Following this interpretation, the sentence from *Genesis* is regarded as an account of a scientific event which took place at some time in the past. It is not regarded as an axiomatic declaration concerning the relationship between God and the world according to which Creation finds its fulfillment in its historical self-realization (268). In classifying this paradigmatic sentence as a cognitive statement it would be immaterial whether a decision for belief expressing itself in such a statement were interpreted in a linear or in a dialectic way. The reference to this possibility of interpretation, according to which the speaker understands himself as being placed within the process of Creation and feels called to concretize the idea of Creation by concretizing his belief expressing the "blik", might be valued only as a tautology because the emotivist interprets the "blik" not as the maintance of a stance, but as a stance itself.

In contrast to those who refer to an eschatological possibility of verification (269) in their reference to this definition, the emotivists have managed to prevent a statement expressing a "blik" like that about God creating heaven and earth from being compared with scientific results. The emotivists' understanding of belief as "blik" offers them the argument to reject the requirement that the value of religious statements should be measured against the progress of scientific research, without exposing themselves to the reproach of immunization. As a matter of fact, their interpretation protects them against the obligation to identify the empirical consequences that can be deduced from the sentence "God created heaven and earth". Yet, it blocks the possibility of a non-scientific explanation for the respective stance in the "blik". In this respect, there is no difference between Hare's "blik" theory and the "blik" interpretations given by Braithwaite and Van Buren. However, unlike theirs, Hare's "blik" theory is not to be taken as a subsequent interpretation of religious statements. Rather, it is the attempt to explain how such statements come about. In this sense, Hare's question about the right "blik" must not be understood as an admonition. It does not content itself with the assertion that a substantiating "because" cannot be given in answering the question "why?". Such a question, strictly speaking, cannot accept Hare's conception of the "blik" as a direct state of the soul that allows an integration of its correctness. With this question Hare comes up against the boundaries of the emotivist linguistic pattern. This makes it impossible to grasp the "blik" as a constituent of all possible explanations. Hare interprets it in a way that does not apostrophize the "blik" as a personal preference, but traces it back to a principle that has become discernable in the stance taken. In other words, he traces it back to the concrete religious decision - the decision for belief. Even if this decision is a personal achievement of the subject speaking or of the community to which the believer belongs, it should be possible to regard it as an achievement that is motivated in the first place by its own matter-of-factness. For this decision, religious language would have to be the reality that consitutes the root of the history of its rational discussion, of its inquiry, its progress in religious insight, and its performance of belief. In this consideration, however, the "blik" concept can no longer be understood in a linear way. In the sense of distinguishing between "believing in" and "believing that" this means that the "blik" can neither be attributed merely to the one nor exclusively to the other of these two momentums. Otherwise, the "blik" would be understood neither as a confirmation of individual events and facts on the basis of a greater or lesser possibility, nor as the abandonment of critical questioning concerning its own contents. Rooted in the "blik", the believer must be concerned by what he believes. In the rational performance of his "blik" (belief) he is so concerned that he risks living his life according to the contents of his belief. However, it was not Hare but Malcolm who tried to defend the ontological argument under these presuppositions. We will discuss this later.

a) The Psychological and Moral Understanding of Sense

Here, the religious statement expresses the recognition of definite moral maxims (270). In the religious context, the maxim is not represented in abstract and direct terminology, but it is veiled and made understandable by means of illustrative examples in "a set of propositions", the so-called

Christian stories. The purpose of such a veiling of moral principles is seen in making people familiar with them, through phantasy, imagination and hope.

> It is an empirical psychological fact that many people find it easier to resolve upon and to carry through a course of action which is contrary to their natural inclinations if this policy is associated in their minds with certain stories. And in many people the psychological link is not appreciably weakened by the fact that the story associated with the behaviour policy is not believed (271).

Braithwaite's quote points out that the belief in the truth of stories with psychological functionality is not necessary but sufficient. It is sufficient:

> ... that the story should be entertained in thought, i.e. that the statement of the story should be understood as having a meaning.
> I have secured this by requiring that the story should consist of empirical propositions (272).

Accordingly, the inherent content of religious propositions is not to be taken as a fact, but rather as a state-of-affairs. Such a view of "Christian stories" may well apply to such parables as that of the Good Samaritan, offering the possibility to accept historical statements on the life and death of Jesus of Nazareth as truly possible. However, this view is not sufficient to interpret, as meaningful, such specifically religious beliefs as the belief in Jesus as the Christ, or those on the Creation and the Last Judgement. This attempt at interpretation is undertaken only when the Gospel is understood as the "way of life". On the one hand, the possibility of verifying religious statements, if they are consistent among themselves, is established by recognizing them as possible states-of-affairs. On the other hand, Braithwaite finds himself at a loss when he depreciates those statements which cannot be verified empirically as "exemplary fairy tales". He evaluates them in psychological terms in order to ascribe to them some kind of sense. According to Braithwaite, the statement that a definite action or a definite way of behavior is in agreement with the will of God is not to be regarded as an assertion of correspondence. In his opinion, it only serves as an incentive and as a psychological help in carrying out a definite activity. The inherently questionable nature of this psychological interpretation has been stressed by William Hordern in his criticism of Braithwaite. He points out the inadequacy of the concept of attitude and rejects the neglect of the inquiry into the truth of the substantial meaning of the statement.

> It is true that the person who makes theological statements normally does reveal something about his own attitudes and behavioral policies. To say that "God created the universe" is to

imply a positive attitude towards the universe. To say that "God was in Christ" implies a desire on the part of the speaker to live a Christ-like life. But down through the centuries Christians have not used such statements solely to express attitudes or behavioral policies. They have used them to express belief about reality. Furthermore Christians have believed that there is a close relationship between the truth of the statement and the attitudes and behavior that normally accompany belief in the statements (273).

In Braithwaite's interpretation of religious statements he attempts to do justice both to the criterion of empirical verification and to take seriously what the believer declares as his faith. This leads to consequences which ultimately, as Braithwaite himself must admit, annihilate the sense of statements of belief that claim to be specific statements and independent of moral implications.

> In this lecture I have been sparing in my use of the term 'religious belief' (although it occurs in the title), preferring instead to speak of religious assertions and of religious conviction. This was because for me the fundamental problem is that of the meaning of statements used to make religious assertions, and I have accordingly taken my task to be that of explaining the use of such assertions, in accordance with the principle that meaning is to be found by ascertaining use. In disentangling the elements of this use I have discovered nothing which can be called 'belief' in the senses of this word applicable either to an empirical or to a logically necessary proposition.
>
> A religious assertion, for me, is the assertion of an intention to carry out a certain behaviour policy, subsumable under a sufficiently general principle to be a moral one, together with the implicit or explicit statement, but not the assertion, of certain stories. Neither the assertion of the intention nor the reference to the stories includes belief in its ordinary senses (274).

This kind of ethics of agape is supported by the fear that the truth-claim of religious statements may disintegrate between the contrasts of a complete irrelevance and a "naturalistic paralogism" (275) of anthropomorphic interpretation. Consequently, the reductionist proposal is not to be taken as an attempt to depreciate religion. Rather it is an attempt with the instruments of early positivism to escape the dilemma of religion. However, in the debate of positivism some doubts arise as to the appropriateness of such a procedure to uncover the logic of religious language and rescue a sense for religious statements. Therefore, the question has repeatedly been put to

Braithwaite whether the attempt to guarantee the claim of sense for belief by rejecting the claim of verification for religious statements, does not mean "eliminating religious language and religion". Similar ideas have been expressed by N. H. G. Robinson in his essay, "The Logic of Religious Language", where he expresses his suspicion that the methods of linguistic analysis may not be adequate for dealing with religious language.

> Does what is recognisably religion remain when religious belief has been eliminated? No doubt to believe in God is to do much more than to believe that certain propositions are true of God, and it may require all the refinements of linguistic analysis to make plain what that something more is; but none the less, is not belief that certain propositions are true of God the indispensable undergirding so that without it religion has ceased to exist? In other words, although belief *in* God is not just belief *about* God, no matter how fully articulated, is it not in and through belief about God that one believes in him, so that without the former either the latter is altogether empty and vacuous or else religion becomes something other than itself, a declaration of moral intent or a number of inspiring stories or both, but not religion? It is the elimination of religious belief that can be true or false that arouses the suspicion - at this stage no more than the suspicion - that the linguistic analyst's account of religious language is doomed to be reductionist in character (276).

b) The Secular Understanding of Sense

Braithwaite has in common with other representatives of the emotive theory the assumption that the sense of religious propositions can be deduced from the principles of behavior.

> The way to find out what are the intentions embodied in a set of religious assertions, and hence what is the meaning of the assertion is by discovering what principles of conduct the asserter takes the assertions to involve (277).

It was characteristic of Braithwaite's considerations that he saw the sense claim of religious statements fulfilled in the context of moral statements. On this point, the secular understanding of religion, in contrast to the psychological-moral interpretation, is more consistent in that it abolishes the difference between religion and morality as well as morals by "reducing theology to ethics" (278). This step is taken in view of the assertion that other realms of life can be scientifically approached.

> Astrology has been "reduced" to astronomy, for example; we have excluded from the study of the stars a cosmological or metaphysical theory about their effect on human life. Alchemy was "reduced" to chemistry by the rigorous application of an empirical method. During the Renaissance, the metaphysical ideas and purposes of medieval painting were excluded, leaving "only" the work of art. In almost every field of human learning, the metaphysical and cosmological aspect has disappeared and the subject matter has been "limited" to the human, the historical, the empirical. Theology cannot escape this tendency if it is to be a serious mode of contemporary thought, and such a "reduction" of content need no more be regretted in theology than in astronomy, chemistry, or painting (279).

The "more" in the sense of a transcendent God of classical Christianity has fallen victim to "the inability to find any empirical linguistic anchorage" (280). The reduction of theology is supposed to overcome the weak point of such a religious interpretation by taking up the psychological observations of Braithwaite.

> If there is a weak link in this chain of reasoning,it is Braithwaite's understanding of the function of the Christian "story" and its relationship to the intention to lead the Christian "way of life". While his psychological observation is correct, his solution does not do justice to the indispensable role of the "story" in the kerygma (281).

The instrumentality of linguistic analysis should go beyond both Barth's and Fritz Buri's (282) critique of Rudolf Bultmann's demythologizing program. This instrumentality was already applied by Braithwaite and is to be further carried out, so that the understanding of the Gospel is no longer possible on the basis of faith without compromising the kerygma and its historical groundwork by an existential interpretation. "Talk of God in the language of the World" is thought of as the mediation of the theses of Bultman: Faith is the presence of the original human possibility of authentic existence; and that faith only become present because of the event of Jesus of Nazareth. Light on the secular relevance of the Gospel is supposed to render conspicuous the function "which history fulfills in the kerygma" (283). The task of carrying further Hare's conception of "blik" should occur in its specifics and in the approximation of the Gospel to this "as an expression of an historical perspective" (284) In doing so critique should be raised which demonstrates that words like "I" and "believe", like those introducing the three articles of the Credo, do not point to an historical fact. Rather, they warn one of the misunderstanding of seeing them as confessional statements which do not talk of contents but of a "blik".

Religion is expressly not classified here according to its self-understanding and the intention of its statements. Rather, it is classified according to the social function that it receives. Accordingly religious statements of the speaker and listener are not seen here as reflexion on creatureliness and sin. On the contrary, they are seen as reflexions on the social conditions of life. This hinders the religious category of transcendence from coming into play, as is impressively demonstrated by Van Buren's interpretation of the Easter event (285).

The word of the resurrection of Jesus is considered by Van Buren to be the perception of Disciples of the dynamic freedom of Jesus which allowed them to become aware of their own freedom.

> Jesus of Nazareth was a free man in his own life, who attracted followers and created enemies according to the dynamics of personality and in a manner comparable to the effect of other liberated persons in history upon people about them. He died as a result of the threat that such a free man poses for insecure and bound men. His disciples were left no less insecure and frightened. Two days later, Peter, and then other disciples, had an experience of which Jesus was the sense-content. They experienced a discernment situation in which Jesus the free man whom they had known themselves, and indeed the whole world, were seen in a quite new way. From that moment, the disciples began to possess something of the freedom of Jesus. His freedom began to be "contagious". For the disciples, therefore, the story of Jesus could not be told simply as the story of a free man who had died. Because of the new way in which the disciples saw him and because of what had happened to them, the story had to include the event of Easter. In telling the story of Jesus of Nazareth, therefore, they told it as the story of the free man who had set them free (286).

According to Van Buren the "blik" of the Christian into the Gospel, finds here its adequate expression. Thereby the uniqueness of the Christian "blik" is unthinkable without standing in relation to the historical person Jesus of Nazareth (287). Due to this "blik" the characteristic freedom of the Christian perspective on life becomes real. Van Buren sees in Jesus the guiding perspective that guarantees the believer an understanding of himself as a free human. It guarantees the believer an understanding of himself as a free person. It guarantees a perspective of history and the world as a perspective in freedom. The statement "Jesus is resurrected from the dead" does not express an ascertainment. Rather the "word of the end of time", "resurrection" can only be assessed according to the behavior of the one who uses it (288). This interpretation of the event of Easter is not without effect on Van Buren's understanding of faith.

In contrast to Braithwaite's psychological interpretation, he understands faith to be an act of positive decision and commitment. The principle of faith, that faith is a gift and not an acheivement, is interpreted as the attainment of a "blik". This means that the decision for a christian world-view is not groundable. Here faith is not understood in the sense of holding something material to be possible, as one could understand Braithwaite's concept of faith. Yet it cannot be seen to be a form of transcendence and a reference to a particular type of reality.

The rejection of a transcendental understanding of faith forces the analysis of the Gospel to limit itself to an empirical based interpretation. It follows that Christian belief of the exclusiveness of Jesus of Nazareth is referable to its unique but thoroughly repeatable historicality. This denies him, for example, divinity as maintained by traditional theology. It consequently follows that Van Buren argues that the freedom of Socrates could become a norm, the lessons of the history of Socrates could become a norm, where the lessons of the history of Socrates have a similar liberating influence to that of the historical Jesus. One can speak of the person involved as being "in Socrates" instead of as being "in Christ" (289).

The interpretation of Holy Scripture is therefore not reconstruction of what is meant by traditional theological exegesis. Rather it is entrance in the social process of emancipation, which it has set in action. Here the religious selfunderstanding of Jesus and that of the authors of the New Testament is seen only in the subjective borders within which an emancipating activity begins. For Christians Jesus is the exemplary case which makes possible the step into the social process of liberation. This is especially true as the unique acheivement of emancipation cannot be forcebly cancelled with the death of Jesus.

When one attempts to interpret a religious statement on the basis of *agape* like Braithwaite, or on a secular basis like Van Buren then one attempts to give a sense to them which does not require a particular religious dimension. Yet one has not explained why they give the impression of constative statements according to their grammatical form. The theory of a secular meaning of the Gospel demonstrates itself to be a hermeneutical theory that lays bare the intentions of the biblical message. However, grammatical findings can only maintain their explanation, if it is discovered that the process of human self-liberation can be established only with difficulty and with resistance from the person involved. It was necessary to use such sentences which could not be immediately seen to be practical and which govern human rationality. This means, their assertive character should raise their effectivity (Braithwaite) as moral statements or emancipatory expectations (Van Buren). In this sense Kai Nielsen believed religious statements were ideological and defined thus:

> An ideological sentence is a sentence which appears to be just an empirical hypothesis but actually functions as a value-judgement. Ideological sentences are primarily used surreptitiously to recommend some action or attitude. They increase the psychological effectiveness of certain value-judgements for some people by making rhem seem to be crucial but mysterious laws of nature. They differ from genuine factual statements that they can in no way be falsified; incompatible evidence is always rejected as inconclusive. The person persuaded by them claims to know them as self-evident truths, through, how he knows this, he will insist, is something which is beyond verbal communication or at least incapable of being shown except by the similarly identified elect (290).

Essential for the effectivity of such sentences is not only that they appear in false clothing (291), but that those who believe in them are also convinced that they are constative.

> For these sentences to be effective they must not be known to be ideological by the person persuaded by them. Further, such a person will always resist any translation of any sentence, so constructed, into an evaluative sentence or into a sentence used to express preferences (292).

Nielsen's interpretation intensifies the concept of a secularization of religion as presented in Van Buren's *The Secular Meaning of the Gospel* (as the title to the original English version implies in contrast to the poor German translation of the title of this work *Reden von Gott - in der Sprache der Welt*), to a religion of secularization.

> God-sentences, I suggest, are like ideological sentences; they express and evoke commitments and they are never taken as just evaluative or as just practical. And, like ideological sentences, they appear to be assertions while remaining anomalous with respect to falsification, they supposedly cannot be fully understood except by the believer, and de-mythologized versions of them are invariably rejected as somehow inadequate. They

function to distort our awareness of what the world is like; and, while they may soothe anxieties, they do so only at the expense of making us believe in the reality of the Emperor's new clothes (293).

In this quote is demonstrated the weakness of such a theory of the secularization of religion, if it must rid itself of the religion which it is assigned to fulfill its program. It becomes contradictory exactly because it is without rest to fulfill its practical function of social emancipation. Undoubtedly, the attempt to mediate a secular understanding of the Gospel is not to be assessed as a political theology of secluarization, even when social and economic consequences are included in its very point of departure. This arises from our investigation of the relationship of the language of the Gospel to the langauge of different types of human experience. In this investigation, the following thesis is proposed.

If no family resemblances were allowed between the language of the Gospel and the way in which we speak of being loved by another human being, we should have to abandon all hope of understanding what the Gospel means (294).

This thesis will be discussed further in the fourth chapter.

c) Sense Claim and Behavioral Practice

In the background of this thesis is the principle of verification with its claim that theological statements are to be characterized as meaningless. They are understood as empirical ascertainments. However, they have sense in so far as they are:

... expressions of a historical perspective with far-reaching empirical consequences in a man's life (295).

Van Buren's secular interpretation has in common with Braithwaite's psychological interpretation the claim that a cognitive treatment of religious language is inadequate according to the stand of logical and theological research. and also measured against the kernal of the Gospel (296). Van Buren's search for secular understanding is founded on the same thesis of a possible understanding of the sense of religious statements as Braithwaite's proposal.

The meaning of a statement is to be found in, and is identical with, the function of that statement. If a statement has a function, so that it may in principle be verified or falsified, the statement is meaningful, and unless or until a theological statement can be submitted in some way to verification, it cannot be said to have a meaning in our language-game (297).

It does not matter which meaning is appointed the "propositional element". The rejection of individual sense goes in every case hand in hand with the settlement of and in consequence of a reduction of the truth - i.e. claim of a statement to understanding within a particular behavioral practice. In the case of our example, the unsaid presupposition of this process is the assumption that the explanation of the sense of "Christian stories" is actually to be taken in sufficient measure from behavioural practice. This claim can refer back to its source in the theory of reduction of late Wittgenstein.

The use of the word in practice is its meaning. ... The meaning of the expression depends entirely on how we go on using it (298).

We are not putting in doubt the agreement of Horden's critique with Braithwaithe, which states that religious statements could have a psychologically motivating and stimulating function. We admit, in reference to Van Buren, that a particular stance toward life corresponds to a particular belief. Consequently we can add to Hordern's question, if this descriptive propositional function can be seen as an exhaustive presentation of the assertive sense of these sentences (299), the question, if the sense of religious statements does not consist in a mutual relation to the mental sense of the statement. In other words, does this consist in the non-reducable behaviorist understanding of the word and the function of this statement in its behavioral context (300). This is a question that will occupy us in a similar manner in the discussion of the analytical theory of understanding. Here it is only important, because the fact, that the assertive sense of a sentence can put in question all previously motivated behavior, is to be explained. It is obvious that Braithwaite and Van Buren have undertaken their interpretations under the influence of the reductionist theory of late Wittgenstein. However, it will be necessary to prove this, if the use of this theory is actually possible for religious statements, as they both presuppose. For such an application it would be decisive that it is not the specifications of the selection of the approached examples which had hardened the correctness of Wittgenstein's theory. In his examples, the dialectical relationship of mutual mediation remains hidden between the paricular sense of a sentence and its function, so the conclusion is allowed that the sense of a sentence or of a word is actually seen in its use in a speech or behavioral situation.

Whatever decision may be made about Wittgenstein's theory and whatever consequences might follow, the validity of the emotive theory of religion can be judged independently from the presence of this decision. The repeated reference to Wittgenstein may not mislead us to believe that the emotive theory is not doomed, because it understands religious language initially as information and communication about religious objects. Rather, it understands it as an expresion of a belief, or a standpoint in life that is not groundable. It must be maintained, that belief must be seen as behavioral motivation as one considers its dialogical function and the religious principle which leads it to become a speach-act. The meta-religous reflection on language is concerned with a normative claim, because the religious sentence effects the belief of others. It attempts to grasp this as a neutral descriptive state of affairs. Language receives a double function: first with its help the standpoint or "blik", according to Hare is determined; and second, it establishes this standpoint towards the descriptive manners of behavior resulting from it. Because the emotive theory of religion has decided to consider this standpoint, i.e. of the "blik" as a fact, instead of seeking in it a unique religious logic it sees itself forced to avoid the question of the justification of the "blik" with reference to psychological assumptions, as in Van Buren's case, or to basic pedagogical perspectives. Here is its decisive weakness. As already mentioned this weakness is determined by the attitudinal meaning which the emotive theory places in importance only next to the constituative meaning which describes a fact. This is different from Wittgenstein's other possibility for understanding the religious statement, for this meaning, in contrast to descriptive meaning, is not seen in the foundational function which it fulfills.

IV. BELIEF AS TRUTH

1. Foundation of the analytical theory of comprehension

Several theories changed in response to Wittgenstein's interpretation of language. The emotive theory rejects the claim that faith is cognitive. This denial takes place by means of a comprehensive analysis of language. It attempts to expose all trains of thought clothed in religious propositions as pseudological and to prove them to be devoid of all assertive power. The criterion of empirical verification supports this evidence for the lack of correspondence with a state-of-affairs or fact. From the point of view of the construction of a theory of intersubjectivity, a language is presupposed which excludes all particular nonempirical use of language, and is a picture of thought. They raise the relative "stability of an individual use of language ... to that of a semantic-syntactical regulated mathematics" (301). In contrast, the emotive theory sees religious language as language which disguises thought in such a way that it is impossible to deduce the disguised form from its external clothing. This is impossible because the external form is designed on the basis of a totally different intention "than to let the form of the body be recognized" (302). Unlike other constative acts of language, the purpose of the religious proposition is not to be found in the propositional content of applied sentences and not to be connected to a truth-claim. Rather, the purpose of the religious proposition lies in a realm which can no longer be rationally grasped. It is a realm which is described emotionally, for which even the question of the corretness of a claim of truth is improper. The abolishment of the linguistic veto and the philosophy of late Wittgenstein have not lost their influence upon the emotive theory, but the representatives of this theory of belief without truth made as little use as possible of the opportunities opened by Wittgenstein's linguistic philosophy. On the contrary, their doctrine of the religious proposition shows dependence on the decisive conceptions of the *Tractatus*. This dependence must be assessed as considerably greater than that on the *Philosophical Investigations*.

In various ways, it has been brought to light that in his late philosophy Wittgenstein substituted the theory of the plurality of language worlds for his theory of the ideal language. He no longer sought the explication of language, but rather sought to enlighten us about its false paths and temptations through a "celebrative language". He requires that language be understood as consisting of regulated language games. The language game of picturing which he appointed the exclusive claim of truth and meaning in his early phase, is now seen as merely one among many. This thesis of the infinite variety of immanently regulated uses of language give boundaries to the scope of the problem of meaning and truth for religious propositions. The analytical differentiation concentrates on the comparison of "known", "unknown", "unsuitable" and "unique" functions of religious language without further considerations of the possible mutuality of the ontological structure of the religious proposition and reality.

On the basis of this procedure and its consideration of the implicitly cognitive character of religious statements, an inquiry arises into the relationship of religious language with other languages:

1. To those languages in which only appointed aspects of experience are expressed.

2. To those languages (e.g. the language of faith) which intend to conceive of the totality of experience (philosophical language) (303).

The determination of the relationship of the religious language to other possible language games in the end is the key to truth. Truth remains postulated as unified truth. Yet it is to be formulated anew due to the re-evaluation of the *Tractatus* and the thesis of the multiplicity of language possibilities.

Indeed, it has been demonstrated that queries such as that of the biochemical language-game about the analysis of the components of bread, are senseless and inappropriate within the religious language game which identifies bread with the body of Christ. However, the intentional or accidental occurrence of the term "bread" in both language games is not explained.

The empiricist exclusion of religious statements (304) in that it was arbitrary in its selection-process displays from an empircal perspective that its predecision was intentional. This implies the danger "that a justified claim to uniqueness of structure and aim in theological language results in an unjustified claim for philosophical immunity, autonomy and self-justification" (305). The countless efforts to secure the cognitive character of theological language at the cost of the truth-claim of so-called scientific language can be regarded as attempts to protect against this danger (306). This is also true for those apologetic endeavours which tend to concentrate on the pragmatic aspect of religious language while neglecting the semantical-syntactical aspect. In this manner, the theory of performative speech offered the advantage of examining the tie between religious language and inter-subjective context, in that one gains a relationship to particular situations without having to deal with the question concerning which criteria justify the truth-claim of religious propositions or to deal with the basic problem of how these religious statements relate to reality. In addition to this, one found oneself close to the analysis of moral language and the discussion of the condition for finding a consensus on moral norms.

There is no disputing that religious propositions only receive their assertional force within the context of language events, or that the determination of their claim to meaning is inconceivable without the pragmatics of the situation of religious speech. The claim of religious propositions expressing themselves in the external form of constative assertion, can be seen "to be true or false ... to give information about God's purpose, nature, intention, and action ... (but) not meant to express the feelings of the speaker" (307). When the believer confesses, "God created heaven and earth", it is possible to question the integrity of this confession. However, it is very difficult to doubt that its propositional content is like that of a constituative act. Undoubtedly performative character suits the words of the believer. A parallel can be drawn between this religious proposition and the words in a parlamentary election with which a commissioner nominates a delegate to be a representative of his district. But this comparison has its limitations. To confess God as Creator is something different than appointing someone to something which he neither previously nor independently could have been (308). As Luther describes this condition, "Faith is the creator of deity, but not according to the person, but rather in us" (309).

The question is appropriate of whether the truth-claim of a religious proposition is opposed to the observations of the *Philosophical Investigations* in spite of or because of the thesis of language pluralism. If this question were not specifically tuned to religious propositions, it could be posed differently. Are not the consequences, which the *Philosophical Investigations* have drawn from the *Tractatus*, in the end, the rejection of an *ontologia generalis*? In line with Wittgenstein, one could define this objection by pointing out that a clarification of the idleness of language, for example of metaphysical language-games, would be unthinkable as a consequence of a mere descriptive procedure. In addition, one would assume "that Wittgenstein understands the differentiation and relativation of languages transcendental logic in language-games in such a way that that which 'merely' shows itself to be the condition of the possibility of all objective description is only accessible in the same objective description (in the sense of an alienation of human self-understanding)" (310). Indeed, Wittgenstein has neither posed nor answered this problem in the *Philosophical Investigations*. However, according to its motive, this problem appears to be present in the history of Wittgenstein's struggle against the bewitchment of an incorrect conception of language. In this sense, the thought of the late Wittgenstein no longer seeks to resolve life's problems. Rather, on the basis of linguistic evidence he shows humankind the way out of problems, by explicating the specific place of this problem in a given language-game. Such a program is obligated either to explain the evidence for the legitimacy of its claim to validity or to explain why such a claim cannot take place. This holds true for religious sentences of the constative propositional form.

Liberation from language's bewitchment occurs when it is proven that propositions of a language are asserted whose treatment would actually belong to another language. Thereby, according to Wittgenstein, the question of the truth of a proposition can only be answered by simultaneously answering the question of the criteria for the truth of this proposition. He believes that these criteria come to light when one describes that language-game in which questionable propositions are encountered. It is another question of whether or not a descriptively oriented deep grammar, following Wittgensteins intention, is enough to justify the truth-claim of religious statements. Furthermore, it should be asked if description is in the position to set free the inner-logic by which religious language is regulated, or whether we stumble here on the limitations of language. In analytical philosophy, the attempt has at least been made, on the basis of the *Philosophical Investigations*, to discuss the truth-claim of religious propositions.

2. The religious language game

The analysis of analytical philosophy proceeds from the assumption of the possibility of true propositions. It tries to come to grips syntactically with a given language, so that some of its propositions can be claimed to be true. As religious propositions cannot be falsified by means of observational propositions, which can be drawn from them, the test of their truth-claim is referred to models.

(a) With their aid a clarification of their status is to be established. The proof of this comes from the fact that all comprehendable theological conceptions are founded on theological models and not on abstract theory (311).

(b) According to this approach, the question of truth can only be posed within a certain linguistic context.

a) Application of Models

In addition to its heuristic function, the interpretation of other models, for example parables etc., should serve to "discover (in religious models) the quest for a unity and coherence in the biblical account as a whole" (312). Its function seems to be "that of laying down guidelines for what may be counted as being real" (313). In contrast to models from other realms of language, it is presupposed that religious models must be able to be considered true because of their heuristic function. Any act of cognitive assent to theology's claims will have a necessary reference to theology's model of reality. But cognitive assent to a claim P, incorporating P into one's scheme of things, is equivalent to affirming that P is *true*. Thus, since every theological truth-claim has a necessary involvement in the key theological model, the *model* in this sense must be judged true or false if any theological statements at all are judged true or false (314).

If one attempts to examine this argument and takes into consideration the truth-claim of, for example, the religious proposition: "God created heaven and earth", then this examination would have to be limited to the definitions of the terms implicated. It could only explain the relationship of these terms in an abstract ('Kalkül'), according to which they would be only a culmination of meaningless signs. Hence, the intelligibleness of the model sentence must be based on models which can be interpreted with the aid of applied terms. In other words they must be translated from a less familiar realm to a more familiar realm of speech. The model should illustrate the rules of the interrelation of speech and act. It should allow these to be ascertained directly unlike certain abstract statements of a higher value.

The model's conceptions as well as the arguments on which they are built speak for themselves. The application of models undoubtedly belongs to the everday life of religious language. Neither theology nor proclamation can afford to dispense with models, especially if one attempts, as Frederick Ferré did following James Jeans to see each parable as a model.

> "Listen! A sower went out to sow. And as he sowed, some seed fell along the path, and the birds came and devoured them. Other seed fell on rocky ground ..." And he said to them "Do you not understand the parable? How then will you understand all the parables? The sower sows the word. And these are the ones along the path, where the word is sown; when they hear, Satan immediately comes and takes away the word which is sown in them. And these in like manner are the ones sown upon rocky ground ..." (315)

Here pictures serve as models for the illustration of religious statements. They are subjected to the theory they exemplify (logical isomorphism); they are universally understandable as they are taken from everyday experience.

The difficulty of employing models lies in the presupposition of logical isomorphism. A pre-fixed interpretation of religious statements is presupposed when the original statement is conceived according to a model that is to be helpful for understanding. Braithwaite has clearly recognized the deficit in this model theory. He reflects on the fact that models make it easier to grasp the logical structure of a theory. However, he points out, this comfortable way makes it easy to overlook the symbolic character of this structure. Hence, Ferré realizes (with reference to Braithwaite's criticism) that "metaphysical models" and theological models of a certain type transcend the boundaries of a fixed language game. They do not always draw appropriate terms from other languages into the process of interpreting the illustration of religious statements. This is the case even though a necessary but insufficient "condition of theological meaning and belief" (316) is presented.

b) Usage of Rules

Along with the issue of truth's reference to models, the linguistic-analytical philosophy considers this question to be limited to a given context of understanding characterized by the situational context and the human form of life. According to Hordern, it is a characteristic of language games that their basic terms are difficult to translate into those of other language games (317). In other words, the truth of a statement is only valid within a certain language game. The method of verification can only be chosen within this context of intelligibility as layed out by Wittgenstein's conception. The intelligibility of the rules which guide this language game were assumed to be a condition for the understanding of the language game. It is the presupposition of its qualification as suitable or unsuitable, and as true or false in the case of an apophantic proposition. Their conclusion was that the propositional truth conditions are to be set equal to the rules of usage of terms that are found in this statement. The analysis of the deep grammatical structure of religious propositions should show whether the truth conditions of a certain statement are fulfilled. When necessary, this can be done by means of models. In other words it can be done by the post-construction of the actual linguistic situation.

The first difficulty encountered by such an assumption is that even if the rules of usage for terms can be gathered from religious language, nothing can be learnt about the form of this usage. This means that the decision remains open, or must remain open, as to what the use and misuse of a rule means.

A use of rules, which is based on a lexicographically regulated convention would offer an alternative. Such a use of a defined use of terms would require training. For its part it could, with its content, never guarantee the amount of certainty and identification intended in a religious statement. However, the condition that linguistic training oversees the language-game is to be maintained. This condition is that language as language always reveals a distinct form of life. Its basis is to be sought in the dilemma that is derived from the various contexts of understanding - for example, the reference to the rules for the usage of the word "bread".

This notion was not foreign to Wittgenstein. Yet analytical philosophy preferred not to take it up. Rather, it chose to face the problems which arose from this, or when necessary, to be content with calling on "intuition" in regard to the proper use of rules (318). For analytical philosophy, the rules of the actual use of language cannot be addressed as rules which guarantee that words can continually be used in the same meaning. However, the thesis of the order of a language game was not abandoned, due to the limited definition of the term "rule". The purpose of such an investigation remains the same: to gain insight into the functional dependency of the truth value of compounded sentences on the truth value of elementary propositions. It is to remind the theologian "that at the center of all his varied utterances there is language about God, which at best is radically analogical or symbolic in character and which at worst may be entirely groundless or even altogether meaninglesss" (319). The best way to understand the logic of religious language is when one is able to specify the "supporting reasons, the manner in which they support, and the situations for which they are devised" (320). To become familiar with these supporting reasons one has to be aware of the "way in which religious utterances function" in "the entire context of religious discourse" (321).

The relationship between various language games presents an approach to the solution of the question of truth. The definition of the internal linguistic relationship receives a special urgency in regard to the claim that the religious language game is that game which is "to orientate the believer to the whole of life. Thus, theological language deals with a person's total commitment" (322). One might go so far as to see the religious language game as the basis for integration, measure of judgement and condition of participation for other language games. The religious game then becomes removed from the other language games in an extraordinary manner. It is placed above these other games and, according to Hordern, apparently functions in a manner similar to that of the Olympic Committee of the Olympic Games.

The Olympic Committee does not legislate the rules of ice hockey, and much less does it train a hockey player how to play hockey. But ice hockey takes its place within the total pattern of the Olympics, and its players must meet the Olympic standards. ... Theological language operates in the life of every Christian. The Christian who is a scientist and has to decide how he will cooperate with the nuclear weapons program, will make his decision in the light of his Christian faith. But there is no evidence that professional theologians can provide him with better answers than he can find in his own prayerful responsibility before God (323).

c) Interdependence of Different Language Games

It is clear that the conception, just presented, exceeds the boundaries of Wittgenstein's theory of a language-game. As long as the thesis of an essential pluralism of immanently regulated language use is maintained in analogy to the relative independence of the various Olympic disciplines, the comparison of Hordern remains preemptory. However, Hordern's comparison supersedes this limitation where an authority is implied which, analogous to the Olympic Committee, insists that *general* norms be observed by individually independent language games. Behind these reflections stands the conviction that it is possible and necessary for one language game to transfer to another. The religious language game is to serve as a guarantor of this transition and, in doing so, guarantees and justifies its truth-claim. Because it is a universal language game, it underlies all other concrete language games. The astonishing part is not the turn away from late Wittgenstein in an attempt to rethink the position of the *Tractatus* on structural linguistic order proposable on the basis of a universal language theory. Rather, the astonishing part that follows from the implications of Hordern's comparison is that structural order is presented in religious language.

Therefore, theology is to be projected as a universal theory of language. This is significant in comparison to the modest position Wittgenstein allotted to theology in the *Philosolphical Investigations* with his casual parenthethical remark, "theology as grammar", made in the context of his discussion of the condition that "grammar tells what kind of object anything is" (324). Here theology receives a demanding task. Under these assumptions, the question posed in regard to the adequate use of the determining rules of language should no longer have to wait for an answer.

Without intending to doubt that religious statements are statements about the totality of the meaning of human experience and are, therefore, statements concerning the meaning of God's revelation, the question of whether or not the function of religious language is not overestimated is nevertheless posed. This issue must be raised. It must be asked to what extent it is justifiable to say that a *language game, which is considered to be constituently meaningful for all further language games* is a language game? To what extent is the structure of such a language game approachable in the sense of the analytical approach of description and exemplification? Does not Hegel's problem of the speculative proposition have to be addressed (325)?

The possibility of the interdependence of various language games is not posed solely under the assumption of the religious language game as the condition for language games. The reflexive relationship of one speaker to his language situation, the problem of translation from one language to another, and above all the interpretation of historical texts in the religious realm, especially that of the exegesis of scripture, raise the question of the relationship of various languages to each other. Whereby this question gains in interest, especially in the cases just mentioned, due to the condition that we "are dealing with situation contexts which in the present are not interwoven with their own language game (as for instance the situation context of the description of the phonetic spelling), but rather belong to the language game in the past which is still to be reconstructed" (326).

In Braithwaite's theory of religious language we find an example of the denial of a relationship between the religious language game and other language games. His analysis and interpretation of religious statements as stories which illustrate maxims necessarily stumbles on the question of the character of the relationship of both of these types of language. Nevertheless, he refuses to recognize such facts. Disputing the religious statements' truth-claim, he states that no logical relationship exists between this and other types of language games. Hereby, he implements "a device of despair to say that the connection is not logical but psychological and causal, as if one fed into the machine raw material that could not be used in a certain way and extracted at the other end something which could be used in that way" (327).

We cannot escape the requirement for an exposition of the interdepencence of the religious language game with other language games. Even in the case of an acceptance of Hare's blik-theory on which Braithwaite's arguments are based, and in the case of the assumption that religious statements have their basis in a decision which cannot be further proven in this or that false blik. We cannot escape this requirement because it does not merely refer to the relationship between the religious language game and other language games, but rather to the relationship between the various religious language games. Along with the truth-claim the inner logical coherence of religious statements would have to be rejected and the various forms of religious language would not only be differentiated from one another. Rather, it would have to be assumed that these religious language games are strictly separated form one another, so that each of these forms of language would *only* be regulated *by its own logic*. This logic would purport nothing other than an inner freedom from contradiction from a set linguistic act. If one does not attach oneself to Braithwaite's theory, but rather counts on the possibility of a mutual reference to various uses between religious languages, the investigation of logical relationships, which exists between the various types of statements, becomes the decisive task of the linguistic philosophy of religion. The abundance of types of language games is, by no means, inferior to the multiplicity of language forms in non-religious contexts. Here one finds the expression of feelings, intentional explanations, instructions, performative utterances, fictions, illustrations and ultimately factual statements. Hereby, a truth-claim does not emerge - at least not explicitly - except for the type of propositions last mentioned. In this sense "explicit" means that something cannot be gathered from surface grammar. In most cases, this becomes obvious due to the condition that these sentences are not indicative sentences, but rather have the form of the imperative or conjunctive, or deal with interrogative propositions or with intentional explanations.

The multiplicity of religious propositional possibilities makes it clear that the logic of religious language cannot merely be comprehended from a possibility of application. As not all religious propositions are of a descriptive character, neither are all discursive. Under no circumstances can expressions of feeling and explanations of intention be regarded as descriptive. Neither can they be allotted to the upper classes of discursive statements, for it is not possible to redeem their claim to validity. Such a possibility can be adopted for commandments and the evaluation of values, but not for factual statements. If this supposition proves to be correct, the disjunction between scientific cognition of descriptive sentences and the irrationality of evaluative propositions becomes weak. This is a result which would agree with the program of the *Philosophical Investigations*. The onesidedness of the experience of certainty of the subjective condition, as is expressed in "blik" could be guaranteed by the objectivity of a cognitive foundational context. It could, thereby, be rendered examinable.

3. Criteria for the religious use of language

a) General Criteria for Intelligibleness

Ferré devides the investigation of language into three parts: syntactics, pragmatics and semantics. These constitute the situation of signification for "theological discourse". Considering these one can hold to three criteria (328) by which the religious statement's claim to validity can be measured.

1. The first criterion is the *intelligibility* of words and propositions voiced in theological discourse:

> ... there is the factor of the language itself, the presence of marks and sounds which *serve* to signify (329).

Ferré starts from the principle that religious language partly consists of expressions. Their "equivalents" can solely be found in the language game of faith. The codex of formal logic can only be applied to "protocol statements" of religion with limitation. Statements of faith rather than theological statements are referred to here. The rules for the application and relation of such expressions are held fast in a non-formal logic of theology.

> Like the language of all other subjects, theological language relies on the formal logical constants to provide the rigid framework for its operations. "And" functions to conjoin expressions within theological discourse in the same manner as in any other statements. "Or" and "not", "some" and "all" - these retain their lofty irrelevance to the content of discussion. Without this common framework in formal logic, the language of systematic theology could neither be credited with any rational rigor nor even be understood.
>
> But in addition to the operation of the formal constants within academic theological discourse, "informal" rules of inference provide this speech with its distinctive syntactic structure (330).

In order to illustrate this reflection, Ferré takes an example from everyday language, which is supplemented by an example from the realm of theology.

> If, on an unpleasant day, I describe the weather by saying, "It's raining and it's not", I am uttering a formal contradiction, but it may be the best possible characterization of the day. If it is, it will not be so merely because I use a form of words which seems to contradict itself but because the expression I use acts as an incentive to increased conceptual precision. Perhaps the English

language is not yet equipped to indicate the more-than-drizzling but less-than-sprinkling condition of the atmosphere. The subject matter demands an increase in vocabulary, a more careful act of attention to what is the case. Again, "She's pretty and she's not", "He's likable and he's not" serve to suggest that further refinement of our concepts of "pretty" or "likable" is needed before an adequate non-paradoxical statement about him or her will be in order. Likewise the apparent contradiction "God is involved in change and he is not" is an indication that further investigation of our concepts of "involvement" and "change" are in order so that we may discover more precisely their theological powers for the inferences which, in theology, hinge on them (331).

Therefore, the intelligibility of religious language in its syntactic dimension depends on the exposition of the linguistic rules of informal logic. It also depends on the exposition of the relation between these rules and the rules of other language games. For Ferré, the principle of analogy is the theological instrument which places these rules in relation to one another.

... the logic of analogy may be appreciated; as laying down guiding rules for the further determination of fundamental theological concepts it offers considerable assistance to the systematic theologian in search of a more adequate syntactic structure for his language. Systematic theology - in contrast to the paradox-ridden "biblical" theology often supported by the logic of obedience - cannot rest in contradiction but improves and refines its concepts in a neverending effort both to retain rational coherence and to respect the fundamental entailment and equivalence rules which distinguish its language from all others (332).

2. The second criterion is formulated in connection with pragmatics. Ferré speaks of the "interpretic function" of language. This criterion implies the *integrity* of subjects which participate in religious discourse...

... the purposes motivating the employment of language use (333).

Undoubtedly, only part of the pragmatic interpretive function of language is indicated by the term "integrity". This part culminates in the question, "Is language about God fraudulent?" (334). The purpose and conditions are questioned under which the speaker makes use of religious language.

One aspect of interpretics concerns the way in which language *affects* its interpreter; the second aspect deals with the circumstances under which the interpreter *uses* his language (335).

Integrity attests to the fact that the speaker does not merely pretend that the needs and feelings which are expressed as well as the determinations and statements, which are made, are felt and intended as they are voiced. Integrity cannot be proven in discourse. Rather it can, at best, prove itself in the interaction between the speaker and that which is being spoken, if this interaction is continued long enough (336). In the special case of the language game of fiction, this means that the mere delusion of the truth-claim of a statement must be known to the speaker as well as to the hearer for it to be a delusion (337).

3. The third and last decisive criterion for the classification of religious statements is that of its *referential character* (338). The justification of the claim of validity for religious statements, and also in a further sense, the claim of correctness for norms and performative statements can only be clarified with the help of this criterion. In both cases, the existence of facts is dealt with - "the 'something' referred to, the content signified". This existence is reproduced in statements whose truth is not merely but actually maintained (339). Thereby, it will have decisive influence for the recognition of the truth-claim of religious statements. The issue is whether or not an understanding of the term "fact" can be attained that is not that of earlier positivists, but which would subject religious statements to empirical verification. Yet one that does not surrender "*ontological* bearing" (340).

> It has also become clear that the sort of "facts" to which theological statements claim to have reference are not the same kind of facts which are discussed in the language of empirical sciences. No straightforward experimental method for verifying or falsifying sentences claiming to state these "facts" seems to be available - or to be desired by those who use the sentences. The explanatory logic of the natural sciences, requiring expansibility, specificity, and regularity, is also inapplicable to these crucial religious "facts". Evidently theological discourse does not intend to refer merely to "natural" facts, if we take the "natural" (as Patrick Nowell-Smith suggests) to include whatever can be dealt with by the experimental methods and explanatory techniques of science (341).

An alternative direction has already been offered by Hare and Wisdom (342). Both reject the positivistic term "fact". According to their thesis, a fact cannot exist independently of thought. Hence, the decision concerning the truth of a statement cannot be made on the basis of empirical verification or falsification, but rather in terms of the whole context of argumentational foundation for discourse (343). In the context of argumentation of such discourse, Ferré attempts to prove the correctness of the intended semantic relation of a religious statement to a metaphysical fact. He draws a parallel between the so-called scientifically demonstrated and metaphysical facts. He contests thereby that the answer to the question of whether or not a statement reproduces a fact is not in the end defined by the recognition that this statement holds in an elaborated schema. Moreover, the question of the truth of a statement appears first where the correspondance to other empirical values or the dignity of the theoretical formulation of this fact is dealt with problematically.

> When we speak of metaphysical "facts", therefore, we need not
> suppose that these are "given" independent of the creative powers
> of intelligence. On the contrary, the "facts" of metaphysics are
> supremely dependent on the conceptual activity of mind (344).

In regard to the examination of the truth of a verifiable proposition, the different conceptions of fact concur with each other under one condition. This condition is that the meaning, which is to be understood by that which is apparently reproduced by this fact, cannot be clarified outside of the foundation of an argument. In other words, that which is to be understood by a fact, is *relative* to the language system belonging to the fact.

> Metaphysical facts, in the last analysis, depend for their
> confirmation on the *adequacy of the system* in which they operate,
> but so must the facts of science ultimately rely on the validity of
> the entire scientific enterprise of which they are part. To convince
> a Hindu mystic of a "fact of science" one must do more than
> perform an experiment before him (345).

Even if one proceeds from the principle that not experience, but the process of discourse in an argumentational system is decisive for the recognition of facts, one fact still remains. This is that the assertion of a scientific fact can gain validity by supporting this thesis by calling attention to its openness in regard to empirical falsification. The reference to experience, for example to an experiment, is offered within the realm of possible interpretation marked off by a system of argumentation. They must be justified within this context. However, this reference contributes to the support of the truthclaim as long as no contradictory experiences can be determined.

In order to support a religious proposition's truth-claim and to claim the existence of a metaphysical fact, criteria can undoubtedly be referred to which allege the legitimation of the correctness of this claim. However, it cannot be determined beforehand to what extent this legitimation will suffice to obtain the necessary validity for the religious proposition. Is it possible to state those presuppositions which must be assumed in order for the relation of religious propositions to facts to be conceivable? Only an investigation into the capabilities and effectiveness of these criteria can display this.

b) Criteria for the Suitability of a Language System

Ferré himself has established four criteria, which are to guarantee the suitability of a theological language system and the religious proposition's truth-claim. He also proceeds from the thesis that the truth-claim of a proposition must always be seen in relation to a certain argumentational background. The question of what a fact is can only be clarified in relation to this. He concludes from a further presupposition, that the assumption of a *metaphysical factum* is justified within the framework of theological discourse. Theological language functions as a metaphysical language. Thus, the discussion takes a turn in that the claim of validity of the religious language, in particular, is no longer being investigated. Rather the validity of metaphysical statements in general is being questioned. This means that should the justification of the truth-claim of metaphysical statements be successful, a further step would be necessary for the justification of religious statements. The first would have to be identified as a certain form of the last.

At this juncture the second presupposition is more important than the first. Proceeding from this presupposition, Ferré attempts to justify the *possibility and suitability* of a metaphysical theory. He hopes to ascertain the criteria, on which their justification is to be based. Consistence and coherence are the criteria immanent of the system. Applicability in experience and applicability in *all* possible experience are those criteria external and transcendent of the system. "That is, it must show all experience to be interpreted without oversight, distortion, or 'explaining away' on the basis of its key concepts" (346).

If one considers that the criteria just mentioned do not merely guarantee the intelligibility of a propositon within a schema of a term or a situation of a language game, but rather that the truth of a proposition is to be demonstrated by the *suitability* of a system of argumentation, then its essence is the "conceptual synthesis" (347). This means that the justification of its suitability consists in producing the context for all facts on the basis of a theoretical model deduced from "facts" (348). Considering this, it becomes obvious that such a plan can only be presented programmatically and cannot be worked out in detail. The successful way seems to be marked with sufficient clarity. In spite of a missing statement, an evaluation may already begin. It is only decisive in that the definition of the four criteria is sufficiently differentiated in order to determine their use and their functionality.

The most important of the four criteria is applicability. One can speak of applicability where, for example, religious propositions possess an enlightening effect on the understanding of experience. (Surely, Ferré refers predominantly to metaphysical syntheses, whereby theological propositions are meant to contrast with propositions of faith.) This effect can be measured by the extent to which it succeeds in clarifying past, present, and - in the sense of the second criterion - future experiential contexts. Conditions for such a comprehensive clarification are:

1. The coordination of various fields of experience with one another on the basis of the creation of their reference.

2. The explication of criteria which permit at least a preliminary determination of metaphysical systematic statements for personal experience.

3. The permission for an inquiry into and a reformation of this system. In this case experiential reflection ceases with the insuitability of our experience. This condition also proves itself to be necessary in the light of the experiential process.

4. The exposition of the superior capability of the metaphysical system in regard to and in competition with other systems.

The explication and perhaps also the prospect of fulfilling these four criteria, their consistence and coherence, found the suitability of a metaphysical system. In such a system a statement's truth-claim is judged. These should not delude us into believing that the central term of such a system, namely the metaphysical factum, is not yet clarified.

To recapitulat: the question of the claim of validity for a religious statement was raised at the beginning. We were referred to models in order to clarify this question. The insufficiency of the term "model" makes it intelligible that such a question can only be posed within the context of religious language. At the same time, this context must be the context of argument. However, the answer to this question presupposes the interdependence of various language games. Consequently, the focus was, first on the inner-logic of religious language. The hope was to find a possibility of transition to other domains of language, by means of comparing the framework of this linguistic context and argumentation. This hope did not go disappointed as, in addition to intelligibleness and integrity, the reference to a so-called metaphysical fact was demonstrated to be a necessary characteristic for the claim of validity for some religious propositions. In regard to the determination of the metaphysical term "fact", it can be assured that this behaves in relation to its specific metaphysical system in the same way as it does to the scientific facts of that system with which it is associated. This insight led to the question which was dealt with in regard to the suitability of a metaphysical language system. Here, instead of attempting to determine the *metaphysical factum* by arriving at the presence of a metaphysical language, it would have been possible to proceed in the opposite direction and proceed from the metaphysical facts themselves. In the language of the theological system, this could not mean that one attempts to determine the perception of God by theoretical predication. Rather, in order to demonstrate the possibilities and meaning of the religious language one would proceed from the perception of God.

Besides, on the basis of the criteria of consistence, coherence and applicability, the examination of the suitability of a linguistic system should also include the relation of the metaphysical language system to another system. However, to be exact , this means that the notion "metaphysical language" can only obtain meaning indirectly by means of an analogy between metaphysical language and other languages. It is not said whether or not this other language must serve as a corrective due to its capability to be false. If one considers that one condition of clarification by "application" is the association of various fields of experience, then the intermediary regulative meaning for metaphysical language can be sought within a much greater realm than merely in the empirical field of linguistic systems. However, the functional analysis of the analogy principle will first show an explication of the question. No matter how the answer turns out, it will have repercussions for the other three conditions just mentioned. At any rate, it has been demonstrated that that which holds true for a term of religious model in a smaller field also is valid for a term of a metaphysical or theological system having a greater field.

Before we turn to the principle of analogy, here is one more remark on Ferré's scheme of justification for the claim of validity for religious propositions. We will attempt to follow argumentational structures representative to a certain extent of the analytical philosophy of language. It is, above all, striking that Ferré introduces terms which would, at best be a curse word in a context of linguistic analysis. With their introduction he intends to do justice to the linguistic analytical differentiation which is present in the distinction between different types of language games and levels of discourse. One can differ as to whether or not the choice of terms was auspicious. However, the attempt to construct the divine (metaphysical fact), demonstrates accordance with the continental tradition of the *Philosophy of the World of Life*, which follows from other presuppositions. This philosophy attempts to construct the divine from the "perception of the world essence". If attempts to determine a perfect type of world essence with the "whole of the world structure" (349). It is expressed similarly in Ferré's *Language, Logic and God*.

> A "metaphysical fact" ... is a concept which plays a key role within the system, without which the system could founder. ... A "metaphysical system" is a construct of concepts designed to provide coherence for all "the facts" on the basis of a theoretical model drawn from among "the facts" (350).

Of course, these estimations allow dissonance to be recognized in execution. However, unity exists in the belief that philosophy should maintain its superiority over religion without simultaneously claiming that philosophy's perception of God is true or that it should replace religion. According to Ferré, the task of philosophy is "simply to display accurately the logical anatomy of the process (religion)" (351) or - in Karl Ulmer's words - to assemble the general structure of the human world and this means

> ... that it develops a general perception of religion and of the godly, which gives each possible religious experience within the world structure its certain place. The religious experience itself, through which the human being, first of all, gains a place in this train of view, cannot be mediated ..." (352).

4. Analogical principle

That which has meaning according to the notion of the analogical principle in Wittgenstein's conceptuality - proceeds from an actual and intelligible language game such as everyday language or an empirical scientific language etc. It should lead to the understanding of a language game for which the manner of functioning and its inner-logic are not intelligible in the same way. If the analogical principle is able to set up this bridge to religious language, it would demonstrate how the truth claim of religious statements is to be justified. It would, thereby, necessarily lead to a religious language as a verifiable language (353). If the bridging cannot occur, then the more modest task of proving whether the analogical principle, renders itself useful in judging the religious language becomes significant. Can it be considered to be *regulative* for the rules which actually constitute the religious language? This question would take the place of the more interesting task of analyzing those rules which do not guarantee predication on the basis of experience and knowledge. Rather, they would do this according to the state of affairs that are founded on belief and by means of predicates which stem from the realm of experience and scientific language. Consequently, our examination will be carried out in three steps:

1. It will demonstrate the type and manner of the acceptance of analogical thought in the analytical philosophy of religion.

2. It will examine the willingness to accept metaphysics implied in the analogical conception, as well as the consequences of acceptance, bound to this, the justification of the claim of validity for religious language.

3. If necessary, it will present the result which the analytical philosophy of religion draws from the analysis of the analogical conception.

However, steps 1 and 2 will not be dealt with separately. One can hardly speak of the type and manner of the acceptance of the analogical principle without considering the implications of its acceptance in its historical form, as well as those contained in its new mode of application.

According to its origin, the concept of analogy as used in the discussion of analytical religious philosophy, refers at least formally to the level of development which this held in High Scholasticism and its doctrine of the *analogia entis*. Leibniz's, Kant's and even Hegel's dialectics have found no resonance.

It is characteristic of the discussion that it originates from the requirement for a syntactical analysis of religious language. Hence, it takes place in the expectation that the analysis of the mode serves to reveal the inner-logic of the language game and disclose its rules. First, the legitimation of the analogical principle is required for the mode of setting the different languages in relationship to each other. The identification of the analogical principle as the rule of translation must occur independently of metaphysics. This is implied in the doctrine of the *analogia entis*. Thus it is required to present this and accept the principle in its purely formal form.

> Can any of us adopt the Thomistic distinctions between the different varieties of analogy and escape the metaphysical consequences with which St. Thomas and in all Roman Catholic theology the logical forms are indissolubly associated? What we want is this logic without that metaphysic, and I have the feeling that we may be crying for the moon (354).

The reason for scepticism cannot merely be sought in the affinity between analytical philosophy and positivism. Although this affinity cannot be denied historically, the reason for scepticism can be found in the fear of compromising the purity of the religious decision. Especially the linguistic, analytical, nondialectical conception of metaphysics or, in more exact terms, the fear that this could deny the mystery of God and could declare that which, according to its approach, cannot be rationally explained to be rational, is the decisive reason for scepticism. The analytical philosophy of religion and the Thomistic conception of analogy meet in their non-dialectical understanding of metaphysics. This appears to be remarkable. However, the difference lies in the fact that, for the latter, the non-dialectical approach is to be understood from the attempt to define the divine - human relationship as proceeding from God. This means, we are to grasp God as the cause and the individual as the caused (effect). In contrast, for the analytical philosolphy the Christian doctrine of creation is no longer the unquestionable presupposition from which all predication ultimately proceeds (355). Rather, its distance to dialectics can be sought in the conception that all contrast can be rationally grasped. From the comparison of two contradictory propositons, one is always classified as true and the other as false. In other words, both can only be considered true under the assumption that they do not possess the same truth value. Under these conditions, a contradiction between two true but contradictory propositions is not possible. Thus, in accordance with a formulation in the *Tractatus*, the expression "contradiction" can only be applied when the combination in all four cases is to be evaluated as false (356).

In the language of the *Philosophical Investigations*, the reasons for contradictions are to be sought in the misunderstanding of rules, which are true for a certain claim. The conciliation, which linguistic analysis offers, rests directly on the interpretation of contradictions, such as a misunderstanding. For the investigation of religious language this question is decisive. "When is a contradiction not a *mere* contradiction, but rather a sublime paradox, a mystery?" (357) This is the basis on which it is decided whether the basis is to be sought as the ultimate goal of life in this world or whether an other worldly piety transcendent of this world is possible, and can be linguistically grasped. If one advocates, as Hepburn in his article "Christianity and Paradox" does, the view that religious discourse for the most part "display vicious muddle rather than revealing improprieties" (358), it is then impossible to comprehend language as a medium of transcendence and to differentiate linguistically religion from worldly piety.

a) The Problem of Contradiction

In order to judge what is implied for the principle of analogy if one sees the cause of contradictions in a false use of rules, the uniqueness of religious statements must be referred to. Unlike here, this uniqueness has been insufficiently expressed in the simple sentence concerning God as the creator of heaven and earth. If one, for example, takes the sentences: "The kingdom of God is in you" and "The kingdom of God is not in you", then the logic sense of the sentence becomes clear. These sentences present a contradiction and that is inadmissible (359). It would be interesting to examine how such sentences, which stand in such a relation are congruent with Ferré's criteria of coherence. The task of ridding religious statements of such logical misfits is also expected from the analogical principle. Therefore a glance at the linguistic and logical evaluation of such an "incorrect confusion" is to be expected from those who see instructive dissonances in this confusion. This is to be done before the question of the acceptance of analogical thought is completely dealt with by the analytical philosophy of religion. It is striking that similar logical insufficiencies in non-religious languages will be referred to in order to clarify paradoxes or religious language.

In order to answer Ronald W. Hepburn, Ian T. Ramsey attempted a topology of contradictory statements, in which he differentiates between avoidable and unavoidable paradoxes. The basis for avoiding paradoxes is not to be sought exclusively in a terminological or argumentative mistake, but rather their avoidability is demonstrated in a new claim which is the result of both original claims. According to Ramsey's view, Kant's antinomies and dialectics, unlike Hegel's dialectics, belong to these. Unavoidable antinomies fall into the categories of logically inapproachable and logically explorable. According to Ramsey's own words, the latter can best be grasped through Hegel's dialectics. In spite of their unavoidability they claim "to have some sort of rational structure". It is noticeable that the solution of a paradox immediately causes another paradox (360).

In the case of the logically inexplorable paradox it continues, but it cannot be judged and controlled as in the previous case. The following sentence is regarded to be an example of an unavoidable paradox, which is not based on linguistic confusion, "I believe in the Holy Catholic Church, and sincerely regret that it does not at present exist." The insight of this paradox, which is expressed in linguistic parallelism to the sentence, "I believe I can cross the equator, but regret that it cannot be seen", rests upon the double meaning of the word "Church", which, according to Ramsey, belongs to "different logical areas". First, the term Church is used for the purpose of a *unio mystica sanctorum* second, in respect to a legally defined visible community (361). Just as avoidable but "positively meaningful" is the paradox in the doctrine of the two natures of Christ. The paradox of the doctrine of the *communicatio idiomatum* lies in the condition that two natures which are separated from each other, the divine and the human, are unified in one person. The positive yield of this paradox is seen by analogy to a scientific example (362), the incompatibility and yet practical necessity of the wave and particle theory of light. The same situation results for the scientific as well as for the religious paradox. Their solution is not to be found in the parallelism of two contradictory theories. Their solution is expected in the currently unclarified logical classification of such "crucial words and phrases" as "light" and "Person of Christ" (363). The result of the explication of the religious paradox is seen in reference to its indepencence from an unavoidable paradox, which takes shape on account of an avoidable paradox. A statement by Evans-Pritchard and its interpretation by Ramsey contribute to elucidate this possibility of a solution. Evans-Pritchard writes in reference to the religious statement of the Nuer that "The twin is a bird":

> It seems odd, if not absurd, to a European when he is told that a twin is a bird as though it were an obvious fact, for Nuer are not saying that a twin is like a bird, but that he is a bird. There seems to be a complete contradiction in the statement; .... But, in fact, no contradiction is involved in the statement, which, on the contrary, appears quite sensible, and even true, to one who presents the idea to himself in the Nuer language, and within their system of religious thought. He does not then take their statements about twins any more literally than they make and understand themselves. They are not saying that a twin has a beak, feathers, and so forth. ... when Nuer say that a twin is a bird they are not speaking of either as it appears in the flesh. ...they are speaking of the association birds have with Spirit through their ability to enter the realm to which spirit is likened in metaphor and where Nuer think it chiefly is, or may be. The formula does not express a dyadic relationship between twins and birds but a triadic relationship between twins, birds, and God. In respect to God, twins and birds have a similar character (364).

This is the theme of Ramsey's interpretation of E. E. Evans-Pritchard's statement. Such a paradox:

> ...only arises if ... we mistake the rules governing the assertions and think of the formulae as expressing a dyadic relationship rather than a triadic relationship. But this does not mean that the example falls into the negative class of avoidable paradox which we considered above. For while it is true that the paradox has disappeared when the correct structure of the formula has been recognized, it has only disappeared on the introduction of another concept, viz., God or Spirit, whose logical behaviour remains unmapped. All we can gather is that such a concept, while it somehow refers to observables such as beaks, twin births, cucumber skin, oxen, refers to more than observables as well (365).

Statements, whose subject is directly or indirectly God, are counted as genuine religious paradoxes, which can neither be avoided nor solved. The only thing which can be attained in regard to such a genuine religious paradox, is the exposition of its structures. This is the proof of the uniqueness of its logical status. Accordingly its nominative is different from all others so that it exposes "more clearly than ever the charactistically preposterous core" (366). The statement that God is transcendent as well as immanent would be regarded as such a genuine religious paradox. As the reference to logical uniqueness is not yet the solution of the gnoseological antinomies of faith and knowledge underlying this, the question is raised if one should not claim the logical insufficiency of religion paradoxes. McPherson and Alasdair C. MacIntyre did this for a while. This would demonstrate the logical conduct of such words. It would connect descriptive and verifiable words without insisting they be verifiable and descriptive. In other words, like a type theory, this requires that should religious antinomies not be absurd, "they must centre on categories which, while they have freedom of association with all type-distinguished categories, are not themselves native to any one language frame" (367).

As such a category, Ramsey names the "I" apart from all descriptive language. This is ultimately the condition and presupposition of language. It constitutes an analogy between the logical conduct of the word "I", whose sense is revealed in so-called "disclosure situations" and the logical conduct of the word "God". In reference to this move into analogy, it remains decisive that the attempt to think "God" is not seen as a presupposition for the "I" - thought. The analogy in this case is nondialectical.

b) Acceptance of the Analogical Principle in the Analytical Philosophy of Religion

We shall once again turn to the first two questions. In spite of agreement in formal structure, the main difference between the doctrine of the *analogia entis* and the modern linguistic analytical analogical theory concerns the fact that the latter is not an analogy of being, but an *analogia linguae*. The analogical principle should prepare those rules of transformation which allow sentences of a self-contained religious language to be transferred to another, commonly understandable language. Here, the attitude toward ontological relevance is ambivalent. Surely, one can argue that within the analytical philosophy of religion, language is seen as all encompassing. Nothing can possibly be external to it as something unspeakable. Language cannot merely stand in a mere external relationship to something. Within this argument's framework the question of the truth of religous statements can be sufficiently answered. In this sense the question of proposition and reality are either contradictory or not. However, this can only occur under the condition that it is possible for this language to develop those rules in the agreement with which it is constituted as a language. Yet, this means that the return to immediacy, posited by Wittgenstein, will be surrendered. This has already occurred in the thought of many analytical philosophers. Questions about the essence of the language game can no longer be left out of consideration.

In my opinion, the surrender of immediacy means a recognition that one has not already offered a sufficient treatment of religion. One has only payed attention to the role that religion plays in the life of humanity. One has attempted a comparison between various views on religion, to discover the meaning of religious grammar; as Phillips did as he compared confessing, thanking and petitioning in prayer with confessing, thanking and petitioning in other contexts. Phillips states, "The religious believer learns ... religious language; a language which he participates in along with other believers. What I am suggesting is that to know how to use this language is to know God" (368). Hick also reproaches these sentences in that he claims that Phillips neglects to pay tribute to the question of the existence of God as opposed to the question of someone's conception of God. The contrast between Phillips and Hick reveals the tension which emerges from the approach of the late Wittgenstein.

Here Hick argues against Dewi Z. Phillips. He claims that the Christian language, the current language of a living community, presupposes the extra-linguistic reality of God. Phillips counters that for the religious language, as it is implemented in devotions, meditations and other religious contexts, the question of God's existence is ultimately the question of the intelligibility of the conception of God. Thereby, as one can perhaps gather from Hick's accusation, Phillips by no means denies the *a priori* existence of God. Rather he refuses to answer the question as he considers it unintelligible. In order to bring to light that which he regards as the incomprehensibility underlying this question, he refers to Wittgenstein "when he asks us to imagine how inappropriate it would be to say to someone who believes in God, 'You only *believe* - oh well ...'" (369). The intra-religious philosophical investigation is justified within the realm expounded here. The analogical problem is to be seen as one of language, rather than as one of being.

In its development, the *analogia linguae* makes use of the present state of discussion of the medieval doctrine. As in this doctrine, it is founded on a double withdrawal. First, from an unequivocal and second from an equivocal manner of speaking. In regard to the truth-claim of religious statements, this means that the same criteria are applied to test their claim to validity as, for example, in the testing of a scientific statement. The religious language could be designated as equivocal, if "in spite of the great degree of similarity" (370) with everyday language, it would be completely different. The words of such a language could hardly be regarded as concepts, but rather as termini. They would possess a majority of meanings completely different from one another.

The difficulty in the definition of the religious language as an analogous language lies in the fact that it must maintain the similarity in dissimilarity and the dissimilarity in similarity with other linguistic possibilities. In contrast to equivocal talk, religious language should not be the mere operation of empty words, as in the "Letternphantasmus" criticized by Gottfried Herder. In contrast to unequivocal talk, the religious language should not only avoid dogmatic anthropomorphism. Following Kant, they should avoid "symbolical anthropomorphism which actually only deals with the *language* and not the object itself" (371). Therewith, there religious language is in a near hopeless dilemma.

> If you assert existence and causality of God in the same sense in which you assert them of finite beings, you are rendering God incapable of fulfilling the very function for whose performance you alleged him to be necessary. But if you assert existence and causality of God in an altogether different sense from that in which you assert them of finite beings, you are making statements about God to which you can, *ex hypothesi*, assign no intelligible content. God therefore is either useless or unthinkable; this would seem to be the conclusion of the matter (372).

The introduction of the analogical principle, and the attempt to interpret the religious language as an analogical language demands nothing short of a dialectical definition. The issue of the question of the possibility of talk about God unites with the question of the possibility of language at all (373). If one avoids this requirement and defines the relationship of religious language to other languages as analytical, then the relationship between religious language and other languages is regarded to be the same relationship as in medieval ontology between God and the world, as Hordern suggests, inspite of or due to the superior status which he ascribes to language. For medieval ontology, the relationship between God and creature was that of *causa* and *causatum*. However, even with such an analytical definition, the dialectical element does not completely disappear. A dichotomy remains between both languages in regard to certain statements. McPherson differentiates between symbolic and semiotical or analogous statements. He claims that the meaning of a symbolical expression could not be explained without losing its meaning (374). The reason for inexplicability is to be seen in the rift. The dichtomy exists between original language (religious language) and representative language (language of the world). It cannot be overcome by a third language or by rules which serve to mediate between these two. McPherson offers the following statement as an example of symbolical language, "God has become flesh in Jesus Christ". He contrasts this with the semiotical statement "God is our father" (375). This dichotomy is explicit in Ramsey's analysis of religious language. In spite of the presupposition that the expression "God exists" is derivable from scientific language, he requires that "the theologian must admit a tentative theology" (376).

Ferré's postulation of a metaphysical *factum* may suggest a presupposition similar to that of the traditional analogical doctrine. The linguistic-analytical philosophy of religion proceeds from the correspondence of the relationship between metaphysical and scientific facts. This is just as relative to the respective metaphysical system as the scientific factum is respectively relative to its given scientific system. Such a turn would grate against the intention of the linguistic-analytical approach of Wittgenstein. This does not render infeasible the recovery of the ontological aspect by means of the analogical principle. Yet this may under no circumstances follow the theoretical rules of correspondence of Wittgenstein's approach, but rather only those of coherence. This means that the legitimation of the sentence "God exists" would be the consensus of all those involved in and possibly effected by this language game. The consensus attained linguistically can be a truth criterion only if the possibility exists to think over or to replace the consensus founded on the legitimacy of the statement "God exists". This would follow Ramsey. The ontological conception on which the statement "God exists" rests is not debatable in the realm of the analytical analogical conception. On the contrary, the concern here has to do with the legitimacy of the application of the word "being". The ontological differentiation of the medieval analogical doctrine presupposes that creator and creature do not agree in being. Rather they only agree in their own respective relationship to there own being. They are different from one another in regard to being. This remains unconsidered. Because this is the case, the attempt to move from a uniform conception of being to one that is not merely an unequivocal predication of God is complicated.

The analytical philosophy of religion like the scholastic, is familiar with the difference between the *analogia attributionis* or *proportionis* and the *analogia proportionalitatis*. The development of the analogy of attribution follows from Franz Suarez's school. There, for example the predicate "healthy" is predicable of Mr. Jones as *analogatum primarium* in the original sense, and of his appearance as *analogatum secundarium* in a derived sense. The second has an essentially different meaning. The healthy appearance is dependent on the health of Mr. Jones. The predicate "healthy" is ambiguous in this example.

This means that a statement is not made about Mr. Jones and his appearance in the same way as the subject of the respective statements do not reach an agreement and are not *univocata*. Consequences for the ontological relevance cannot be deduced from them.

> Thus when we say that God and Mr. Jones are both good or that they are both beings, remembering that the content which the word "good" or "being" has for us is derived from our experience of the goodness and being of creatures, we are, so far as analogy of attribution is concerned, saying no more than that God has goodness or being in whatever is necessary if he is to be able to produce goodness, and being in his creatures. This would not seem necessarily to indicate anything more than that the perfections which are found formally in various finite modes in creatures exist *virtually* in God, that is to say, that he is able to produce them in the creatures; it does not seem to necessitate that God possesses them formally himself (377).

The analogy of attribution no doubt advocates similarity in dissimilarity. However that which it intends to illustrate does not follow from it. Rather this rests on the presupposed dependence between creator and creature, as well as on the application of the predicate "health" to the skin color of Mr. Jones. It is only legitimate in that it is an indication of his health which was not caused by fever. In the analogous attribution of God, God is not fixed as the *analogatum primarium*. Rather this is attributed to the human because this is the analogy in which God, as the *analogatum secundarium*, is granted a predicate. The relationship, on the basis of which God is granted a predicate, is that between creature and creator. This is the ontologically reversed relationship, which sees God as *analogatum primarium* and the human and the creation as *analogatum secundarium*.

A further difficulty of the analogy of attribution lies in the fact that it is presupposed *a tertium* that both members of the analogy, creature and creator (or Mr. Jones and his skin color), are in agreement. If the analogy of attribution is transfered to the relationship of an individual to God, the difficulty arises that the *tertium*, in which both stand in agreement, must be thought of as simpler than the simple being of God.

This form of analogy developed by Thomas Aquinas was certainly rejected under the influence of Cajetan and his school of thought. The analogy of proportion was eliminated from the school of Suarez. Therefore, these two conceptions have drawn closer to each other - a condition reflected in the analytical evaluation of analogical forms.

The proportional analogy assesses the relationship between God and the individual differently than attributional theology does. The analogical predicate is declared by both *analogata*. However they are materially defined by the *analogatum* that is respectively designated to them. In regard to the analogy of being, this means that God and creatures are not in agreement in being, but rather in the respective relationship which each one has to its own being. This relationship does not lie in *a tertium* (being as superior and simple concept or the concept of health which in the subject of both sentences finds a different manner of application), but rather in similarity and dissimilarity. The difficulty of the analogical form lies in this condition. The lack of *a tertium* does not allow the human - God relationship to appear to be rational.

> If the agreement would lie in *a tertium*, the relationship between God and creature would then be rational. The *convenientia in aliquo uno* would be the agreement in an ideal or category: the distance between creature and God would be that one of the finite form to the infinite but it would lie within the same ideal or categorical diminsion. Therefore the agreement lies in the relationship itself. As the relationship in both members is as different as the being, which in itself is referred to its carriers (God and creature), is radically different (*esse a se, esse ab alio*), agreement and opposition simultaneously, identity and contradiction, *similitudo* and *dissimilitudo* simultaneously lie in the relationship. However, this means that the relationship is dialectical (378).

To be more exact the dialectics of similarity and dissimilarity in its relational abstraction is the basis of the difficulty of the understanding of the analogical form. Similar problems do arise for proportional analogy as for the attributional analogy in regard to a presupposed theism. However, due to the dialectical definition of relationship underlying it, the attributional analogy could only be insufficiently grasped within the linguistic-analytical reflective horizon. Therefore Paul C. Hayner's attempt to avoid dialectics (379) requires that a predicate attributed to God agrees at least with the application which it takes in regard to humanity. This means in exact terms that he requires the agreement *in tertium* in which both predicates are identical in one respect and in opposition in another respect. The various relationships of predicates to this *tertium* would allow this dialectic to be avoided by similarity and dissimilarity. The possibility exists for the different respects to exist beside each other. This is different than if identity and contradiction would be placed in a single relationship. However, the following stands in contradiction to Hayner's suggestion that that which he regards to be the coexistence of similarity and dissimilarity is equivocation. This is true in spite of Hayner's assurances to the contrary. Using Hayner's example the claim that God and humanity are in agreement in a predicable aspect, yet in other basic aspects do not agree, expresses nothing other than that God and humanity participate in the predicate "love" and share the full meaning of this predicate. It can then be fully and completely said of neither of them. From humanity and not from God and from God and not from humanity, therein lies the difference!

> The suggestion here proposed is that, in order to employ analogical predication in religious discourse, we must hold that any two entities standing in an analogical relation to each other, including the Deity, must have a minimum of one property in common. "God is love" is analogically true, for example, only if all entities, including God, of which "love" is predicated share at least one property. We may thus avoid agnosticism by the view that what may be truly asserted about God may also be truly asserted, at least in part, about things other than God.
>
> One question which is sure to arise at this point is whether such a view of analogical predication does not entail anthropomorphism. I believe that this consequence is avoided by the stipulation that terms which are analogous in meaning always have overlapping significations. As Rudolph Otto has pointed out, in illustration of a similar point, the statement, "he loves me," has the same verbal form when uttered by a child of its father and by a girl of her lover. Nevertheless there is a qualitative, and not merely a quantitative, difference between the love of the father for the child and the love of the lover for the girl. At the same time, however, we would probably agree that there is some sense in which the word "love" means the same thing in both cases. In other words, there is an analogy, but not identity, of meaning for the term "love" as used in these two cases. In somewhat more technical language, there is a difference in signification to be noted in these two uses of "love" in the sense that the *combination* of properties signified by one is different from the combination of properties signified by the other. Hence the meaning (i.e. the signification) of these two terms is not identical, or univocal. But neither are they completely equivocal. And because they are not completely equivocal, we are justified in using the same term, "love," in both cases. They are not completely equivocal because *some* (at least one) but not all of the properties signified by the term in the first case are identical with some but not all of the properties signified in the other.

What is more, if necessary, we could designate the common properties signified by both terms (380).

Opposed to this solution is that a predicate can be true of God only in an absolute and complete, but not in a limited sense (381).

5. Intelligibility and truth

The analogical principle should guarantee the intelligibility of religous language. Aside from the issue of its actual performative ability, the question can be raised whether the intelligibility of religious statements, the suitability of the language system in which they are treated, is a sufficient stipulation for the truth of religious statements. Is the fulfillment of further stipulations necessary for the verification of truth?

From Wittgenstein we learn that a proposition such as "God created heaven and earth", as well as a simple sentence such as "It is raining", are not means-of-communication as long as such statements are not defined according to their modal function. He teaches that a proposition is intelligible only if one can gain insight into the whole of its behavioral practice. That which could be intended by such a thesis can be presented from the *Philosophical Investigations* (382). Wittgenstein has a construction worker call to his colleague, "A brick!" or "the sheet there!". In order to understand what this construction worker means he recommends watching exactly "what happens". This means one should observe how the workers behave during the execution of the language game. Hereby it seems that the total meaning of these words did not become clear until the situational context communicated it. The meaning of the words makes it clear that the worker could also have said, "Please give me a brick now!". This example gives the impression that the meaning of a proposition can only be taken from the respective entanglement of the use of word and sentence with the way it conducts itself in the situation in which it is expressed. Karl-Otto Apel's critical question (383) has already been referred to. He asks if Christ's sentence "The kingdom of God is at hand" can be sufficiently comprehended on the basis of the performative practice. The intelligibility of the meaning taken from its performative practice is decisive for the illustrative value of the example of the construction worker. It is not a matter of claims and theoretical determinations. That which was presented to us is the language of command and of the carrying out of a command. However, in the case of a proposition such as the religious statement executed, its valid character is not indisputably evident. We are not merely dealing with communication such as in an advertisement where the listener may be able to adjust. In this case, the listener does not immediately reach for the sheet and pass it on nor does he pick up an umbrella when he leaves the house. He only does this when the speaker and the listener find themselves in a certain linguistic situation where the valid character of those sentences compare with a sentence of request, such as the sentence "I have run out of plates", or in the case of the sentence "It is raining". The sentence is unquestionably recognizable. Only this understanding enables the impartial listener to make out a correct use of the word and the manner of conduct belonging to it without great effort.

The construction workers use their language to give very definite orders which are necessary within the realm of their work. However, in order to understand the meaning of the applied words and the appropriateness of the sentences that appear, it is presupposed that these sentences and expressions can be applied in situations which correspond to other situations. The condition that the construction worker in this language game may follow or even break rules, which may be easily recognizable in this case, does not necessarily mean that these rules have a definite meaning. They may be understandable beyond and above the course of their immediate function. Applied to the religious proposition, this does not mean that the inner consistence of the course of a church service, guaranteed by a great number of rules, identified the propositons which are voiced here as meaningful and understandable. This is true as long as the language game of the church service is seen as a ritual speech and conduct. It is isolated within itself and set apart from all other connections. Whatever meaning one may attribute to the parable of the construction worker and whatever conclusions one may draw from it, that which is immediately observable in Wittgenstein's theory is that he claims that each language is a family of language games. However, he says nothing concerning whether or not the same language is spoken in the various types of language games. This does not mean that all the sentences used in different language games are of the same type. A statement can contradict this by advocating that each language game could be a complete language (384). This means that in spite of the specification of its subject, notions of belief "cannot at all be understood if their relationship to other forms of life are not taken into consideration" (385).

As true as such a claim may be, the claim raises the question of whether in the understanding of a religious proposition the ontological content of this statement has also been taken into accout. This occurs in addition to the question of the qualification of the analogical principle, that establishes or at least reveals a connection between the religious language game and other languages games. As in non-religious statements, here such an assumption proceeds from the fact that the verifiable content of a statement is sufficiently founded in the use of language. This means that the consideration of the difference between word and thing is actually superfluous because the functional language game is understandable as "an own, perfected reality" (386). In this reality the relation to the other players as well as to the other language games and ways of life is unquestionably established.

However, the previously posed question can be formulated more precisely. The same is actually meant when one posits that a sentence with verifiable assertive content is just as understandable as when one posits that it is true? Intelligibility means, in the first case, the intersubjective agreement of that which is involved in the language game. In contrast the truth-claim posits a type of relationship between the statement of the sentence and the fact stated. For the claim that a statement is true implies a right to validity which is not to be confused with a right which alleges the capability of control over a certain competence of a rule. This makes it possible to utilize those systems of rules and to bring forth or understand a statement. Whether the truth conditions of the statement "It is raining" are fulfilled or not can as little be tested as the statement "God created heaven and earth" can. This could only be accomplished by comparing the rules of application with the rules of a corresponding reconstructed situation or by the construction of the rules of conduct generated in similar situations. Such a test would only be successful when the truth conditions of a statement are defined by the rules of application of the linguistic expressions present in this statement. However, this is a presupposition proceeding from the fact that the truth conditions are not only defined in the rules of application, but rather they are already fulfilled. Then the truth-claim of a statement would consequently no longer require further justification.

Even if the statement "It is raining" can be expressed in the indicative form or as Wittgenstein suggests as question and answer, "It is raining?, Yes" (387), its truth-claim is not yet sufficiently confirmed on the basis of intelligibility. It is not the intelligibility of this statement, but rather the recognition of its claim to validity that produces a certain manner of conduct. This is due to something as simple as a convincing glance out of a window or a relationship of trust with other persons. The atheist does not allow himself to be motivated by the statement, "God created heaven and earth", because this statement is intelligible to him (because he considers this statement intelligible) or because he knows that this statement does not express a scientific program. Rather he is motivated because he does not recognize its truth. If he should reject this statement because it is not at all clear to him what is meant by it, then he would more or less be rejecting it on the basis of logical error. Faith would be the necessary result of the correct use of the language's immanent rules. The intelligibility of a statement is merely one of the conditions which leads to recognition of its claim to validity. There can be many reasons for the recognition itself, which do not constitute the justification of the claim underlying the recognition. The purpose of the act that results from a claim is the sole guarantee of recognition, e.g. taking along an umbrella, taking down the laundry or - in the case of the religious statement - Braithwaite's renowned optimism (388).

Indeed, in late Wittgenstein the analytical concentration on the structure of language and its intersubjective meaning opens up the possibility of the notion of pluralistic linguistic worlds. These differ from one another according to the given manner of speech, be it that of the scientist, the philosopher or the theologian. However, such a classification of language does not render the question of truth superfluous. Its truth-claim legitimates not on the basis of the fact that a statement is ascribed to a certain language game of a combination of language games. With the choice of a definite "language clothing" (389), that is of a definite context of language games, we appoint a statement that requires explanation. For example we could choose to appoint the assertion that the world was created by God to a definite realm of language and material. However, this appointment does not establish the relation of the proposition to reality. The rules of language clothing regulate only those statements which are grounded within their context of argumentation. Whether or not a statement is true is determined solely on the basis of the existence of the factual situation which the statement professes to express. Only those terms which are necessary to form this statement are taken from the language clothing. The appropriateness of such language clothing can only be measured indirectly by the standards of true statements.

The appropriateness of a certain language clothing initially cannot be determined for statements whose truth has yet to be examined. If truth and appropriateness are not one and the same, then appropriateness as the guarantor of the intellgibility of a statement is only one of the conditions of its truth. The sentence stating the chemical components of bread within the context of religious language games becomes meaningless, because the religious language context lacks the appropriateness necessary for its intelligibility. Consequently, it is not verifiable. This is similar to the sentence "The sun is rising" within the realm of a modern astronomical theory that is not false but meaningless. However, for Wittgenstein, the same sentence is not only meaningful but also verifiable in the context of a language game involving farmers and tourists (390). Claims which lack explanation cannot find the necessary terms and predicates for their justification within language clothing appropriate to them.

One condition precedes the definition of truth and its reference to a coherently theoretical basis which correctly equates intelligibility and truth.

The argument cannot refer to an accord between language clothing and reality. In this case the question of which language system is appropriate to the discussion of a certain statement would be arguably redeemable. One could argue this within the realm of the reflective foundation of the presupposed relationship of proposition to reality in the form of a universal criticism of language. For analysis would no longer merely depend on a rhapsodic collection of statements. The appropriateness of language clothing could be measured by the degree of clarity reached. The measure would be the clarity that is permitted by the given material. As in Aristotle's *Nichomachian Ethics* the claim of exactness would thereby not be raised for all scientific problems in the same manner. Just as in Aristotle the logically trained listener requires of handmade artistic production as much clarity and exactness as the matter allows. It is just as absurd to accept probabilities from mathematicians as it is to requires proofs from preachers. Exactly *this* condition characteristic of *these* propositions, remains for the proof of religious propositions. Religious propositions speak of matters of belief (metaphysical facts, God, eternity) and states of affairs that are believed (God created heaven and earth). Consequently, their proof will have to be carried out under consideration of this feature. In the process of argumentation and legitimation a statement concerning such a state of affairs should not be stealthily altered into a statement concerning a known state of affairs (391). To deny a proposition's truth merely because it speaks of such states of affairs and not of formal-analytic or empirical-synthetic generated states of affairs would mean to withdraw from the reflective foundation of the relationship of language to reality. Undoubtedly, the truth of a religious proposition can be judged as little as the truth of an empirical statement solely on the basis of the appropriateness of language clothing. In regard to the appropriateness of the proof of a statement, it must be possible to question this appropriateness in a fundamental reflective process that attaches a statement to another or to a modified language clothing. Only this exchange itself must be founded. In this sense, one would no longer seek to verify the phenomena of rain within relgious language clothing. Knowledge exists of the physics of the atmosphere and Zeus is no longer regarded to be the cause of rain.

It is the prerequisite of a fundamental reflective process that the language itself is the medium in which the experience of its synthesis with reality is executed. In language, the affinity of the language system with reality is assured. In his late philosophy, Wittgenstein himself posited the unity of reality and language and viewed the analytical reference to reality to be decisive for description. Although no longer metaphysically considered this unity is limited to the postulate of a possible agreement between different language clothings. He rejected further linguistic analysis of its difference and reference. The guarantor is merely agreement in the sense of distributive rules of agreement and honesty.

If one proceeds from the fact that propositions of faith include statements about matters which are believed then they are revisable on the basis of knowledge just as propositions of probability are. However, they cannot be contradicted or confirmed on the basis of trust in the conduct of others. In this way, it becomes evident that an agreement between the logic defining this agreement and that of other language systems is only possible when one can demonstrate the ontological difference of a prerequisite reference to language. The turn from *analogia entis* to *analogia linguae* hides this difference, rather than restricting it. Therefore, as its greatest concession only interreligious meaning can be attributed to the analogical principle. However, the analogical principle cannot be recognized in its function as a mediator between the religious language system and other language systems.

The question raised earlier of the procedure which the analytical philosophy draws from the analogical conception, can now be answered with the following statement.

> If we insist on the use of the "material mode" of speech, requiring analogy to provide us with information about real properties of supernatural entities, little can be salvaged. But if we allow ourselves to examine the logic of analogy as *one means of providing criteria for the disciplined use of ordinary language in theological contexts*, looking for its value on the "formal" rather than the "material" mode of speech, much that may be of interest to us remains (392).

Following the syntactic-formal limitation of the analogical conception, its task is the explication of rules. This places limitation on the practice of using words, which originate from a non-religious context, in their application in religious statements. The exposition of such rules should prevent a non-qualified application of expressions in religious language. However, it guarantees the proper use of certain words in these very statements.

> Seen thus, the analogy of attribution states the rule: A word from a secular context may be used theologically *where there is already a ground* in the theological "universe of discourse" (authoritative doctrine, dogma, creed, or proposition entailed by one of these) for holding that this quality is derived from God's uniquely characteristic activity. But this rule also warns that the quality designated by the word in question is not to be assumed "formally" applicable to God but only "virtually", as a reminder

that within the theological conceptual schema God is taken to be its ultimate source (393).

Supplementing attributional analogy, the proportional analogy posits that the transference of words from every day language into theological language is *only* possible when their use in this language can *only* take place on the basis of axioms and rules which define theological language. Because Ferré stipulates that the mode of application of the analogical principle is not founded on the ontological presupposition of the identity of God and humanity, there can then be no objections to it. This is true because it is no longer susceptible to objections to the scholastic conception of *analogia entis*. However, the question of the ontological relevance of a religious statement which the analogical conception was designed to clarify remains unanswerable.

V. BELIEF AND TRUTH

1. The foundation of the linguistic analytical theory of truth

The positivist emotive theory of religion denied the cognitive truth claim of religous statements. However, the analytical philosophy of religion stemmed from this theory. Insight into the multiple non-cognitive functions of religious language according to which the relationship of truth and faith was seen in the alternative of truth *or* faith. Here truth is attributed to knowledge and faith to feeling. In the question of the possibility of the justification of the religious standpoint as an attribute of "blik" it is evident that religious faith cannot be localized in a range between insufficient objective and subjective certainty. Neither the certainty of knowledge, nor a deficient rigor in speech that is unable to identify meaning, can be attributed to religious faith. The classification of the religious statement as an expression of an emotionally motivated perspective, which is incapable of legitimating a verifiable claim, and yet raises this claim, has shown itself to be questionable in Hare's "blik" theory and in the various attempts to reinterpret the ontotlogical claim of religious statements.

In connection with late Wittgenstein's linguistic theory, the linguistic analytical theory of intelligibility acknowledged the cognitive character of religious statements. It does not contest their capability of truth. It regards as sufficiently guaranteed the evidence for the authorization of the validity of such statements on the basis of intelligibility within the context of the language game or the language system.

The urgent problem for this theory is not the question of the conditions for the verification of religious statements, but the study of the structures and motivating strengths of those forms of life in the context of religious expressions.

> To ask a question, then, about the reality of the physical world, is not to ask whether the physical world exists (what would that mean?) but to ask for an elucidation of the concept of reality in question. Similarly, the question of the reality of God which is of interest to the philosopher is a question about a *kind of reality*; a question about the possibility of giving an account of the distinction between truth and falsity, sense and nonsense, in

religion. This is not a question of experimentation any more than the question of the reality of the physical world, but a question of conceptual elucidation; that is, the philosophers want to know what is meant by "real" ("exists") in the statement "God is real (exists)" (394).

Theoretical reflections seek to comprehend the exposition of the conditions for the possibility of understanding religious statements. However, they do not seek to inquire into the constitution of such statements; even if it is uncontested that the possibility of the intelligibility of religious statements should be regarded to be affirmed along with the legitimation of religious statements. Indeed this second problem cannot solely, be handled analytically. Linguistic analysis merely locates the previously constructed deep grammatical structures, without characterizing more closely the relationship between language and reality. It is undoubtedly the merit of the linguistic analytical theory of intelligibility to have drawn attention to the multiple modes of linguistic application (395). Thereby, however, it invalidated the difference between belief and truth and attributed this too as truth. Any possibility other than that of securing truth through intelligibility within the family of religious language games concerned would mean the application of semantic criteria which are indeed more comprehensive, but also *heterochthonous*. Again this could not guarantee the intelligibility of religious statements.

The third and last direction of analytical philosophy to be discussed arises in part from the positivist thought of Wittgenstein's early work, especially of Wittgenstein's *Tractatus*, as well as from theories rooted in the *Philosophical Invertigations*. Together with the analytical theory of intelligibility this third direction focuses on the cognitive character of religous statements. However, it agrees with positivist thought that it must be possible for cognitive statements to set conditions of verification beyond that of intelligibility within the context of a certain language game (396). Certainly - and herein lies the difference from emotive religious philosophy - it speaks of verification only as it simultaneously emphasizes that religious statements are to be structurally differentiated from those statements which are based on scientific knowledge. This means that one attempts here to consider the uniqueness of religious statements for the verification process without immediately succumbing to the temptation to eliminate the relationship between reality and language from reflection. Belief and truth are neither thought of as alternatives nor as identical. But rather one attempts to consider their relationship within the difference between belief and knowledge. As opposed to the alternative belief *or* truth and to the identification of belief *as* truth, the relationship of both can now be defined as *faith and truth*.

The proof of the cognitivity of religious statements was sought within the framework of the analytical theory of understanding with the help of the analogical principle. This attempt achieved only minor success. The analogical theory starts from the principle that religious statements say something about God. In these sentences predicates are applied which have their special meaning in relationship to the subject. In recognition of the particular character of the subject of the sentence, the particular meaning of the predicates in statements about God is to become clear as one considers the normal application of these predicates. In this way, the function of disclosure in regard to the subject of the sentence would offer them. The second attempt to understand and prove the truth of religious propositions and the supposition of their cognitivity does not proceed from the analysis of the predicate, but rather from the perception of the subject. In this manner it chooses the direct way already called to mind in the criticism of the analogical principle. In demonstrating that a theism underlies this principle, it seeks to transcend the realm of experience in order to make statements about God. In regard to the analogical principle, it has been shown that the principle is only capable of arriving at what is expected of it and demonstrating that religious language is an intelligible language, if it succeeds in producing unequivocal evidence of God the Creator.

Certainly the word has gotten around among linguistic analytical philosophers that these proofs of God's existence are not so easily established, as perhaps some of its expressions appear to be at first glance. But that is not the question here. Linguistic analytical investigations concentrate more on the logic of proof concerning the already existent. It deals, to a great extent, with the metaphysical-philosophical and not the theological discussion. The prominent questions are:

1. On the basis of which type of experience should one proceed in order to best establish a proof for the existence of God: experience of order, chance, beauty or religious experience?

2. Which grammatical structures underly the key words (such as: "necessary existence") and the central propositions of such a process of proof? What result does the analysis of logical models bring forth, i.e. the logical models upon which such proofs are based?

The positivist criticism of religious statements claimed that in these cases one is only apparently dealing with synthetic statements. Yet these are in reality analytical. Therefore, the proofs of God, as central religious propositions, are especially suited to cast light on the unique function of religious language and on the clarification of their actual logical status. The difference between theories of verification and of comprehension is not, as their discussions and mutual critique often lead one to suppose, that the former has given up the perception of necessary existence. Rather the opposite is the case: its view of the relationship between language and reality does not allow God to be thought of other than as necessarily existent. The question of the existence of God remains, as such, superfluous. In order to defend the claim just mentioned, that the question of God is not the question of whether God exists but merely the question of His "kind of reality", Phillips attacks Hick as a proponent of eschatological verification. He writes:

> Because he (Hick) misconstrues the philosophical issues at stake, Hick misunderstands the point of my comparison of the philosophical treatment of the reality of physical objects with the philosophical treatment of the reality of God. He says that whereas we are all agreed about the reality of the physical world, we are not all agreed about the reality of God. But when *did* we agree about the reality of physical objects? What would it be like to disagree? I know what it means to agree that it is a tree and not a lamp-post that we see in the fog. But when I am facing the tree in normal conditions do I agree that it is a tree? What if everyone else said that it was not a tree? Would I say that I must be mistaken? No. I should think I was mad! We are familiar with situations where we say, "This is a tree", "Here is a torn page", "Here is an ink-bottle" and so on. Our confidence in saying so is not based on evidence. No, such situations are examples of the kind of thing we *mean* by talking about physical objects. Should our confidence in such situations be undermined, the result would not be greater caution on our part, but radical changes in our use of the words "physical object". There is no question of justifying the criteria for our use of "physical object": that is how we *do* use the concept. The comparison with the reality of God was meant to be at this grammatical level. In each case there would be no question of a general justification of the criteria for distinguishing between the real and the unreal (397).

The reason for changing the question of whether God exists into the equally decisive question of His type of existence lies in the lack of a differentiation of language and reality. Only under this supposition does the question of the mediation of reality in the perception of God make sense. The ontological proof was given in order to provide this mediation for which a need only exists when the differences between language and reality has become a problem beforehand. The analysis of intelligibility has never allowed the problem of the mediation of language and reality to be valid. Thus, for example, Ferré also defends John N. Findlay's attempt to prove the logical impossibility of the existence of God as a necessary existence. He attempts to overcome the objection that here one is merely dealing with a twisted ontological argument. He does this although he is, by no means, a follower of Findlay's reflections in a broad sense.

> To this objection I believe that Findlay has a valid reply. His argument, he might say, is intended to show that the true logic of the word "God" is such that the issue of existence cannot even be *raised* about its referent (398).

The differentiation of synthetic - analytic was not given a special position. It focuses on language "as a 'natural growth' that leads to a corresponding emphasis on the essential sociality of language. It is only in and through society that language may be said to have 'grown naturally'" (399). Here language does not remain limited to the differentiation between synthetic - analytic, but rather it is said to have other manners of use, which decrease the significance of this first differentiation.

> *Language, ... is a complex social product with many legitimate uses* (400).

Against C. B. Martin's reproach that a statement such as 'God is good' is purely analytical (401) stands the claim that this only holds true for the use of this statement within systematic theology.

> Given a religious rather than a systematic use, the latter statement - which, ..., springs out of an act of commitment and is itself part of the speaker's continuing disposition to commit his life to a theistic model by which to envisage reality - is far from tautological. It is a judgement which both reflects and deeply affects the whole life of the person who utters it in its religious use. The history of religious development and the facts of the religious life illustrate the non-tautological function of "God is good" once this form of words is removed from the systematic language of academic theology. It is all too easy to forget, in our day and culture, that "God" has not always been understood in Christian terms. But it was in fact only after millennia of fear and superstition in which the gods were believed arbitrary, bloodthirsty, and vengeful that the belief in a God of love and goodness gradually entered the world. Such a concept did not arise because philosophers decided to define a term in a certain way; it came, for Western civilization, through the historical experiences of a nation and - supremely for Christians - through the death of a man on a cross (402).

The situation for verificative analysis is different. Here the question of the reality of God stands central. The discussion of the analogical problem ends with the generally binding insight that here God could only be recognized as the one who withdraws from all speech. The transference from religious language to everyday language or to a scientific language failed due to the fact that the analogical principle, as the *terminus ad quem*, to proceed from ordinary language makes this transference possible. However, if preference is due religious language, then the thesis of the equality of language games is to be corrected in this regard. The ontological argument, which begins directly with the concept of God, seems to be more appropriate for legitimizing the claim to the validity of religious statements, than the argument which proceeds from the predicate term of the religious sentence applying the analogical principle. The ontological proof does not begin by reflecting on the word and then transfering it to God. This differentiates it from the cosmological, teleological and physio-theological proofs. Rather for this proof, God is the first in *ordo essendi* as well as in *ordo cognoscendi* It proceeds from the fact that:

> ...thought, when it follows its own bent most completely and sets itself the task of thinking out the idea of an object that shall completely satisfy the demands of reason, may appear to be constructing a mere *ens rationis*, but in fact is never devoid of objective or ontological reference (403).

Seen in this way, the ontological proof is not merely one way which may lead to insight into the truth of religious statements, but rather it becomes the basic question of philosophy altogether (404). If religious language is understood to be the basic principle of all speech, then the ontological proof does not merely provide the foundation of just an obscure religious truth. Rather the legitimation of the claim to validity of statements for all other language games can first be thought of when one proceeds from this ontological truth. In this sense, E.E. Harris writes in defence of R.G. Collingwood and in critical response to Gilbert Ryle:

> No proof of existence is ever anything but the satisfaction of a demand of the intellect. We have seen that mere sense perceptions cannot prove matters of fact. Such proof requires, at least, the comprehension of sense data into a system from which we can infer to the existence in question. It is only by such inference that any exis-tence can be unassailably established (even when the thing in question is present to our senses). Any such inference, to be valid, must satisfy the demands of the intellect, and the conclusion of such inference is no more nor less than what the intellect demands in the face of the evidence

produced. If, then, our experience is such that, for it to have any recognizable character at all and be more than mere meaningless chaos, our intellect demands an absolutely whole system of reality, and if the satisfaction of this demand is the *sine qua non* of the validity of all arguments, including proofs of existence of finite things, then the absolutely complete system of reality must be.

On this view it follows, also, that we may not argue, as Mr. Ryle does, that because the proof of existence of a finite thing requires premises of the same kind. For any operation in thought upon any premises requires and must rest upon the existence of God in the manner explained. Apart from the Absolute, no proof or argument would be intelligible (let alone valid) (405).

Considering this claim it becomes clear why the discussion of the ontological argument is not limited to the circle of analytical religious philosophers interested in religious problems. The advocates of this proof seek to convince us that the ontological argument is much more deeply interwoven in the problems of the theory of knowledge than its discussion within the framework of religious themes of metaphysics demonstrates. This view is certainly not new and does not pretend to be. The reference to Anselm, René Descartes and Hegel is openly admitted. The arguments which justify the connection of the problem of knowledge with onto-theology are borrowed from these three thinkers.

All formulations of the ontological proof of God agree in the conviction that the certainty of God's existence follows from a definite conception of God. In these formulations God is considered to be the *highest being* or the *ens necessarium*. The analytical philosophy of religion discusses the proof of Anselm of Canterbury whom they consider a representative of this first form of proof which attempted to conceive God as the "*ens quo maius cogitari non potest*" (406); and the definition of the perception of God as *ens perfectissimum* according to Descartes. Descartes also serves as the guarantor for the second type of formulation as does Kant although he rejected ontological proof.

2. Is existence a predicate?

The systematic basis of proof was not developed by the representatives of linguistic analysis. Rather they merely legitimized, emphasized new accents, or defended them against incorrect objections. In a similar way their criticism is also dependent on historic predecessors, Gaunilo, Petrus Gassendi and, above all, Kant. Because apology and polemics change according to historical relations they do not agree in their respective line of argument. The most frequent objection presented against the ontological proof is the reference to a radical difference between perception and being. This is especially apparent in the discussion of the postulation of Kant that being is not a real predicate.

a) Russell

In the cases of Russell and George Edward Moore the discussion of this question is carried out on a purely logical level. The issue is not raised of how this question arose. They discuss the question: "Is existence a predicate?" without any allusion to the proofs of God's existence. Proceeding from general statements such as: "All Greeks are men", Russell emphasizes that such a statement does not imply the existence of Greeks. One would be dealing with a statement of existence if the following supplement "and there are Greeks" were added to the first statement.

> If you include the fact that there are Greeks, you are rolling two propositions into one, and it causes unnecessary confusion in your logic, because the sorts of propositions that you want are those that do assert the existence of something and general propositions which do not assert existence (407).

The combination of both statements would lead one to believe that the statement, "All Greeks are persons", as well as the statement, "No Greek is a person", would be true if there actually were no Greeks. Russell's argumentation for this is as follows:

> All statements about all the members of a class that has no members are true, because the contradictory of any general statement does assert existence and is therefore false in this case (408).

Here Russell resorts to the differentiation between a statement and the function of a statement. He limits the use of model categories; "necessary", "possible" and "impossible" to the functions of a statement. Applied to the ontological proof this means that God's existence can neither be accidental nor conditioned. Thus in this proof an erroneous positing of absolute necessity is made of a statement instead of a function of a statement.

> Much false philosophy has arisen out of confusing propositional functions and propositions. There is a great deal in ordinary traditional philosophy which consists simply in attributing to propositions the predicates which only apply to propositional

functions, and, still worse, sometimes in attributing to individuals predicates which merely apply to propositional functions. This case of *necessary, possible, impossible* is a case in point. In all traditional philosophy there comes a heading of "modality", which discusses *necessary, possible* and *impossible* as properties of propositions, whereas in fact they are properties or propositional functions. Propositions are only true or false (409).

At best, a predicate can be derived from a subject by means of logical ground rules only with logical, and not with actual necessity. However, real necessity must be attributed to an essence whose existence cannot be eliminated. The restriction of the modal categories to the function of statements can be contrasted with the explanation that a statement can only be true or false. According to Russell, one can now recognize that the logical structure of statements which claim existence prohibits *a priori* truth to be posited of them. According to Russell's theory of description, if someone says, "Human beings exist" or "That is a human being", then he says nothing other than that the function of a statement is true in at least one case, for example:

> "Horses exist but dragons don't exist" is not to say of horses that they possess, and of dragons that they do not possess, a special characteristic, namely existence. It is to say of the concept of a horse that this concept has instances, and of the concept of a dragon that it has no instances (410).

In that existence is not a characteristic that can or cannot be attributed to something, the logical level of argumentation cannot attribute this predicate to the highest being.

b) Moore

In his essay "Is Existence a Predicate?" (411) Moore comes to a similar conclusion with other arguments, although he sees no reason why existence could not be a predicate. Moore proceeds from the usage of the word "exists" and compares the two sentences "Tame tigers exist" and "Tame tigers growl". He asks if the difference between these two propositional predicates is other than the difference between the latter and a sentence with the predicate "to scratch". ("Tame tigers scratch.")

While the examples of the sentence predicates "growl" and "scratch" have a double meaning, as in these sentences:

> "All tame tigers growl (scratch)"

"Most tame tigers growl (scratch)"
"Some tame tigers growl (scratch)",

the sentence "Tame tigers exist" always means, "Some tame tigers exist". The difference becomes even clearer in the negative form:

"Some tame tigers don't growl".

The meaning of this sentence is obvious. Yet the meaning of the sentence

"Some tame tigers don't exist"

is not clear and evident in the same way.

A meaning for the last sentence can only be accepted if the word "exists" does not have the same meaning as it does in the positive form of such a sentence. From the circumstance that "exists", in contrast to the attributes "growl" and "scratch" alters its mode of usage according to the type of sentence it is in, Moore draws the preliminary conclusion that existence cannot be viewed as a predicate in a logical sense.

However, Moore recalls this judgement in that he ascertains that the sentence, "Some tame tigers do not exist", can also mean, "Some tame tigers are imaginary", or "Some tame tigers are not real". Proceeding from the differentiation between thought or imaginary existence or existent existence, he then turns against Russell's claim that existence is only a predicate of functions of statements. It is possible to claim that to exist is synonymous with: occasionally being true.

Considering the various applications of predicates in sentences like, "Some tame tigers exist" and "Some tame tigers growl", he conceeds the possibiltiy that existence is not a predicate. However with the aid of other uses of this word he also attempts to prove that such a claim is basically incorrect.

> To point at a thing which you see and to say "This exists" seems to me to be meaningless, if "exists" is the singular of "exist" in the sense in which it is used in "Tame tigers exist"; but I cannot help thinking that in the case of anything to point at which and "This is a tame tiger" is significant, it is also significant to point at it and say "This exists" *in some sense or other*. My reason for thinking this is that it seems to me that you can clearly say *with truth* of any such object "This *might* not have existed", "It is *logically possible* that this should not have existed"; and I do not see how it is possible that "This might not have existed" should be true unless "This does in fact exist" is true, and therefore also significant. The statement "it is logically possible that this should not have existed" seems to *mean* "The sentence 'This does not exist' is significant"; and if "This does not exist" is significant,

"This does exist" must be significant too. Now I cannot help thinking that in every case in which I point at an object which I am perceiving and say significantly "This is a tame tiger", "This is a book", my proposition is in fact a proposition about some sense-datum, or some set of sense-data, which I am perceiving, and that part what I am saying is that this sense-datum (or these sense-data) is "of" a physical object. That is to say, I am saying of some sense-datum that it is "of" a physical object in the same sense in which it is true to say of an after-image which I see with my eyes shut that it is *not* "of" a physical object. And I think that part, at least, of what we mean by "This exists", where we are using "this" in the same way as when we point and say "This is a book" is "This sense-datum is of a physical object", which seems to me to be certainly significant (412).

If one, following Moore, proceeds from the fact that one can assert that a sense-datum exists, then from the very beginning it is uncertain that the predicate "exist" must refer solely to a physical object. If of sense-datum as well as of an imagination of a dream it could be said, "This might not have existed", then this is only possible under the presupposition that the sentence, "this does in fact exist", is true and meaningful. From the various modes of application of the word "exist", Moore concludes now that one is actually dealing with a predicate. This is a claim which, indeed, could not have a fruitful effect on the discussion of the ontological proof, because only the abstract preconceived difference between thought and existence makes the recognition of the validity of the claim possible. Only then could one recognize existence as a predicate. However, the content of that which is unique in the concept of God, that the determination of the existence of God is present in this, cannot be grasped by this type of differentiation. It does not consider the ontological difference on which the use of the predicate "exist" in the respective various statements is based. The reflections of Moore, as well as those of Russell, 18 years earlier, on the question if existence is a predicate have not, thereby, promoted the discussion, but rather have blocked it.

3. The ontological proof of God

a) The Conditions of the Validity of the Proof

Charles Hartshorne and Norman Malcolm can initially be counted as defenders of the ontological proof. Both proceed from Anselm's form of proof in their apologetics and both claim to have discovered in this proof two different trains of thought which contrast one as possessing conclusive truth over against the other (413). According to Malcolm, the first version of the Anselm argument is founded on the false belief that existence is a perfection. This would imply that something is somewhat greater when it exists than when it does not exist, as is claimed in the *Proslogion*.

> I said further that if a thing exists even in the mind alone, it can be thought to exist also in reality, which is greater. If, then, it (namely, 'that-than-which-a-greater-cannot-be-thought') exists in the mind alone, it is something than which a greater *can* be thought. What, I ask you, could be more logical? For if it exists even in the mind alone, cannot it be thought to exist also in reality? And if it can (be so thought), is it not the case that he who thinks this thinks of something greater than it, if it exists in the mind alone? What, then, could follow more logically than that, if 'that-than-which-a-greater-*cannot*-be-thought' exists in the mind alone, it is the same as that-than-which-a-greater-*can*-be-thought (414)?

In his criticism of this form of proof, Malcolm refers to Kant. He construes similar examples as a means of illustration such as that of the 100 talars (415). However, with his objection Malcolm does not mean to touch the nerve of the ontological argument, but rather to critique a form of argumentation that upholds the difference between perception and existence exactly at the point where existence must be viewed as belonging to the concept. The premise of this formulation is that the concept of existence must be thought in the concept of God. Malcolm sees a *petitio principii* in Anselm's first form of proof which regards existence as a characteristic of perfection. In his opinion, this can be observed in the example of a king's inquiry into who is the best chancellor. It is possible to perceive God as perfection without thinking of him as existent. He does not discover a similiar dichotomy in Anselm's second form of argumentation. Here Anselm does not try to list "existence" among the haphazard characteristics of God, listed. Rather the proof of God's existence is established on the basis of the perception of His essence. Malcolm regards *Proslogion 3* to be the decisive passage for this form of proof.

> And certainly this being so truly exists that it cannot be even thought not to exist. For something can be thought to exist that cannot be thought not to exist, and this is greater than that which can be thought not to exist. Hence, if that-than-which-a-greater-

cannot-be-thought can be thought not to exist, then that-than-which-a-greater-cannot-be-thought is not the same as that-than-which-a-greater-cannot-be-thought,which is absurd. Something-than-which-a-greater-cannot-be-thought exists so truly then, that it cannot be even thought not to exist. And You, Lord our God, are this being (416).

Malcolm's own reasoning proceeds from the use of the word "God" and divides Anselm's proof into two reflections: the first purports that a being whose nonexistence is logically impossible is "greater" than a being whose nonexistence is possible. The second line of thought proceeds from the argument that God as such is a being beyond which no greater being can be conceived. Here Malcolm with his reference to the use of the word "God" infers that the argument that regards the assertion that God is the greatest of all beings or the most perfect and the highest being, is in full agreement with this usage. Consequently he concludes that statements about God are logically necessary truths in the same sense as statements that a quadrangle has four sides.

Malcolm sees the difference in Anselm's first line of argumentation, where it is claimed that existence is a perfection. This form of proof merely asserts that the logical impossibility of nonexistence is a perfection, i.e., that necessary existence is perfection. In order to explain what can be understood by necessary existence, Malcolm refers to causal axioms and specifies as follows:

If we reflect on the common meaning of the word "God" (no matter how vague and confused this is), we realize that it is incompatible with this meaning that God's existence should *depend* on anything. Whether we believe in Him or not we must admit that the "almighty and everlasting God (as several ancient prayers begin), the "Maker of heaven and earth, and of all things visible and invisible" (as is said in the Nicene Creed), cannot be thought of as being brought into existence by anything or as depending for His continued existence on anything. To conceive of anything as dependent upon something else for its existence is to conceive of it as a lesser being than God (417).

In addition to "independence" Malcolm refers to "superiority", "eternity" and "infinity" as characteristics of an essence *"aliquid quo nihil maius cogitari possit"*. Like Anselm he concludes that when we can think of a being in this way and a being would not exist, if it then should exist, its nonexistence would be possible. In such a case of its existence it would not be independent, but rather depend upon others. This means that God's existence is either

a) logically necessary or

b) logically impossible.

According to Malcolm's conception, Anselm proved that the concept of an incidental existence or of an incidental nonexistence cannot be applied to God. The only possible way to refute such a line of argumentation is offer the proof that the concept of God as a being beyond which nothing greater can be conceived is either self-contradictory or senseless. Malcolm referred to Kant in regard to the rejection of the proposal that existence is perfection. He referres to Descartes in regard to the claim that *necessary existence* is perfection. In answer to Gassendi's objection to Descartes who appears to be wavering in the classification of existence as perfection, however, he leaves no doubt that necessary existence must be viewed as perfection.

> Here I do not understand of which type the existence of the things should be according to your viewpoint and why it cannot be denoted to be characteristic just as the omnipotence as one can use the denotation characteristic for any given attribute or for all that what can be said about a thing, as it can be grasped here altogether. Yes, the necessary thing is really characteristic in God, which must be grasped in the narrowest sense, because it is befitting of God alone and in God alone designates a part of being (418).

Malcolm's reference to Descartes is not incidental. His demonstration of the statement that God, the most perfect being, is a logically necessary truth in the same way the four sides of the quadrangle posit a truth, may have called for renewed recognition of Descartes. However, the agreement in their line of argumentation appears to be of a merely formal nature. In the fifth meditation Descartes wrote that there is contradiction in "conceiving God as a highly complete being, who is lacking being and who lacks a certain completion" (419). Descartes' proof is conceived as "a case of applying the method of distinct recognition" (420). He introduces it in connection with a mathematical illustration. Descartes claims that it belongs to the nature of God to exist in the same way that one may prove a figure or a number. With careful reflection we can convince ourselves "that being can be separated from the essence of God just as little as the fact can be separated from the essence of a triangle that the sum of its angles is 180 degrees (421).

That which is decisive in Descartes' line of argument is that this is a case of the methodological application of clear knowledge. Consequently, in his estimation one does not proceed on the basis of arbitrary conceptuality. Just as Pegasus does not become a being who is clearly and distinctly conceivable when one imagines a horse with wings, "Nec" and his brothers "NEc" and

"NEC" - as Paul Henle pleads against Malcolm (422) do not correspond to the requirements of clear and distinct knowledge as is required for the conception of a being that is absolutely necessary. Henle's argument ignores Malcolm's line of argument as well as St. Thomas' critique of Anselm. The attempt to deduce the existence of God from a name, fails the formulation of Descartes. Irrespective of the fact that the notion of perfection or the highest being did not seem to be sufficient in Malcolm's eyes, he included such attributes as "necessary eternity, necessary unlimited, necessary omniscience, necessary omnipotence" (423). Yet decisive for his interpretation of Anselm's proof is that he does not, as Henle says, proceed from a normal definition of a "Nec". This only can be thought of as necessarily existent, but in no way as extraordinary. "Nec", as it is presented by Henle, is nothing other than a product of the imagination.

> Let us designate by "Nec" a certain being who has necessary existence but who is otherwise less remarkable. He has a certain amount of knowledge, though nothing extraordinary, and certain power, though he is unable to cause motion. As a necessary being, of course, Nec's nonexistence is inconceivable and he does not depend on anything. Nec is limited in the sense that his knowledge is exceeded by that of other beings, but it is not limited in the sense in which an engine is limited by its fuel supply; in this latter sense, which is very like dependence, he is unlimited. Clearly Nec cannot exist contingently since he is a being whose nonexistence is inconceivable. He cannot, therefore, merely happen to exist, nor can he exist temporally. It follows that Nec must exist necessarily or else it is impossible that he exist at all, and assuming what seems plausible, that there is no inherent contradiction in his nature, Nec must exist (424).

b) The Correspondence of Language and Reality

For Malcolm the existence of God cannot be deduced from a name. Undoubtedly he agrees with Descartes who held that only that "of which can be seen clearly and evidently that it can be said of this thing that it belongs to the true and unchangeable nature or form or essence of a thing" (425). In the fifth meditation Descartes believed that he had clearly and distinctly analyzed the inner connection of the idea of the essence and being of God on the basis of the criteria of truth. Malcolm regarded this investigation of the linguistic use of the word "God" to be proven. The reference to linguistic usage should demonstrate the justification of the premise that God's essence and existence are to be thought of as one, i.e. that existence is a necessary perfection. On the contrary, the premise which underlies the proof of existence of the family "Nec" is arbitrary. The conception of its necessary esixtence is not native and secure in the language game context. However, such a claim is a metaphysical invention in Wittgenstein's sense and therefore represents a misuse of language.

Malcolm has not escaped the argument opposed to the ontological proof of God put forward by his own camp of analytical philosophy. In this confrontation the difference with Findlay in the judgement of the ontological argument is of special interest. Findlay proceeds from the question, "Can God's existence be disproved?", and his ontological proof of the nonexistence of God. He regards the day on which Anselm's famous procedure of proof occured to him to have been a bad day (426). Findlay claims that the ontological proof attempts to build a bridge between mere abstract perception and concrete existence. In his interpretation as well as in Malcolm's positive attitude toward the ontological argument, the understanding of language is decisive. The antithesis between both is not a specifically religious-philsolphical or theological kind. Rather it has its basis within the realm of fundamental philosophy. The striking agreement in regard to Findlay's characterization of the religious attitude and the language bound to it only superficially conceals a basic difference underlying their implied language theories. In his defense of the ontological argument, Malcolm firmly advocates that an analysis of the concept of God makes clear the necessary unity of essence and existence. Findlay sees in this proof a risky and an unjustified additional predication of a presumed plurality of predicates. Findlay's own characterization of religious language forbids such an addition.

> The true object of religious reverence must not be one, merely, to which no *actual* independent realities stand opposed: it must be one to which such oppostion is totally *inconceivable*. God mustn't merely cover the territory of the actual, but also, with equal comprehensiveness, the territory of the possible. And not only must the existence of other things be unthinkable without Him, but His own non-existence must be wholly unthinkable in any circumstances. There must, in short, be no conceivable alternative to an existence properly termed "divine": God must be wholly inescapable, as we remarked previously, whether for thought or reality. So we are led on insensibly to the barely intelligible notion of a Being in whom Essence and Existence lose their separateness. And all that the great medieval thinkers really did was to carry such a development to its logical limit (427).

For Findlay the ontological argument does not proceed from the internal evidence of the concept of God. It has its application in language characterized by it. Rather it proceeds in a questionable way from a "barely intelligible notion of the being in whom Essence and Existence lose their separateness" (428). For this concept the necessary unity of existence and essence cannot be preconceived as it is in Malcolm's theory, rather this unity must be added to Findlay's conception.

In regard to Malcolm's argument one can say that in confrontation with the philosophy of the *Philosophical Investigations*, the difference between reality and language is thought of as eliminated in the performance of a language game. Therefore one can presuppose the unity of essence and existence. Opposed to this, Findlay basically rejects such an understanding of language and reality.

> Those who believe in necessary truths which aren't merely tautological, think that such truths merely connect the *possible* instances of various characteristics with each other: they don't expect such truths to tell them whether there *will* be instances of any charteristics. This is the outcome of the whole medieval and Kantian criticism of the Ontological Proof (429).

Following this quote from Findlay the realm of "eternal truth" certainly corresponds to the nominalist thoughts of medieval philosophy, and to a certain extent to Kant's rejection of ontological proof. One has no other choice but to understand this truth as formal truth limited by logical impossibility. Indeed the attempt of a proof of the existence of God is as senseless as it is contrary to religious consciousness. In order to substantiate the separation between essence and existence as a contrast of the idea of the embodiment of a predicate with the real thing Findlay cites medieval nominalism. Accordingly this disjunction "so to speak by means of God (through theology) had been brought along its way" (430). Consequently this led to an understanding of language which disregarded the relation to reality intended in the attitude of recognition. It formally transfered the question of existence from metaphysics and ontology to formal logic. In this way nominalism in its formal transformation, originally an off-shoot of the separation of existence and essence, becomes the witness of the correctness of this separation (431).

In the heterogeneity of linguistic understanding lies the difference of the understanding of the ontological proof between Malcolm and Findlay. Findlay believes it to be the case that:

> ...necessity in propositions merely reflects our use of words, the arbitrary conventions of our language (432).

Nothing can be proven insofar as an ontological proof of God begins from the name of a necessary essence. Indeed, Findlay remains indebted to the fact that the ontological proof of God necessarily proceeds this way. Thus, Malcolm also consents to the "modern view" propagated by Findlay. He believes that necessary truths are only the expression of the usage of words under the presupposition of a limited "*logical*" truth. This occurs prior to their characterization as "necessary truth". At the same time he admits being unable to comprehend why such a view should lead to the conclusion, "the Divine Existence is either senseless or impossible" (433). In contrast, Malcolm asserts:

> The correct reply is that the view that logical necessity merely reflects the use of words cannot possibly have the implication that every existential proposition must be contingent. That view requires us to *look at* the use of words and not manufacture *a priori* theses about it (434).

The proof of the impossibility of the existence of God cannot depend solely on the unintelligibiity of its necessity. This must be able to be substantiated. In fact it should not only be accomplished concerning logical necessity, but also concerning actual necessity. On the one side of the argument is the formal-logical concept of necessity. Religious language that predicates "existence" in reference to God must be declared inconclusive, because it assumes something to exist which contradicts its presuppositions. In this case the opposite claim of the impossibility of the existence of God, is just as difficult to comprehend. On the other side the formal-logic idea of necessity is considered to be insufficient to establish statements about existence. Malcolm's reasoning proceeds from that which he believes to be the correct linguistic event of the concept of God. In contrast, Findlay doubts that this concept has a natural linguistic home. He claims that there is a contradiction in this which Catherus and Kant had already revealed. Here Malcolm objects that the claim of contradiction has only been surreptitiously substantiated by falsely equating the statement, "God necessarily exists", and the statement, "If God exists then He exists necessarily". The latter statement presupposes that it is possible that God does not exist (435). The insufficient intelligibility of the statement, "God necessarily exists", is both analytically and synthetically founded. The fact that it could only have contingent character in this case is taken by Malcolm as positive evidence of its claim to have meaning. The proof that God's existence as such is unintelligible does not permit the conclusion that there is no God. Rather it concludes that God's existence cannot be proven by means of formal logic or empirical verification (436).

Statements like Ryle's assertion, "Any assertion of the existence of something, like any assertion of the occurrence of something, can be denied without logical absurdity" (437), or J. J. C. Smart's, "There can never be any *logical contradiction* in denying that God *exists*", and "Existence is not a property", (438) by pass Malcolm's reasoning. They do this in the case of God's existence which is claimed to be a necessary predicate as this cannot be the case for those things which obtain proof of their existence by synthetic judgement. It follows from this that God does not exist in a nominal way. Therefore a statement of His existence does not hold the same meaning as a statement about the existence of an empirical object. For late Wittgenstein, the criterion of the truth of a statement does not lie in the explanation of its langugae game, but rather in the perspective as an original phenomenon. The weight is on the *confirmation* of a language game and the *proof* that *this language game is being played* (439). Malcolm contrasts this criterion of truth with all the criteria of ontological proof in reference to Wittgenstein and the 90th Psalm.

> In the Ninetieth Psalm it is said: "Before the mountains were brought forth, or ever thou hadst formed the earth and the world, even from everlasting to everlasting, thou art God." Here is expressed the idea of the necessary existence and eternity of God, an idea that is essential to the Jewish and Christian religions. In those complex systems of thought, those "language-games", God has the status of a necessary being. Who can doubt that? Here we must say with Wittgenstein, "This language-game is played!" I believe we may rightly take the existence of those religious systems of thought in which God figures as a necessary being to be a disproof of the dogma, affirmed by Hume and others, that no existential proposition can be necessary (440).

This is the strongest argument for linguistic analysis following late Wittgenstein which can be plead against the critics of ontological proof. At the same time, however, this reveals the central problem of the treatment of the relationship between language and reality for the entire linguistic theory as developed under the influence of the positivism of early and late Wittgenstein. The arguments of Findlay, Ryle and others against ontological proof cannot refute this. However, their reservations out of which they have grown due to the silent tension between language and reality are, by no means eliminated (441). The main objection against the notion of being beyond that of which nothing greater can be conceived or against an *ens necessarium* remains in so far as these notions cannot be defined. Malcolm expressly agreed with Findlay's characterization of religious language (442).

The reference to the truth-function of the statement, "God necessarily exists", does not escape those critical reflections and inquiries which have already been made in connection with the discussion of the relationship between language games. Malcolm conceded that existence is not a predicate. However, he denied "existence" the character of predicate.

4. Criticism of Ontological Proof

Hick's criticism of the ontological proof is of interest. He and Crombie can be counted as the most striking advocates of the thesis that religious statements are verifiable and ontologically relevant. The ontic foundation of the ontological proof of God is not sufficiently guaranteed for either of them. Consequently they seek the legitimation of religious propositions by means of the idea of eschatological verification.

Here, in his criticism of the ontological proof, Hick proceeds from the second form of proof in Anselm's *Proslogion* in a similar manner to the interpretations of especially Hartshorne and Malcolm. Here, it must be considered that the same idea of *ens necessarium* does not underly their interpretation. Hartshorne understands the idea of necessary existence logically, where Malcolm proceeds from ontological or factual necessity (443). In order to judge both of these interpretations, Hick proceeds from Findlay's application of the idea of logical necessity to the problem of God's existence. In the sense of analytical philosophy and therefore, also in Findlay's sense only analytical statements are logically true or logically necessary. Their truth consists of the definition of termini which constitute a statement. Here Hick practices criticism. In agreement with Malcolm, he calls it an unidentified presupposition of logical empiricism that logical necessity could only be attributed to analytical statements and not to statements of existence. Like Findlay the claim that God must be conceived as necessary in regard to His characteristics and existence, appears to be a contradiction in terms of the presupposition of the exclusive inner necessity of analytical statements. In matters of principle, Findlay allowed this contradiction to be legitimate in his later work. He did this even under the influence of Hartshorne in the book *Language, Mind and Value*. He modified his original standpoint to the effect that he admits that if God exists he would also necessarily exist (444).

Hick recognized only conditionally the premise of logical empiricism. He believes that assertions of existence cannot be attributed analytical truth. However, he rejects the further premise that the claim of the necessary existence of God is the claim of the logical necessity of the existence of God. Findlay saw a misuse of language in the claim of the logical necessity of the existence of God. According to him, such a claim is to be regarded to be equivalent to those claiming that a circle is round. He now requires that the claim of the necessary existence of God be eliminated from language, because it is contradictory on account of its analytic structure. Hick claims that a notion which is itself contradictory could not be one which finds its application in religious language within the context of a performance of religous faith. With this argument Hick goes a step beyond Malcolm. He places before himself the task of explaining the actual mode of the usage of the notion of God. He asks which experiences are decisive in developing the notion of God as an *ens necessarium*. He declares the Judeo-Christian tradition to be the realm of this experience (445).

Hick emphasizes that the question concerning the necessary existence of God can certainly not be directly answered in reference to Scripture. The notion of an *ens necessarium* is not an explicit aspect of the biblical conception of God. However, he believes that even the biblical authors did not regard His existence to be contingent.

> They were so vividly conscious of God that they were unable to doubt his reality, and they relied so firmly upon his integrity and faithfulness that they could not contemplate his becoming other than they knew him to be. They would have allowed as a verbal concession only that there might possibly be no God; for they were convinced that they were at many times directly aware of his presence and of his dealings with them. But the question whether the nonexistence of God is *logically* inconceivable, or *logically* impossible, is a philosophical puzzle which could not be answered by the prophets and apostles out of their own firsthand religious experience (446).

Like Malcolm, Hick rejected the logical necessity of the existence of God as a notion such as that advocated by Findlay. This notion is missing the *fundamentum in re*. Therefore, it is to be seen as nothing other than a poorly formulated product of reflection. For Hick, God's existence is not a logical but rather an ontological necessity (447). This differentiation clears up some matters that are not taken into account by arguments against the existence of God. They are still unconvincing. It is not yet said how the ontological or factual necessity is thought of as differentiated from logical necessity.

Only conditional support can be expected from a reference to Kant's justification of the differentiation between logical and ontological necessity (448). Kant distinguishes material necessity in being from the mere formal and logical connection of concepts. However, he adds the idea that "the necessity of existence can never be known from a notion but rather always from the connection between that which is perceived according to the general laws of experience" (449). Like Kant, reason does not explain the essence of such a being on the basis of the mere modal definition of "necessary being".

Reason had to "have an idea at its disposal which contains the necessity of being and of which the content is simultaneously defined" (450). The thought of *omnitudo realitas* would be such an idea. This is the case only on the premise that it is possible to prove the existence of being from this notion. However, this would presuppose that the conditional evidence for the ontological proof of the inner necessity of causality upon which the idea of the *omnitudo realitas* rests is not empirically perceptible.

The reference to Kant merely illustrates the event of the differentiation of formal and logical necessity. However, the notion of ontological necessity has not yet been legitimated. This is the case even if one may deduce from Kant's reflections that "the identification of the *indefinability* of the necessity of God is the identification of God's existence as an *infinite being*; (451) that is if one accepts the inability of the notion of an *ens necessarium* of finite things to be defined.

Kant's radical differentiation of idea and being was not decisive for late Wittgenstein's view of the relationship between language and reality. Rather the opposite can be said of the performance of the language game. Here the difficulty lies in the fact that the correspondence between language and reality is being prematurely advocated. Kants "bow" before the reality of God, which wishes to say the "God does not appear in any notion which humanity has made of God until now" (452), yields too easily to the view that one can speak of God exactly in the same way that one can speak of finite, i.e. by linear predication. Wittgenstein's extensive abstension from cautious treatment of religious themes may be an expression of an uneasiness due to an omission of reflection on the correspondence of proposition and reality in religious questions.

The reason why Hick, in his discussion of ontological proof, proclaims Kant to be a witness of the difference between logical and ontological necessity can only be seen in connection with his disputation with Findlay's so-called ontological counter evidence and his own way of verifying religious statements. It lies far from Hick's intentions to continue attempts to prove the existence of God. Like those of Anselm, Malcolm and even Hartshorne, he is solely concerned with illustrating that God's existence must be thought of as an ontological rather than a logical necessity. This is the reason for the reference to Kant. He intends to argue that the notion of God's ontological necessity has not disappeared as a result of a failure in the logical line of argument (453).

Hartshorne's line of argument is contradicted by this differentiation. Hartshorne is indeed aware of the limitation of a purely logical argument because the concept of God is not a concept of formal logic.

The technical difficulty with regard to the argument is that the idea of God is apparently not a conception of formal logic. Hence, even if the idea implies the necessity of a corresponding object, so that the denial of such an object is contradictory, still the whole question seems to fall outside the basic rules of any language . However, the matter is not so simple. There ought to be a formal rule concerning the division between necessary and contingent statements, and as we shall see, by some reasonable criteria for this division, the statement "Divine Perfection exists" falls on the side of necessity. Moreover, there may well be an aspect of the idea of God which is formal in the logical sense. If, for instance, "deity" connotes, among other things, "the sole individual definable *a priori*" (distinguished *a priori* from all others, actual or possible), is this not a formal characterization? Or suppose it follows from the meaning of "God" that it can only refer to an individual "such that, given any statement about any other individual whatever, this statement can be translated without loss of meaning or truth into a statement about God" (454).

Here Hartshorne apparently gives inspiration to the idea that the notion of ontological necessity, which is a part of the notion of God, be introduced to an artificial theological language by applying a postulate of belief. Apart from the fact that Hartshorne does not extend this and does not formulate a postulate of belief such an attempt is problematic. That the statement, "God exists", could be true in regard to an introduced postulate of meaning, is in my opinion correctly criticized by Hick (455). Following Carnap, to whom Hartshorne refers in regard to the introduction of a postulate of meaning, this cannot include an "existential qualifier". However, a postualte of meaning which serves the legitimation of ontological proof, could not proceed without this qualifier. Yet one could counter this with the argument that the justification of the application of a postulate of meaning is for Carnap, not a question of knowledge. Rather it is "a matter of decision" (456). Aside from these difficulties, it is not a matter of demonstrating the truth of the ontological argument in an artificial language; rather its rigor is to be demonstrated in natural language (457).

The second proof which Hick discusses, is that of Malcolm. He rejects it as an error. Certainly he recognizes a line of argument similar to that of Hartshorne. Yet he overlooks that it does not even intend to argue on a formal basis. Malcolm is concerned with the roots of the idea of God in religious language. Consequently, as a result of his consideration of ontological proof, Hick formulates:

Once again what is thus proved is that God is not a contingent being, or more precisely that he does not contingently not-exist. In being other than a non-existent-which-might-exist, he *either* exists *or* is a nonexistent which could not exist (i.e. whose existence is impossible). But what is not proved is that he exists (458).

5. Eschatological Verification

After a verification of the basic religious assertion of the existence of God failed due to deficient evidence for the self-contradiction of an opposed claim, and prior to the attempt to clarify the cognitivity of religious statements under the presupposition of a correspondence between language and reality that did not lead to the result which was hoped for, Hick and Crombie (459) attempted to legitimate the truth claim of religious statements. They begin with the evidence that even though these are in principle verifiable that which is foremost in establishing the conditions for verification is an eschatologial future (460). This evidence proceeds from an investigation of the nature of faith (461) and leads to the result that, in an anticipatory sense, religious statements are part of a total interpretation of our experience. Their ultimate verification can first occur when this process of experience has been concluded. However, past and present experience permit preliminary criteria to be developed which render it possible for persons now living to make a decision on the congruence of religious statements and reality. In this sense, verification means eliminating those reasons which allow doubt to arise in regard to the truth of a statement, and which place the correctness of a statement's truth-claim in question. This claim can be neither true nor false. Rather it is either entitled to this claim or not. There can be many reasons that a statement should be determined to be entitled to a claim of truth. Their recognition varies according to the respective subject of this statement. If, however, the truth-claim is recognized as justifiable, its dependability must then be proven, i.e. that it fulfills the expectations placed upon it.

a) Conditions of Verification

Hick proceeds on the basis that an indicative sentence only expresses a factual assertion that the situation of the universe would be different, if the alleged claim could not correctly be characterized as true (462). The justification of the claim of validity results from the dependability with which the predictions concluding from or included in statements are fulfilled.

Here verification is spoken of on two levels. First on a logical and second on a psychological level according to Hick's labels. In one way, the statement purports, that *p* is verifiable - that a certain state of affairs exists. In another this statement is a statement that someone can confirm the legitimacy of the justification of the claim of *p*. In the last case it is implied that the justification of the truth-claim of *p* is recognized. In consequence of this use of language, it can be said that "'Verification' is thus primarily the name for an event which takes place in human consciousness" (463).

The differentiation of logical and psychological is implied here in the concept of verification. On one level, it has to do with the claim of a true statement; on another with the metalingual establishment that the requirement of truth is correctly imputed to the statement. This is supported by the condition that a statement, as far as it represents a fact that exists must correspond to this fact and not visa versa. "My contention is going to be that 'God exists' asserts a matter of objective fact." (464). Argumentatively, one can only arrive at it when it is seen as metaphysically established and then only if the claim to validity, which is bound to the statement, is discussable. However, the basis of this claim of validity is the "objective fact", "which is basically suited to be *experienced* by anyone" (465) The claim of God's existence reproduces an experience and this experience serves as information about discourse concerning the correctness of the claim of the requirement for the validity of the statement "God exists". The necessity of this experience at hand is attributed to the psychological aspect. However, the logical aspect determines the extent to which an experience is *suitable* to verify a particular statement. Experiences can only be suited to verify a statement. They themselves cannot be true or false. In contrast to this, the truth purported by this proposition, that verification is an event of human consciousness, is a characteristic of statements. Therefore, the claim of validity of this statement can only be solved on the basis of argument.

According to this view, a statement is recognized as true if one is interested in its valid character. The question is, can one have the same or similar experiences under the same conditions which another person experiences and which build the foundation of the valid claim of this statement? If so then the truth conditions of a statement are:

1. The ability in principle of experiences to be experienced. These experiences must yield those expectations or predications which are derived from the statement to be examined.

2. The agreement in principle of those involved on the valid claim of the statement in question in regard to the evaluation or clarification of this experience.

Not until both conditions are fulfilled can the statement's verifiability be considered as a criterion for their factual meaning. The conditions under which a particular statement is verifiable are defined by the specific subject ascribed to a statement.

These conditions are not specifically tuned to the verification of religious statements. Rather they are of a general nature. They are valid on all epistemological levels. Even the simplest perception of the senses is not without *interpretation*. As is well known, the logical empiricists failed here with their idea of protocol propositions. That which generally holds true for knowledge, especially holds true for knowledge of God according to Hick. For him the correspondence of proposition and reality is unexplainable. However, he believes the verification of a statement to consist in the argumentability of its legitimation. Thus a given possibility of interpretation on the basis of experience.

> There is in cognition of every kind an unresolved mystery. The knower-known relationship is in the last analysis *sui generis*: the mystery of cognition persists at the end of every inquiry - though its persistence does not prevent us from cognizing. We cannot explain, for example, how we are conscious of sensory phenomena as constituting an objective physical environment; we just find ourselves interpreting the data of our experience in this way. We are aware that we live in a real world, though we cannot prove by any logical formula that it *is* a real world. Likewise we cannot explain how we know ourselves to be responsible beings subject to moral obligations; we just find ourselves interpreting our social experience in this way. We find ourselves inhabiting an ethically significant universe, though we cannot prove that it *is* ethically significant by any process of logic. In each case we discover and live in terms of a particular aspect of our environment through an appropriate act of interpretation; and having come to live in terms of it we neither require nor can conceive any further validation of its reality. The same is true of the apprehension of God. The theistic believer cannot explain *how* he knows the divine presence to be mediated through his human experience. He just finds himself interpreting his experience in this way. He lives in the presence of God, though he is unable to prove by any *dialectical* process that God exists (466).

This conception attempts to avoid two mistakes. The first is that of early positivism. It assumed that there are facts which can determine magnitudes for the unquestioned basis of a statement. The second is the disregard of the relation to reality because one is convinced that this already exists in the performance of a language game. Consequently theoretical criteria of coherence suffice to determine the truth of a statement. Both of these procedural modes conjoin here; even if it does remain unclear how this synthesis is supposed to occur. The last sentence of the quotation above makes it clear that it does not dialectically occur. This does not initially become a problem, because the claim that the statement "God exists" possibly expresses an objective fact. Rather it is also a problem for any other statement which is viewed as the affirmation of an objective statement. Furthermore, under the supposition of a non-diallectically conceived synthesis, the issue of a correspondence theory of truth seems altogether to be argued *ad absurdum*. The experiences which underly the interpretation of a statement may support this interpretation, but are never its basis. This is true in that a statement's truth-claim is understood in a linguistic-logical manner. At least Hick's proposition, that verification is an event of human consciousness, begins here. He is only conditionally serious about the intelligible dialectic of reality and language; only in as far as he admitts that there can be no knowledge of the senses of thought, i.e. without interpretation. However, from the insight that truth is only linguistic truth, and further from the insight that it is not language itself but rather the reality implied by language, Hick did not draw the opposite conclusion. He did not argue that the subject of this language, in whose consciousness verification should occur, grasps something *other* than itself. It discovers oneself in this process of mutual definition. Flew's ironic question, "Can a man witness his own funeral?" (467), is contrasted to those (468) regarding immortality to be an empirical hypothesis and those promising verification or falsification of religious statements by following the instruction, "Wait until you die". This opens the wounds of Hick's notion of "I" and "consciousness".

In this connection, the question of what the attribute "in principle" means in the formulation of both conditions of truth for a sentence, seems to me to be on the same level as the question whether the truth theory at hand is oriented toward a coherence or a correspondence theory. This question is relatively easy to answer for a statement like, "The sun will rise within 24 hours". First of all, "in principle" here means that the interested individual must conduct those acts necessary for verification. Secondly, the existence of experiences and agreement in the interpretation of those involved in the experiences is also to be expected in the future (469).

If one understands religious statements to be part of a total interpretation for which a verification can basically only occur in an anticipatory sense, then "in principle" means, first of all in the case of other statements, that the person who wishes to verify such a statement must conduct the necessary courses of action. One may then hope for argumentative empirical agreement. In the sense of a total verification, this means that its conditions cannot be fulfilled "post-mortem-existence", or as it is called in a later formulation "*post resurrectionem*" (470). Such a verification cannot call only on the totality of a prior existing experiential process, but rather is one for which the experiential process has concluded.

The foundation of the theory of eschatological verification is the differentiation between three levels of human experience, 1) of the appearance of the senses; 2) of moral obligations and social experience; and 3) of religious experience which can be described as follows:

> ... the primary religious perception, or basic act of religious interpretation, is not to be described as either a reasoned conclusion or an unreasoned hunch that there is God. It is, putatively, an apprehension of the divine presence within the believer's human experience. It is not an inference to a general truth, but a "divine-human encounter", a mediated meeting with the living God (471).

This mediated encounter of God and humanity is not thought of as an experience beyond the other two levels of experience. Rather it is a realized awareness of God's action in and through the experience of the world. From the standpoint of the theory of knowledge, this is "an interpretation of the world as a medium of divine presence and intention" (472). Therefore, the theistic interpretation of the world as other attempts of a total interpretation includes all empirical-scientific, moral, aesthetic and religious factors in its understanding of the world. This is the case although:

> ...the universe as envisaged by the theist, then, differs as a totality from the universe as envisaged by the atheist. This difference does not, however, from our present standpoint within the universe, involve a difference in the objective content of each or even any of its passing moments. The theist and the atheist do not (or need not) expect different events to occur in thee successive details of the temporal process. They do not (or need not) entertain divergent expectations of the course of history viewed from within. But the theist does and the atheist does not expect that when history is completed it will be seen to have led to a

particular end-state and to have fulfilled a specific purpose, namely that of creating "children of God" (473).

b) The Relationship between the World and the World of Resurrection

It is evident that not before the end of all history can ultimately be decided about the dignity of an interpretation of the world, and about the reality of God. Accordingly, the claim to validity of a single or even a number of religious statements can expect no final confirmation. However, if religious statements are only "in principal" and not in practice verifiable, it is indispensible to present those criteria which at least identify their valid claim in its preliminary state.

In the sense of an interpretation of totally, this means that the religious claim must be superior to the claims of other theories in the strength of its interpretation. It may not fall behind the level of critical awareness which has already been attained. In this way, the valid claim of religious assertions must be immediately resolvable. Like eschatological expectations which can also be derived from religious statements, the claim of meaning for the theory of eschatological verification rests on an expectation of the resurrection of the dead. The answer to two further questions also belongs to the verification of religious statements.

1. How can the relationship between world and resurrection be conceived.

2. How can the identity of the resurrected with his person as an individual in this world be conceived.

It is necessary to answer these questions, for the concept of eschatological verification should close the gap in the proof of the claim to validity of religious statements. The closing of this gap failed in the attempt to guarantee the intelligibility of religious language by means of translation into another language. Calling upon the ontological proof of God was just as hopeless. Indeed, Findlay's objection to the logical impossibility of such a proof could be overruled. Yet the question of whether the ontological argument is of logical or ontological nature remained unanswered. In any case, the concept of eschatological verification grants it only logical demonstrative strength. Thus from the *logical* perspective the proposition of the existence of God is not self-contradictory and therefore, excluded from a *possible* verification. Turning this around, this means that that which is applicable for each proposition on the existence of God, also holds true for the empirical. In both cases, one is dealing with sentences which can be verified factually and not with logically necessary truths. Therefore, verification does not mean the demonstration of the logical impossibility of the incorrectness of a religious proposition. Rather "such weight of evidence as suffices, in the type of case in question, to exclude rational doubt" (474). This means the differentiation between logical and psychological verification. Meaningful for this type of differentiation is the inclusion of the linguistic subject in the semantic definition of the religious statement.

The second of these two questions discusses an individual's self-confidence. The possibility is given in the eschatological situation to dispose of doubt concerning the truth of a given proposition. The discussion of both questions including the question of how the relationship between this world and the world of resurrection is to be thought proceeds in constant reference to parables. They are told in order to render intelligible the conception of eschatological verification that lies within the boundaries of logical possibility. They show that a verification of the sentence "God exists" leaves the field of experience in favor of another type of experience. The subject, that verifies, is also bound to those rules of the new field of experience which with strict logic lead to verification. That means that God, of whom the sentence to be verified speaks, is thought of here as existing in another world. This is necessary for experience but not for logic. The impossibility of proving His logical necessity does prevent the attempt to reveal God in the form of a general demonstrative relation. However, at the same time it does not render the question of God's existence to be logically possible. The conditions for the verification of the proposition of God's existence cannot be thought of as existent; yet in every case as being capable of existing. A condition for the possibility of the verification of a religious statement appears to stand firm: the logical validity of the realm of eschatological experience (world of resurrection) and the logical compatibility of religious statements with the logic of statements that are based on life's experiences. However, the problem of the verification of religious statements has, by no means, been rendered debatable on the basis of the fulfillment of this condition (475).

According to the second condition, the *differentiation* between this world and the world of resurrection is brought to consciousness by means of this eschatological experience. In order to fulfill this condition the question, "What does death mean, what meaning falls share to death as the temporal end of our days?", must first be answered. The experience of death in this life is not sufficient. It is only the experience of death in the sense of observing the death of other creatures. "Death is not an event of life. Death is not lived through" (476).

Hick's parables and pictures fail in the case of death in spite of distinctness. Not only does its reality not allow itself to be presented in them, but also the question of post-mortem-existence, which results from it, does not find an answer. Hick says that the difference between the first two and the third parable lies here. The logical possibility of the verifiability of the sentence, "God exists", which, for eschatological verification, does not exclude the logical possibility of overcoming death, is not to be thought of as the legitimation of an understanding of death. One is not following Epicurus here and positing events in the spectrum of time. If death is seen as a linear exchange of bodies, as in Hick's parable, this view certainly cannot explain how someone could come to knowledge of himself as dead or alive.

> In these circumstances (i.e. finding himself resurrected) how does Mr. X know that he has been resurrected or recreated? He remembers dying; or rather he remembers being on what he took to be his death-bed, and becoming progressively weaker until, presumably, he lost consciousness. But how does he know that (to put it Irishly) his "dying" proved fatal; and that he did not, after losing consciousness, begin to recover strength, and has now simply waked up?
>
> The picture is readily enough elaborated to answer this question. Mr. X meets and recognizes a number of relatives and friends and historical personages whom he knows to have died; and from the fact of their presence, and also from their testimony that he has only just now appeared in their world, he is convinced that he has died. Evidences of this kind could mount up into the point at which they are quite as strong as the evidence which, in pictures one and two, convince the individual in question that he has been miraculously translated to Australia. Resurrected persons would be individually no more in doubt about their own identity than we are now, and would be able to identify one another in the same kinds of ways, and with a like degree of assurance, as we do now (477).

The answer, which Mr. X receives from one who is apparently deceased is not self substantiated. On one hand there is a *consensus communis* about a type of new being and its identity. However, the knowledge they all have died has accompanyed the newcomer from a former life. The uselessness of such a conception of death and of such conceptions of immortality even when they are wrapped up in reference to Paul's Christian resurrection faith, demonstrate the conception of eschatological verification as applied to the problem it was designed to solve. The question of the resurrection of the world has neither been given an answer beyond that of a supposition of a necessary relationship between them, nor has the question of the criteria for identity of the person been answered. Here remains the mere assurance of identity. However, it has an impeding effect on the clarification of the legitimacy of the truth claim determined by the linear understanding of death.

This would be impossible in a post-mortem existence, for such a condition would, as Hick admits, not enable the resurrected one to verify the proposition of God's existence at all.

> For survival, simply as such, would not serve to verify theism. It would not necessarily be a state of affairs which is manifestly incompatible with the non-existence of God. It might be taken just as a surprising natural fact. The atheist, in his resurrection body, and able to remember his life on earth, might say that the universe has turned out to be more complex, and perhaps more to be approved of, than he had realized. But the mere fact of survival, with a new body in a new environment, would not demonstrate to him that there is a God. It is fully compatible with the notion of survival that *the life to come be*, so far as the theistic problem is concerned, essentially a continuation of the present life, and religiously no less ambiguous. And in this event, survival after bodily death would not in the least constitute a final verification of theistic faith (478).

The difficulty to conceive a definition of contents of this other-worldly experience confronts religion with its claim of reliable knowledge of the life to come. An analysis of religious statements must not waste its time drawing pictures of the existence of resurrection, only then to abandon them. In them the religious ambiguity of our present life would only be extended. They can only turn to the question of whether one can conceive of experience after life which *would* serve the verification of theism (479).

Religion prepares us for such experiences, as Hick adopts such statements originating in religion his manner of argument changes. If the first condition is formulated so that the result of expectations is necessary in order to affirm a statement based on this-worldly experience, then the direction of argument changes. Hick's designation of psychological as opposed to a logical verification as the basis of the valid content of an eschatological experience is not questioned here (480). Rather this question is raised: How can verification affirm that this content is eschatological? Those experiences are described as having eschatological content which pose religion as such:

> There are, I suggest, two possible developments of our experience such that, if they occurred in conjunction with one another (whether in this life or in another life to come), they would assure us beyond rational doubt of the reality of God, as conceived in the Christian faith. These are, *first*, an experience of the fulfillment of God's purpose for ourselves, as this has been disclosed in the Christian revelation; in conjunction, *second*, with

an experience of communion with God as he has revealed himself in the person of Christ (481).

Belief in religious propositions establishes the possibility of their verification. The agreement between personal experience and those promises proclaimed in religion would hold true for the believer as evidence of the reality of God. The thesis of logical positivism, that statements for which no verifiable conditions can be given are to be judged as meaningless, could not be applied in this way. However, the view that verifiability is confirmed by tracing it back to sensual data would, by all means, be contradicted. However, this would not be a specific characteristic of religious propositions. Such a contradiction would only indicate that the truth conditions for such statements are different from those for which propositions of theoretical validity are subject. If one tries, as Hick does, to name the conditions of the verification of religious statements, then one immediately finds oneself in a dilemma. The conditions attained claim that faith *fides qua creditur* cannot be justified within the logical structure of our thought. The claims of religious statements can only be made evident through an experience which is beyond our experience. The justification of the condition by calling on the conditional character of all predictions misjudges the unique character of religious promises. Their truth does not consist in the method of their verification. Rather, it consists in the presupposed belief in the truth of such a proposition, in other words, in the belief in its agreement with reality.

The sentence, "A table is standing in the next room", contains a conditional prediction: "If someone goes into the next room, he will see, etc. but no one is forced to go into the next room". What is the corresponding condition of the verification of the proposition "God exists"? According to the conception of eschatological verification as post-mortem verification, this condition could not be faith, but death or the end of history. However, in the light of the unavoidable necessity of a decision concerning the claim of meaning for religious statements for contemporary persons, criteria must be developed which make a preliminary decision possible. Yet if the "and" in the formula "Faith and Truth" represents death so to speak, then it must be asked how, in the case of this dichotomy, the explanation of the criteria of meaning of religious statements can only be possible in a preliminary sense. This must be asked if the claim that faith is verifiable by faith is justifiable.

EPILOGUE

The title of this investigation reads: Truth and Belief: The Interpretation and Criticism of the Linguistic Analytical Philosophy of Religion. The first phrase brings the systematic intention of the work to light, and the second defines the historical framework within which the attempt was undertaken to define the relationship between faith and knowledge and to develop a theory of religion. Here it must be taken into consideration that, according to the linguistic analytical approach, it is possible to conceive of several competitive forms of religon. Actually, at least three different main directions of theories of religion can be demonstrated which are existentially discordant in regard to the possibility and the actual accomplishment of the verification of religious statements. The charm of these investigations, that the analytical philosophy of religion is a movement which has not yet reached a conclusion, is at the same time a problem. The attempt was made to place its motivations and its solutions to problems in the total context of religous philosophical endeavors.

In order to properly understand the development of the linguistic analytical theory of religion it was necessary to refer to its relation to positivism and the type of the inquiry and debate influenced by this relation. It became reasonable for the analytic understanding for it to be, by all means, non-positivistic. This can only be conditionally said of emotive theory. Indeed, it also accepts the uniqueness of the religious language and moves away from the thesis of meaninglessness without, however, also wanting to recognize the cognitive character of religious statements.

In the background of the effort of the linguistic analytical philosophy of religion to bring the cognitive character of religious statements into focus, i.e. demonstrate and justify their truth-claim, stands the unsolved question of how the relationship between language and reality is to be conceived. A dispute which should have been carried out on the ground of fundamental philosophy now shifted to the area of debate about the truth of religious statements. Between the belief that religion is in the end only the semantic illusion of a "brilliant way of our intelligence to place our language in the service of emotional needs" (482) and the claim that religious language is the transcendental condition for the possibility of speech, it was persistently attempted to approach and successfully explain the relationship of language to reality, tossed about by the insight that reality can neither be regarded as equivalent to the world of objects, nor can it be reduced to that of the subject.

On the contrary, reality cannot be conceived without these two being interwoven. However, without being unreflective of how this interweaving should be conceived, analytical theory developed a certain scepticism against the so-called scientific attempt to solve the problem.

The reason that the approach of generative grammer, as developed by Noam Chomsky found hardly any resonance in the analytical philosophy of religion, may be sought in this scepticism. Indeed, the persuance of formal systematics in linguistics has not lost its fascination for the linguistic analytical philosopher. Rather, his experience in the discussion of religious issues (analogy, proof of God, death, etc.) has made him cautious concerning a clarification of the truth-claim of religous statements by means of a theory of linguistic competence. This attempt saw its task to be the reconstruction of a system of rules according to which linguistically competent speech built and remodeled such sentences. The reference to the creativity of the linguistic subject as a possibility for constructing a desired number of sentences as demonstrated by generative grammar, does not confront the question which concerns religious philosophy. If linguistic competence is only understood as an inborn predisposition for rules and regulations which produce the abstract syntactical schemes of deep structure, then the problem which Wittgenstein calls deep grammar is by no means solved when he posits that theology is grammar. In the question of truth, religious statements deliver "the principles of the universal grammar indeed ... a highly restrictive schema, with which every human language should be in tune as well as specific conditions for which the grammar of a certain language can be used" (483). However following Kant, one could say that those structural relations which are to be found in language and which can be abstractly investigated by linguistic structures are still not the "testing stone" upon which the truth of religious statements could be identified (484).

In that this investigation is not solely concerned with the interpretation of the development of the philosophy of religion in connection with positivism and late Wittgenstein, but also is interested in testing the skill of linguistic analytical methods to solve philosophical problems, a closing remark is necessary. The choice of religious philosophical inquiry in order to test the analytical method may, at first sight, appear to be an unjustified procedure. In a way similar to the construal of positivistic verification criteria, it seems to prejudge the result of such a test. However, this procedure is justifiable in that religious philosophical inquiry is not being consulted. Rather it stops at the application of analysis and, in this way, became the measure of this method by its own initiative.

The attempt to acquire a theory of religion by means of an analytical method has only conditionally succeeded. The proof of the legitimacy of consulting linguistic analysis in solving philosophical problems has, therefore, only been a limited success. In the context of the explication of details, one has referred, in different ways, to its reasons. Initially, the understanding of reality has been made responsible within at least the horizon of language communication.

A positive assessment can be made for the linguistic analytical method. As opposed to the positivist methodology it, above all, succeeds in proposing and, in many cases, formulating philosophical problems. If one proceeds from the fact that, in the future, the linguistic analytical theory of religion will neither be oriented towards generative linguistics, nor will it primarily see the religious statement as an object of investigation for religious sociology and socio-linguistics, an attempt which has been suggested by some in order to understand the language-game as a whole as speech and life forms, then the possibility exists that, in the future, analytical philosophy can seek exchange with the continental European tradition, in particular Kant and Hegel. In this way, it may find itself in a position to develop beyond a mere analysis of words and sentences.

This is not the place to prognosticate about the path of analytic linguistic religious philosophy in the future. Here it can be said with certainty that the connection has not yet been made. It is obvious in the development of this theory that it proceeded from an approach which, from the very beginning, did not intend to give an unsurpassed answer to the question about the claim of meaning and truth of religious statements. It denied those inquiries legitimacy and discontinued to treat their problems in the course of their development which have occupied religious philosophy and metaphysics from the beginning, even though these were considered to have already been eliminated or solved. Thus, many surprises can be counted on in the future.

FOOTNOTES

1) Cf. Simons, "Das Dilemma der Theologie"; here one also finds further reference to the problem.

2) This influence is most evident in the respective treatment of the problem of verification and falsification.

3) Cf. Peukert's translation of the edition of High, *New Essays on Religious Language*; Dalferth, *Sprachlogik des Glaubens*; Martin, *The New Dialogue between Philosophy and Theology*; Ladrière, *Rede der Wissenschaft - Wort des Glaubens*; Grabner-Haider, *Semiotik und Theologie*; Etges, *Kritik der analytischen Theologie*; Bayer, *Was ist das: Theologie?*; Just, *Religiöse Sprache und analytische Philosophie*. Also to be named is the dispute between Albert, *Traktat über kritische Vernunft*, and Ebeling, *Kritischer Rationalismus?* as well as the answer of Albert to Ebeling: *Theologische Holzwege*; Rokita, *Ist Theologie notwendig?*: further the collection which has been edited by Sauter: *Wissenschaftstheoretische Kritik der Theologie*, and Pannenberg, *Wissenschaftstheorie und Theologie*.

4) One example is J.S. Morris, "Religion and Theological Language". In his opinion, belief statements cannot be proven. All such attempts fail as alleged arguments would respectively only turn out to be attempts to justify an attitude. Morris does not allow this restriction to be valid for theological language, a language of the second order in comparison to the language of belief, as it is a translation and interpretation of language of the first order into a philosophical system: "... there is a long discourse... and in this claims are made which are open to the kind of justification one expects for cognitive claims, it protests concern and commitment. Theology, on the other hand, translates the values expressed in the commitment into categories of a philosophical or other conceptual language."
Morris' distinction between the language of belief and theological language seems problematic in that the latter is considered to be only an interpretation or translation and these are denied any inherent importance, i.e. they have neither a directive nor a critical force.

5) In regard to the problem of the true statement, in reference to the truth antinomy see Hofmeister, "Semantische oder transzendentale Sprachkritik?".

184

Chapter I

6) Stegmüller, *Hauptströmungen*, p. XXXII.

7) Cf. Toulmin, *Einführung in die Philosophie der Wissenschaft*.

8) Cf. Sauter (ed.), *Theologie als Wissenschaft*.

9) *Erkenntnis*, I, p. 8.

10) Carnap, *Logische Syntax*, p. III f.

11) Kraft, *Wiener Kreis*, p. 21.

12) Ibid, p. 23.

13) Wittgenstein, *Tractates*, 5.634.

14) Carnap, *Erkenntnis*, II, p. 433.

15) Ayer, *Language, Truth and Logic*, p. 79.

16) Schulz, *Philosophie in der veränderten Welt*, p. 49 f.

17) Ibid, p. 50.

18) Cf. Peukert, "Zur Einführung".

19) Cf. Charlesworth, *Philosophy and Linguistic Analysis*, p. 130 f.

20) To be exact Ayer applies (ibid, p. 37) the term "weaker" and Charlesworth speaks of "broader". Cf. Lazerowitz, *The Structure of Metaphysics*, p. 117 ff.

21) Bridgman, *Reflections of a Physicist*, p. 97. Cf. the essay by C.J. Ducasse, "Verification, Verifiability and Meaningfulness". He attempts to develop the criteria of the claim to meaning of statements.

22) Charlesworth, *Philosophy and Linguistic Analysis*, p. 131.

23) Ayer, Language, Truth and Logic, p. 35.

24) Carnap, *Scheinprobleme*, p. 48.

25) Kraft, Wiener Kreis, p. 40.

26) Cf. Wittgenstein, *Tractatus*, 4.12. The sentence is able to present the whole reality but it is not able to present what it has to have in common with reality to be able to present it - the logical form. In order to be able to present the logical form we had to be able to stand outside of logic with the sentence, i.e. outside of the world.

27) Kraft, *Wiener Kreis*, p. 40.

28) Wittgenstein, *Tractatus*, 2.1.

29) Stegmüller, *Hauptströmungen*, p. 543.

30) Wittgenstein, *Tractatus*, 2.141.

31) Ibid, 4.022.

32) Ibid, 5.5563.

33) Ibid, 4.1212.

34) Ibid, 4.002.

35) Ibid, 6.522.

36) Ibid, 6.44.

37) Ibid, 4.121.

38)   Ibid, 6.4311-6.45. From letters to Ogden which comment on the translation of the *Tractatus* into English, it becomes apparent just what difficulties Wittgenstein himself had with the term "the mystical".

39) Wittgenstein, *Tractatus*, 6.41.

40) Cf. Ibid. 6.42-6.421.

41) Schulz, Wittgenstein, p. 41.

42) Ibid.

43) Lüthi, *Theologie als Dialog*, p. 46.

44) Wittgenstein, *Tractatus*, 6.432.

45) Ibid, 6.54.

46) Ibid, 7.

47) Charlesworth, *Philosophy*, p. 100.

48) Wittgenstein, *Diary*, 6.11.1916: "The meaning of life, that is the meaning of the world, we can call God."

49) Ibid, 7.8.1916.

50) Wittgenstein, *Tractatus*, 6.52.

51) Ibid, 4.12.

52) Benedikt, *Wissen und Glauben*, p. 253.

53)   Popper, *Logik der Forschung*, p. 61; *The Logic of Scientific Discovery*, p. 95f.

54) Cf. Apel, *Idee der Sprache*, p. 29 and the notion of faith by R. Demos, "Are Religious Dogmas Cognitive and Meaningful?". He defines faith as "belief which rests on no evidence whatever empirical or a priori" (p. 71). Of interest is the discussion of this definition by the symposium: "Are Religious Dogmas Cognitive and Meaningful?", which is printed in *Journal of Philosophy*, LI, 1954, p. 145-171. Within the framework of this discussion Demos repeats his claim and he comes to the conclusion that science as well as religion would have cognitive significance from the statement that a belief also axiomatically underlies science.

55) Popper, *Logik der Forschung*, p. 224; *The Logic of Scientific Discovery*, p. 280.

56) Cf. Weizsäcker, *Die Einheit der Natur*, p. 124.

57) Bartley, *Flucht ins Engagement*, p. 73 f.

58) Bartley quotes this from Tillich, *Wesen und Wandel des Glaubens*, p. 20, on p. 108. Bartley in *The Retreat to Commitment*, p.100 (German: *Flucht ins Engagement*, p. 108). Quotes from Tillich, *Dynamics of Faith*, p. 10. (German: *Wesen und Wandel des Glaubens*, p. 20).

59) Tillich, ibid, p. 72; Bartley, ibid, p. 109, Tillich, *Dynamics of Faith*, p. 58ff; *Wesen und Wandel*, p. 72. Bartley *Retreat*, p. 101; *Flucht*, p. 109.

60) Cf. Pannenberg, *Wissenschaftstheorie*, p. 45.

61) Bartley, *Flucht*, p. 111.

62) Ibid, p. 100.

63) Cf. Pannenberg, *Wissenschaftstheorie*, p. 45.

64) Cf. Ebeling, "Theologie", column 763; Schupp, *Kritische Theologie*, p. 13.

65) Popper, *Conjectures*, p. 267.

66) Popper, *Logik der Forschung*, p. 71.

67) Bartley, *Flucht*, p. 16.

68) Cf. Schäfer, "Über die Diskrepanz zwischen Methodologie und Metaphysik bei Popper", p. 856 ff.

69) Pannenberg, *Wissenschaftstheorie*, p. 56 f.

70) Ibid, p. 46 f.

71) For an interpretation of Tillich's theology see Kolar's Vienna dissertation, *Das Methodenproblem in der Religionsphilosophie Paul iTillichs*.

72) Tillich, *Gesammelte Werke V*, p. 243.

73) Tillich, *Wesen und Wandel des Glaubens*, p. 72; Bartley, *Flucht*, p. 109. Tillich, *Dynamics of Faith*, p. 58ff; *Wesen und Wandel*, p. 72. Bartley, *Retreat*, p. 100f. *Flucht*, p. 109.

74) Rahner, *Mysterium Salutis* II, p. 415.

75) Cf. Carnap, *Introduction to Semantics*, above all p. 246.

76) Savigny, *Analytische Philosophie*, p. 55.

77) Schulz, *Philosophie*, p. 71.

78) Kraft, *Wiener Kreis*, p. 37.

79) Ibid.

80) Carnap, *Symbolische Logik*, p. 70 f.

81) Cf.Ch.W. Morris, *Signs, Language and Behaviour*.

82) Cf. Fahrenbach, "Sprachanalyse und Ethik".

83) Cf. Charlesworth, *Philosophy*, p. 5.

84) Stegmüller, *Hauptströmungen*, p. 566.

85) Ibid.

86) Wittgenstein, *Philosophical Investigations*, § 255; cf. § 309: "What is your aim in philosophy? - To show the fly the way out of the fly-bottle." Wittgenstein always differentiated philosophical therapeutic from psychotherapy. Cf. e.g., Malcolm, *Ludwig Wittgenstein*.

87) Wittgenstein, *Philosophical Investigations*, § 38.

88) Ibid, § 112.

89) Cf. Wittgenstein, *Philosophical Investigations*, § 89. To Augustine see Mader, *Die logische Sturktur des personalen Denkens*.

90) Ibid, § 116.

91) Lübbe, "Wittgenstein - ein Existentialist?", p. 124.

92) Ibid.

93) Cf. Kerényi, "Die griechischen Götter", p. 15.

94) Wittgenstein, *Lectures*, p. 95.

95) Ibid.

96) Cf. Wagner, *Existenz, Analogie und Dialektik*, p. 164 f. Concerning the problem of *analogia entis* see especially Heintel, *Hegel und die Analogia entis* as well as "Transzendenz und Analogie" by the same author.

97) Wittgenstein, *Lectures*, p. 94. In spite of the difficulty of determining the character of a statement in some cases, as Hudson emphasizes in his essay "Some Remarks of Wittgenstein's account of Religious Belief", Wittgenstein holds fast to the special character of religious statements: "The basis of Wittgenstein's position... does certainly seem to be that religious belief is logically distinct from any other universe of discourse. ...Referring to those who argue that religious beliefs can be treated as though they were scientific hypotheses, he says: '... if this is religious belief, then it's all superstition'. But he is careful to add that they deserve ridicule, not because their beliefs are based on insufficient evidence, but because they are cheating themselves. On the other hand, any unbeliever who thinks that he can refute religion by showing that the evidence adduced for its belief, if compared with anything in science which we call evidence, is not good enough, will be overlooking the fact, as Wittgenstein put it, that 'for a blunder that's too big'. He explained: 'If you suddenly wrote numbers down on the blackboard, and then said: "Now I'm going to add", and then said: "2 and 21 is 13", etc. I'd say: "This is no blunder".'... Wittgenstein's point is that

in such a case you would be up to some queer arithmetic, not making mistakes in the ordinary variety; or at least one would be wise to suspect that you were. The 'blunders' in religion are too big for it to be simply bad science." (p. 43).

98) Schulz, *Wittgenstein*, p. 60.

99) See Wittgenstein, *Lectures*, p. 87.

100) Ibid, p. 94.

101) Ibid, p. 106.

102) Ibid, p. 90.

103) Ibid, p. 106.

104) Wittgenstein, *Philosophical Investigations*, § 373.

105) Paton, *The Modern Predicament*.

106) Anscombe, "Misinformation: What Wittgenstein Really Said", p. 373, quoted from Charlesworth, Philosophy, p. 101.

107) Wittgenstein, Philosophical Investigations, § 432.

108) Ibid, § 43.

109) Matthew, 26/26.

110) Heintel, *Sprachphilosophie*, p. 14.

111) Apel, *Idee der Sprache*, p. 23.

112) Benedikt, *Wissen und Glauben*, p. 250.

113) Wittgenstein, *Tractatus*, 5.473.

114) Apel, "Wittgenstein", p. 71 ff.

115) Wittgenstein, *Philosophical Investigations*, § 371.

116) This contradiction did not remain without having an enduring effect upon the attempt to justify religious statements in the analytical philosophy of religion. Especially the representatives of an emotive theory of religion rejected the possibility of justifying religious statements.

117) Wittgenstein, *Philosophical Investigations*, § 219.

118) Ibid, § 217.

119) Ibid.

120) Ibid, § 307.

121) Cf. the problem of individual language in: v. Kutschera, *Sprachphilosophie*, p. 266 ff.

122) Heintel, *Sprachphilosophie*, p. 144.

123) Wittgenstein, *Philosophical Investigations*, § 71.

124) Ibid, §23.

125) Ibid, § 90.

126) Ibid § 7.

127) Ibid, § 71.

128) Ibid, § 98.

129) Ibid, § 7.

130) Apel, "Entfaltung der 'sprachanalytischen Philosophie'", p. 288.

131) Winch, *The Idea of Social Science*, p. 107 ff.

132) Oeser, *Begriff und Systematik*, p. 446.

133) Heintel, *Sprachphilosophie*, p. 163.

Chapter II

134) Flew, "Theology and Falsification": "Once upon a time explorers came upon a clearing in the jungle. In the clearing were growing many flowers and many weeds. One explorer says, 'Some gardener must tend this plot'. The other disagrees 'There is no gardener'. So they pitch their tents and set a watch. No gardener is ever seen. 'But perhaps he is an invisible gardener'. So they set up a barbed wire fence. They electrify it. They patrol with bloodhounds. (For they remember how H.G. Well's The Invisible Man could be both smelt and touched though he could not be seen.) But no shrieks ever suggest that some intruder has received a shock. No movements of the wire ever betray an invisible climber. The bloodhounds never give cry. Yet still the Believer is not convinced. 'But there is a gardener, invisible, intangible, insensible to electric shocks, a gardener who has no scent and makes no sound, a gardener who comes secretly to look after the garden which he loves.' At last the Sceptic despairs, 'But what remains of your original assertion? Just how does what you call an invisible, intangible, eternally elusive gardener differ from an imaginary gardener or even from no gardener at all?'"

135) Wisdom, "Gods".

136) Popper, *Conjectures*, p. 37.

137) Flew, "Theology", p. 97.

138) Popper, *Conjectures*, p. 264.

139) Ibid, p. 261.

140) Flew, "Theology", p. 99.

141) Cf. Blackstone, "Crombie's Defense of the Assertion-Status of Religious Claims".

142) Cf. Popper, *Logik der Forschung*, p. 7. *Logic of Scientific Discovery*, p.31ff. These four criteria are definitely not formulated by Flew with striking clarity. The abruptness and thesis character of his essay does not allow for reflections on theoretical recognition. It is not difficult to see from the text that these criteria find application in the claim to meaning of religious statements. In his work *Flucht ins Engagement*, Bartley expressly took over the criteria of Popper. Rokita *Ist Theologie notwendig?*, p. 171 f. Rokita holds similar views from a systematic viewpoint.

143) Popper, *Logik der Forschung*, p. 32. *The Logic of Scientific Discovery*, p. 59f.

144) Popper, *Conjectures*, p. 117.

145) Flew, "Theology", p. 98.

146) Ibid, p. 97.

147) Crombie, "The Possibility of Theological Statements", p. 47.

148) Certainly, the demarcation through "falsifiability" does not constitute a definition of metaphysics. It would be wrong to define all non-falsifiable sentences as metaphysical. In this manner, universal there-are-sentences, such as "There are white ravens" are not falsifiable.

149) Cf. the relationship of philosophy and natural sciences especially in Ulmer, *Philosophie der modernen Lebenswelt*, Vol. III, §§ 37-41 as well as *Von der Sache der Philosophie* by the same author.

150) Ebeling, *Kritischer Rationalismus?*, p. 60.

151) Albert, *Traktat über Kritische Vernunft*, p. 50.

152) Popper, *Logik der Forschung*, p. 13. *The Logic of Scientific Discovery*, p. 38f.

153) Albert, *Traktat*, p. 50.

154) Dantine, *Der Heilige Geist*, p. 197.

155) This statement does not intend to dispute that a critique of religion which stems from "outside" can also be seen as useful for religion. However, it must be taken into account that religion may not be transformed according to such requirements, but rather the critique can only be fruitful if it is integrated into its own structure of religious consciousness. Hereby, the philosophical religious criticism receives the task to "first of all annihilate all attempts of religion to make itself 'tolerable' through accommodation, but rather to cultivate a reflective attitude within religion, toward its hermeneutical-critical task" (Schaeffler, *Religion*, p. 312).

156) Schelling, Werke VI. p. 407. Certainly, such a notion of faith corresponds to that which L.E. Llewelyn says about the biblical authors. According to his conception, for them faith is "a way of knowledge, a way of finding out, but not a way of knowing" (Three Conceptions of Faith", p. 244).

157) To claim that religious statements are exempt from questioning the unconditional belief in the divine truth that characterizes the statement of the believer, would mean overlooking what each empirical consideration of religious history easily allows to be recognized: "Not only Socrates unconditionally entrusted himself to that saving good to 'know' that he was so unassuring that exactly the confession of his own lack of knowledge is his whole 'wisdom'; and not only he sees in his lifelong criticism of the oracle of Delphi (actually a criticism of human speech in which God's word is only accessible to him through the oracle) his 'service deity'. On the contrary, it belongs to the essence of religion everywhere to regard godly truth to be greater than the form in which it is presented to us and therefore to question each type of knowledge of the divine in order to keep trust in divine truth pure" (Schaeffler, *Religion*, p. 270).

The conception that religious statements are exempt from any criticism which is often heard from believers misses - no matter who it is advocated by - the difference which is decisive for religion between the divine truth asserted in the religious statement and the manner of statement which requires criticism as doxa. In his essay "The Factual Reference of Theological Assertions", Clifford holds a disputation with this problem in regard to the arguments of Flew and Nielsen. Hereby, he blames both for the fact that it is misleading to assume "that assertions like 'God loves us' or 'God is merciful' are simply subject to counter-evidence, such as the experience of suffering, and to complain that theists leave themselves all sorts of loopholes by refusing to admit any evidence of this kind as decisive" (p. 345). As opposed to this, he asserts that religious statements are neither more nor less easily proven false than other statements and the opposing arguments merely rest on the condition that Flew and Nielsen haphazardly limit the evidence which speaks for religious statements. Hereby, the positive insights which Clifford cites for the truth of religious statments do not seem to be as stringent as when he argues as follows: "If the universe were completely chaotic, if all human suffering were destructive of personality, if man laid claims to no sense of the numinous, if there were no allegedly revelatory events, if, in short, those aspects of human experience on which religious belief is grounded were missing, then there would be no reason to believe in God or his providence. All the evidence would be against such belief, and indeed it would be difficult to see how it could even arise" (p. 344).

The fact that the arguments cited can be used against the claim of God's non-existence, may not be assessed as proof that belief in God is also meaningful.

158) Albert, *Tractates*, p. 48. Cf. concerning Albert's criticism of theology: Ebeling's reply *Kritischer Rationalismus?*, as well as Albert's criticism of *this* critique *Theologische Holzwege*.

159) Cf. MacIntyre, "The Logical Status of Religious Belief", p. 195 ff.

160) Toulmin, "Contemporary Scientific Mythology", p. 16 f.; cf. Wagner, *Existenz, Analogie und Dialektik*.

161) Toulmin, "Contemporary Scientific Mythology", p. 16.

162) Wellmer, *Methodologie als Erkenntnistheorie*, p. 29.

163) Hick, "Theology and Verification", p. 155.

164) Flew, "Theology", p. 96.

165) Ibid, p. 98 f.

166) Srzednicki, "Are Statements of Religion Really Worth Discussing?". He considers religious statements not worth discussing. He is undoubtedly correct when he states that belief in God is the core of any Christian's religion. However, this seems to be the only thing in which he is correct. When he continues to ask if the statement "There is a God" presents a genuine religious reflection and wants to answer his question by comparing the religious statement with a statement such as the following, "I took the statement for a walk", his attitude toward religious statements becomes understandable; but this raises the question of the extent to which academic seriousness falls share to this comparison. As easy as the clarification of the claim to meaning of the above passage is, this is certainly not the case with religious statements. For when "statement" finds application in the sense in which this word is normally used in the English language, the statement becomes without a doubt senseless. However, if it were called my cat and not my goldfish - for one can hardly take a walk with a goldfish - "statement", meaning undoubtly falls share to the sentence. According to Srzednicki, the mode of application of the word "God" in religious sentences corresponds more readily to the word "goldfish" than to the word "cat".

Concerning the discussion of Srzednicki's thesis see Wilson, "The Meaningfulness of Religious Statements" and Londey, "God is the (a) Necessary Being".

167) Emmet, *The Nature of Metaphysical Thinking*, p. 180.

168) McPherson, "Religion as the Inexpressible", p. 132. My agreement with McPherson only exists in regard to his question and not to his answer. He

seeks a synthesis between Otto's notion of the numinous and Wittgenstein's notion of the mystical, there he completely accepts the positivist position of the meaninglessness of religious statements.

169) Cf. Clarke, "Linguistic Analysis and the Philosophy of Religion", p. 179: "There is a clear and intelligible distinction which can be made between logically true propositions and factually true propositions, but it is not the fact that one 'asserts nothing' and the other does not, nor it is the fact that one 'reflects our use of words' and the other does not. They both assert something and they both reflect our rules. The differences lies in how we determine whether or not they are true."

170) Campbell, *The Language of Religion*, p. 42.

171) Zuurdeeg, *An Analytical Philosophy of Religion*, p. 14.

172) In this sense Kaufmann, "Philosophy of Religion: Subjective or Objective?", determines: "Since the meaning of the term 'religion' thus determines the character of one's investigation *a priori* in certain very critical ways, it is of great importance to have some understanding of religion even before beginning the investigation" (p. 58). For Kaufmann religion is the attempt "to express a solution to the problems of human finitude" (p. 68). He comes to the conclusion "that materialism, rationalism, humanism and other forms of Western philosophy - as well as such social movements as communism and nationalism - must, from the point of view of the philosophy of religion be interpreted as religion and evaluated accordingly, just as certainly as Christianity, Buddhism and Hinduism" (p. 69).

173) Campbell, *The Language of Religion*, p. 42 f.

174) Clarke, "Linguistic Analysis", p. 169. The influence of the neutrality thesis upon the development of the analytical philosophy of religion cannot be denied. However, this is only characteristic of the analytical philosophy of religion to a certain extent. Especially during recent years many advocates of the neutrality thesis have clearly recognized the normative character of analysis. Here the analytical conception of religious philosophy was revised only in that it was unnecessary to simultaneously revoke the relinquishment of a priori structures defining that which can be viewed as a religious proposition. In correcting their course the insight into their own normative procedure was less decisive than the condition that analysis, which confronts propositions by which the believer attempts to justify his faith, must take a position in regard to those propositions.

175) The attempt to rework religion to match reason, as a result, demonstrated, for the most part the disintegration of the inner structure of religion, through which religion stood with even less protection against the

arguments of criticism. Philosophical criticism of religion proves to be a danger for religion as it "tempts this to pursue an apologetic way which is amiss, so that the apologetically 'purified' religion is condemned to be unfirm" (Schaeffler, *Religion*, p. 311). Cf. Wagner, *Existenz, Analogie und Dialektik*, p. 23.

176) MacIntyre, "The Logical Status of Religious Belief", certainly is correct when he maintains: "to *accept* religious belief is a matter not of argument, but of conversion" (p. 209). On the other hand, he confuses the decision and the religious confession with reflection on such a decision and such a reflection. The question of justification is not a *logical* one, as MacIntyre asserts. In this case he would be totally correct, but rather it is one, in the sense of Kant, of *transcental* logic. Cf. p. 88.

177) Zuurdeeg, "The Nature of Theological Langugage", is of a different opinion. For him confessional and theological language build forms of "convictional language" which are differentiated from indicative language. For Zuurdeeg the question of truth falls away with this categorization. Cf. Thompson's criticism of Zuurdeeg in: "Philosophy and Theology: A Reply to Professor W.F. Zuurdeeg". In regard to this estimation of analytical philosophy by Zuurdeeg, see his essay "The Implications of Analytical Philosophy for Theology".

178) Morris, "Religion and Theological Language", is not willing to recognize the situation of dialectical conversation. He conceives of theology the translation of religion, but denies it a critical influence on statements of belief. Yet he wants to be critical within the theological system.

179) MacIntyre, "The Logical Status of Religious Belief", p. 172.

180) Fahrenbach, "Sprachanalyse aund Ethik".

181) Cf. Hare, "Theology and Falsification".

182) Heintel, *Labyrinthe*, p. 205. Cf. "Sokratisches Wissen und praktischer Primat" by the same author.

183) Binkley, "What characterizes Religious Language?", p. 18.

184) Ibid.

185) Ibid.

186) Hick, "Comment", p. 23.

187) Gellner, *Words and Things*, p. 91 ff.

188) Robinson, "The Logic of Religious Language",p. 14f: "The recognition of the linguistic situation does not permit the philosopher of religion to play fast and loose with the logic of this or that area of language, but it may enable him to see where a given account of the logic of moral or religious

language, for example, is too narrow and has become something of a strait-jacket in which neither religion nor morality can breathe freely. This, I suggest, is precisely what has happened in the treatment of morality as consisting of nothing other than prescriptions and in the treatment of religion as a combination of expressions of intent, performatives and fictional elements; and it has happened because the linguistic situation has been ignored or discounted, and because accordingly it has been assumed that the almost impersonal idea of a self-contained language, ownerless and anonymous, is perfectly adequate and not in the least misleading. It is not to be thought that the linguistic situation and the social context of language have been completely ignored. It is more likely that they have been immobilised by being given a place within the language. I who speak to you and you who listen to me have become 'he' and 'she' and 'they' within the language. We have become what might be called logical subjects, and we function within the language as logical subjects. It is clear, however, that this is not, and cannot be, the whole story. We who function as logical subjects within a language are those who create and use the language, and inevitably therefore stand outside and above it; and we stand outside and above it, not in isolation, but in personal relationship - otherwise there would be no language. By the very nature of the case I am not just a possible 'he' in the language which I use, nor are you; and the first- and second-personal pronouns effectively break through the barrier which a self-contained interpretation of language would erect."

189) Gellner, *Words and Things*, p. 96.

190) Crombie, "The Possiblity of Theological Statements", p. 39. Cf. Alston, "Religious Language", p. 169: "We may say that the difficulties in understanding other forms of religious language all stem from obscurities in statements about God."

191) Crombie, "The Possibility of Theological Statement", p. 43.

192) Whether the question "Who is Tom?" is really already answered with the reference "That is Tom"; and to what extent philosophical problems do not also - for the understanding of this sentence - have to begin with the question of what existence means for a subject and, that therefore, the simple answer: "this is Tom", falls prey to a nominalistic empiricism, will not be further handled here. Rather should it be noted as a question.

193) Crombie, "The Possibility of Theological Statements", p. 40.

194) Ibid, p. 41.

195) Ibid.

196) Kraft, *Erkenntnislehre*, p. 95.

197) Crombie. "The Possibility of Theological Statements", p. 41 f.

198) Wittgenstein, *Philosophical Investigations*, § 71.

199) Crombie, "The Possibility of Theological Statements", p. 42.

200) In the discussion of the special position of the predicate, I hold mainly to the statements of Crombie as in the case of the first characterization.

201) Ibid, p. 47.

202) Ibid, p. 45.

203) Warnach, "Was ist exegetische Aussage?", p. 106.

204) Heintel, *Labyrinthe*, p. 539.

205) Luther is interesting in this regard. For him it was certain that "*omnia vocabula in Christo novam significationem accipere in eadem re significata*" (Disputatio de divinitate et humanitate Christi II 94, 17/18). "In this theological principle, the general hermeneutical experience is expressed that words draw their meaning from the context in which they are used. Therewith (i.e. in God) an eschatological new context is given in regard to all contexts in which words are otherwise used, which necessarily gives all words used in *this* context a new meaning" (Jüngel, "Metaphorische Wahrheit", p. 77).

206) Thomas, *Summa Theologica*, Qu. XIII, Art. V.

207) Apel, "Entfaltung der sprachanalytischen Philosophie", p. 242.

208) Hartshorne, "Is God's Existence a State of Affairs?", p. 26.

209) Cf. Blackstone, *The Problem of Religious Knowledge*.

210) Price, "Faith and Belief", p. 11.

211) Ibid, p. 10.

212) Barth, "Das Wort Gottes als Aufgabe der Theologie", p. 167.

213) Price, "Faith and Belief, p. 23.

214) Cf. Schelling, *Werke* I, p. 92 f.

215) Price, "Faith and Belief", p. 11 f. Cf. Litzenburg's criticism in his article "'Faith-in' and 'Infaith' - Reply to Professor H.H. Price". He means the difficulties which Price encounters in his relationship between "believe in" and "believe that" can at best be overcome when the term "in faith" is used instead of "believing in". Thereby he emphasizes that faith "is *not at all* a matter of my *believing-in someone* but, rather, a matter of *being met by someone*" (p. 252) and concludes "it makes as little sense to love a God one has never met (encountered or been confronted by) as it does not continue believing in (in the reducible sense of believing-that) a God one meets" (p. 254).

216) Price, "Faith and Belief", p. 24.

217) Whereby, as Gollwitzer, in *Denken und Glauben*, p. 47, emphasizes, concerning the use of the verb *pisteuein* in the New Testament, it is apparent that the construction with the dative or with *epi* and the dative is used in reference to God. Whereas *eis* is used with the accusative when referring to Jesus. Concerning the relationship between thought and faith by Augustine see Mader, *Die logische Struktur des personalen Denkens.*

218) Gollwitzer, *Denken und Glauben*, p. 48.

219) Crombie, "The Possibility of Theological Statement", p. 32; compare to this also Blackstone's dispute with this question, ibid.

220) Malcolm, "Is it a Religious Belief that God exists?", p. 106 ff.

221) Gadamer, *Wahrheit und Methode*, p. 314. *Truth and Method*, p. 290f.

222) Phillips, "Religious Beliefs and Language-Games", p. 21 f. Cf. Klein, *Vernunft und Wirklichkeit* I, p. 103 f. The rejection of a placing before or behind does not necessarily result in the thesis of inseparability, as advocated by Palmer, "Understanding First". With the mere rejection of an order of precedence of "believing in" and "believing that", nothing is said about the type of logical relationship between the two. This is also the case in the affirmation of the statement that religion has its own logic and it is a form of life, which is carried out according to autonomous rules. These are the criteria named through which religion is differentiated from all other social forms of life. The question of a coexistensive logic does come up actually here. However, the question of the relationship between "believe in" and "believe that" is specific only to the total problem.

223) Cf. Heintel, "Gottes Transzendenz", p. 292 f.: "All thinking faith - and this alone is meaningful - proceeds from an "a priori of meaning" in regard to the revelation which is binding for God and humankind in the same way. So understood the 'word' of God formulates nothing other than the supposition of all motivatational understandings of God's message directed to humankind. In it the movement of belief proceeding from mankind and God's self-definition in revelation encounter each other. Therefore, this apriori of meaning is common for humankind and God, because in no other way could the movement of belief lead to a definite belief and gain meaning. From here it is demonstrated that certain revelation must always be historical revelation from which, of course, belief in the reminding repetition of God's central act of salvation in time knows itself to be above time and in this consciousness enjoys the 'reconciliation' (transcendence which has been removed by God himself)." Cf. by the same author "Glaube in Zweideutigkeit. R. Musils 'Tonka'".

Chapter III

224) In this way, for example, Schmidt comes to the conclusion that there is no such thing as religious knowledge ("Is there a Religious Knowledge?"). He differentiates only between "formal knowledge (logic and mathematics) and empirical knowledge (p. 529). Furthermore he writes, "I discover that religious claims do not fit in any of these kinds".

225) For the mode of application of the term "emotive" see Alston's article "Emotive Meaning". An exact definition is hardly possible, as Alston emphasizes, because "many writers on the subject make free use of the phrase, they in fact talk mostly about kinds of uses or functions of language and do little or nothing to exhibit any basis for using the term 'emotive' to label a special kind of meaning" (p. 491).

226) It is known that ethics, aesthetics and all those areas of life, which could not be subjected to the demands of mathematical systematics, were dealt with in a similar way: "Positivism tossed them into the waste basket of 'emotive language'. This meant that ethical, aesthetic and theological language were thrown indiscriminately into a heap that contained such other language forms as commands, ejaculations, statements about other minds, and nonsense verse." Hordern, *Speaking of God*, p. 34.

227) *Philosophical Investigations*, § 22: "Imagine a picture representing a boxer in a particular stance. Now, this picture can be used to tell someone how he should stand, should hold himself; or how he should not hold himself; or how a particular man did stand in such-and-such a place; and so on. One might... call this picture a proposition-radical."

228) Ibid.

229) Braithwaite, *An Empiricist's View of the Nature of Religious Belief*, furthermore: Van Buren, *The Secular Meaning of the Gospel*, and Hepburn, "Demythologizing and the Problem of Validity".

230) In this context we also refer to Austin's theory of performative language which he later modified by differentiating between the locutional and non-locutional aspect of the act of speech. This had a lasting influence on theological language models. The attempt to introduce the emotive - as opposed to the constative - mode as well as Austin's differentiation between performative and non-performative propositions fell into the difficulty that a criterion cannot be given in a grammatical sense through which these could respectively and clearly be differentiated from one another; so that Austin came to the conclusion that a locutional aspect must be differentiated from a non-locutional one in all linguistic acts.

For the application of Austin's theory to religious language see especially Just's study *Religiöse Sprache und analytische Philosophie*, p. 131 ff. Just comes to the conclusion that for religious, even non-locutional acts of language the question of truth is not irrelevant. The linguistic act (for example Jesus) can only be seen as successful when it is true that Jesus is the Messiah.

231) Stenius, *Wittgenstein's Tractatus*, p. 224 f.

232) See Wittgenstein, *Notes on Logic*, p. 188 f.

233) Cf. Ayer, *Language, Truth and Logic*, above all Chapter VI: Critique of Ethics and Theology; furthermore: Hare, *Language and Morals*, and by the same author *Freedom and Reason*; and Stevenson, *Ethics and Language*.

234) Kaulbach, "Stand der Sprache, praktische Vernunft und Handeln", p. 494.

235) Trillhaas, *Religionsphilosophie*, p. 223 f.

236) Hare, "Theology and Falsification", p. 99 f.

237) Charlesworth, *Philosophy and Linguistic Analysis*, p. 141.

238) Stenius, *Wittgensteins Traktat*, p. 224.

239) According to Van Buren, the public proclamation of a Blik-exchange finds its expression in baptism. He explains that in the Christian tradition "this rite represented the dramatic change which Christians felt to lay between their past bondage and their present liberty, between the world as it had appeared before and the world as it was seen with their new perspective." *The Secular Meaning of the Gospel*, p. 185.

240) Braithwaite, *An Empiricist's View*, p. 431.

241) Ibid, p. 433.

242) Van Buren, *The Secular Meaning of the Gospel*, p. 40 ff. and 82 ff. Cf. Ramm, "Karl Barth and Analytic Philosophy". For a correct estimation of Barth's significance for analytical philosophy, Robinson's article "Karl Barth's Empiricism" is also of interest in that he also goes into Zuurdeeg's Barth-interpretation. There he writes: "... even Professor Karl Barth, although he does not explicitly consider the contentions of Logical positivism, none the less reveals a certain common ground between that position and his own when he describes 'the world of man' as that 'in which everything is problematical, everything must first be tested with the result that it is identical with God' [Doctrine of the Word of God, p. 513]" (p. 362). "Certainly, radical Protestantism is... primarily radical *empiricism* in theology, if this word be used to indicate that which is given and not just which is given to sense" (p. 364).

243) Hare, *Religion and Morals*, p. 182.

244) Bendall-Ferré, *Exploring the Logic of Faith*, p. 216 ff.

245) Flew, *God and Philosophy*, p. 182.

246) Bendall-Ferré, *Exploring the Logic of Faith*, p. 101.

247) Cf. above, p. 37 ff.

248) High, *Language, Persons and Belief*, p. 77 f.

249) Apel, "Wittgenstein und das Problem des hermeneutischen Verstehens", p. 87; and Pannenberg, *Wissenschaftstheorie und Theologie*, p. 182 f. *Theology and Philosophy of Science*, p. 182f.

250) Apel, "Wittgenstein", p. 87.

251) Gill, "Wittgenstein and Religious Language, p. 66.

252) Ibid.

253) Ibid, p. 68.

254) Ibid, p. 67.

255) Charlesworth, "Linguistic Analysis and Language about God", p. 156.

256) Wittgenstein, *Philosophical Investigations*, § 116.

257) Hare, "Theology and Falsification", p. 103.

258) Cf. Hume, *A Treatise of Human Nature*, above all book I. See also Flew, *Hume's Philosophy of Belief*.

259) Hare, "Theology", p. 100.

260) Ibid, p. 101.

261) Ibid, p. 101.

262) Ibid, p. 102.

263) Hare, "Religion and Morals", p. 187.

264) Ibid, p. 192.

265) Hare, "Theology and Falsification", p. 102.

266) Ibid, p. 100. The criticism of Duff-Forbes also sets in at this claim of Hare's ("Theology and Falsification Again"). On the one hand, he suggests that for Hare not only the insane person has a 'blik' but rather those who qualify the insane person to be sick. On the other hand, he asks: "On what grounds is one said to be insane and the other sane? Surely this, that the graduate holds to his theory in the face of any and all observations that can be made concerning the behaviour of dons (this is why he is said to be a lunatic), whereas his friends do allow the behaviour of dons to count. And if the behaviour of dons had been other than it was (if dons had been creeping around after dark with guns and knives and pots if poison) then the opinion of the lunatic's friends would have been other than it was. This is why they are said to be sane. But then what *they* say about dons is falsifiable, and if *that* is so, then they, unlike the lunatic, haven't a 'blik'

about dons *at all. They make factual claims*. The right 'blik' turns out not to be a 'blik' at all" (p. 145).

Therefore, Duff-Forbes comes to the conclusion: "If *both* the graduate and his friends have a 'blik' about dons, that is to say, if the theories of both are compatible with anything and everything that can be observed about the behaviour of dons, then no state of affairs can count as between them. But then the ground for saying that one is a sane 'blik' and the other an insane 'blik' has gone. The language of 'lunatic', 'obsession', 'insane' used of the graduate is simply the language of *our* 'blik', as the language of 'simple-minded', 'stupidly trusting' and so on, used of us by the graduate, is the language of *his* 'blik'. Hare has robbed himself of the ability to draw a distinction between the right and the wrong 'blik'. Or, at least, if he draws the distinction in the way he does he is left with only one 'blik', the lunatic's, and, if he insists that *both* the lunatic and his friends have 'bliks' about dons, he is deprived of the distinction he requires. Hare cannot, it seems to me, hold that *all* have 'bliks' *and* say that one is better than another, one is right and the other wrong: or if he can hold this he has not shown that he can" (p. 146).

267) When Sontag, "The Platonist's Concept of Language", scolds the analytical philosophy of religion because it regards language as an object and therefore transforms propositions into things, so should one agree to this criticism: "... language must never be taken for its own object and confused with the independent object of language. ... Without reference to the structure of the things themselves, the purpose behind the structure of language cannot be made evident" (p. 830). However, the conception of language which Ross offers, for example, to understand language as sign is to be rejected as well because it does not do justice to the language's own value.

268) Cf. Tillich, *Systematische Theologie* I, p. 295. *Systematic Theology*, p. 250f.

269) Cf. Chapter II/3.

270) Cf. Riser, "Toward the Philosophical Analysis of Theological Statements". He advocates the cognition of religious statements. Religious statements are primarily categorical value judgements which cannot be falsified: "They are not falsified by facts because they go to define what is to be taken as a fact in the first place" (p. 388). "Theological statements, then, provide systematic accounts of value-impregnated experience, and the mystic symbols appearing in these statements are expressions indirectly referring to features, or configurations of features, in such experience" (p. 393). In order to explain the difference between religious and moral statements, Riser refers to the necessity of a philosophical anthropology.

271) Braithwaite, *An Empiricist's View*, p. 437.

272) Ibid, p. 436.

273) Hordern, *Speaking of God*, p. 73.

274) Braithwaite, *An Empiricist's View*, p. 437 ff.

275) Cf. Moore, *Principia Ethica*, and by the same author, *Ethics*.

276) Robinson, "The Logic of Religious Language", p. 7.

277) Braithwaite, *An Empiricist's View*, p. 432.

278) Van Buren, *The Secular Meaning of the Gospel*, p. 197.

279) Ibid, p. 198.

280) Ibid.

281) Ibid, p. 96.

282) Cf. Buri's reception in the Anglo-Saxon philosophy in Ogden's works, and especially in Hardwick, *Faith and Objectivity, Fritz Buri und the Hermeneutical Foundations of a Radical Theology*. In this first great work on Fritz Buri, Hardwick does not only try to describe Buri's theology, but also to develop his basic theological statements by means of lingustic analytical philosophy.

283) Van Buren, *The Secular Meaning of the Gospel*, p. 99.

284) Ibid, p. 143.

285) Ibid, p. 126 ff.

286) Ibid, p. 134. Cf. Luther's explanations in "Von der Freiheit eines Christenmenschen". He deals with the question of man's freedom or constraint facing God's will. This publication is the answer to the question:... Is God just a projection of man? Cf. Gottfried Fitzer, *Was Luther wirklich sagte*, p. 59f.

287) Cf. the conception of freeedom in the New Testament in Niederwimmer's work of the same name as well as Schwarz, *Was Jesus wirklich sagte*.

288) Van Buren, *The Secular Meaning of the Gospel*, p. 131. According to Van Buren, words which point to "the end and goal of all existence" inform the hearer of a certain attitude of the speaker. A statement like "The Kingdom of God is at hand" cannot be verified empirically but the attitude expressed by such a statement is open to verification by considering the conduct of the one who makes the statement. Van Buren's abbreviation of the religious meaning of this proposition is clearly shown when he states the following in regard to the speaker of such a statement: "Presumably he

would rather 'live for the present' than make careful plans for his old age".
Cf. Morris, "Religion and Theological Language", p. 19.

289) Van Buren, *The Secular Meaning of the Gospel*, p. 139. Herewith, Van
Buren is expressly in contradiction to the interpretation held by all
Christian-Church institutions for whom the confession of the deity of
Christ or to his godly nature - as it was formulated by the Fourth
Ecumenical Council of Chalcedon in 451 - was recognized as a basis of all
belief. In spite of the differences in thought and expression there reigns
unity in regard to the "identification of God's historical will of Salvation
with the historical appearance of Jesus of Nazareth! As far as the formula
of 'vere deus' in strict connection with 'et vere homo' wishes to express
nothing else, it remains 'unrelinquishable' for the Christian faith", as
Dantine writes. In the problematic of the divinity and humanity of Jesus
the question arises of whether "'God' can be spoken of at all, and if this
question is affirmed, 'how' can God be spoken of?!" (Dantine, *Jesus*, p.
112).

290) Nielsen, "On Talk About God", p. 889.

291) On this point Nielsen does not reiterate Van Buren's opinion. Cf. Van
Buren's essay "On Doing Theology", especially p. 55. In this sense, Nielsen
theology can only be seen as a high-styled theory of cheating. According to
Van Buren theology is "that activity of men struck by the biblical story, in
which they undertake to revise continually the ways in which they say how
things are with their present circumstances, in the light of how they read
that story" (p. 53).

292) Nielsen, "On Talk About God", p. 889.

293) Ibid, p. 889 f.

294) Van Buren, *The Secular Meaning of the Gospel*, p. 199.

295) Ibid.

296) In the essay "On Doing Theology", Van Buren has removed himself from
the distinction "cognitive/non cognitive": "I find that the distinction
'cognitive/non cognitive' is not helpful in getting clear about how Christian
faith is a matter of how the world is, and I regret having once been seduced
into picking up that stone axe as an appropriate tool for opening up this
delicate bit of watch-works. The issue is not, as that distinction leads us to
suspect, that we have an agreed frame of reference, an agreed way of
carving up the world into tables and chairs on the one hand, and our
attitudes or dispositions towards tables and chairs on the other, and that
faith must lie on one or the other. Christian faith, on the contrary, proposes
another way to do the carving up in the first place. And in so far as how we
carve up the universe of our experienced world sets the terms for further

speaking and understanding, how we do that carving is fundamental for cognition. Only we do this in more than one way, and in each way in which we do it, we are embarked on a cognitive enterprise, in which questions of truth and questions of matter of fact are very much in order" (p. 66).

297) Van Buren, *The Secular Meaning of the Gospel*, p. 104 f.

298) Wittgenstein, *The Blue and Brown Books*, p. 69.

299) Cf. Etges, *Kritik der analytischen Theologie*, p. 83.

300) Apel, *Die Idee der Sprache*, p. 34.

Chapter IV

301) Simon, *Sprache und Raum*, p. 269.

302) Wittgenstein, *Tractatus,* 4.002.

303) Martin, *Philosophische Sprachprüfung der Theologie*, p. 149.

304) Cf. Chapter II/3.

305) Martin, *Spachprüfung*, p. 149.

306) Cf. Hordern, *Speaking of God*; Evans, *The Logic of Self-Involvement*.

307) Hordern, *Speaking of God*, p. 181.

308) Robinson, "The Logic of Religious Language", p. 1 f.

309) Luther, *Weimarer Ausgabe*, 40, I, p. 360.

310) Apel, "Wittgenstein und das Problem des hermeneutischen Verstehens", p. 77.

311) Cf. Ferré, "Models", p. 83 (p. 79).

312) Ibid, p. 76 (p. 73).

313) Ibid, p. 81 (p. 77).

314) Ibid p. 91 (p. 87).

315) Ibid p. 72; Jeans, *Physics and Philosophy*.

316) Ferré, "Models", p. 85 (p. 81). Braithwaite causes one to think that models are the most *comfortable* way to reflect upon the structure of a theory (*Scientific Explanation*, p. 92 ff). Cf. in regard to criticism of the application of models in order to explain religious statements, Hepburn, "Demythologizing and the Problem of Vaildity".

317) Hordern, *Speaking of God*, p. 82.

318) Ferré, *Language*.

319) Robinson, "The Logic of Religious Language", p. 2.

320) Blackstone, *The Problem of Religious Knowledge*, p. 33.

321) Ibid, p. 34.

322) Hordern, *Speaking of God*, p. 86.

323) Ibid, p. 87. MacIntyre holds another conception ("The Logical Status of Religious Belief"). He considers a transition from a religious language game to a non-religious one or vice-versa to be basically impossible. "It is noteworthy that in our account of religion we have nowhere found a place for point at which a transition can be made from non-religious to religious language. One can accept religion in its own terms or reject it; there is no way of justifying it by translating it into other terms. ... Religion is justified only by referring to a religious acceptance of authority. And it means, if you like, that religion as a whole lacks any justification" (p. 202).

324) Wittgenstein, *Philosophical Investigations*, § 373.

325) Cf. Heintel, "Der Begriff des Menschen und der 'spekulative Satz'".

326) Apel, "Wittgenstein", p. 79.

327) Robinson, "The Logic of Religious Language, p. 10.

328) Ferré, *Language*, Chapter 12.

329) Ibid, p. 146.

330) Ibid, p. 152 f.

331) Ibid, p. 153.

332) Ibid, p. 154.

333) Ibid, p. 148.

334) Cf. Ferré's article of the same name: "Is Language about God Fraudulent?"

335) Ferré, *Language*, p. 155.

336) Cf. Mitchell's parable in "Theology and Falsification", p. 103 ff.

337) Cf. Hofmeister, "The Problem of the Lie in Kant" and "Truth and Truthfulness".

338) The applied termini for the designation of the criteria of religious statements are not explicitly found in Ferré's thought.

339) Cf. Ferré, *Language*, p. 146. In the following I will base my work upon Ferré's analysis of the religious proposition because it is the most applicable and the most meaningful.

340) Ibid, p. 164. In the essay, "Is Language about God Fraudulent?", Ferré certainly already defended the cognition of religious statements, but inasmuch as he totally rejects the differentiation of the emotive from the cognitive, he plays down the ontological reference of religious statements.- Instead, he operates with the conception of responsive truth which he formed in connection with Stevenson's "persuasive definition"; and thereby

he differentiates the truth of religious statements from empirical and logical statements.

341) Ferré, *Language*, p. 160.

342) Cf. Chapter II.

343) Above all, this is emphasized by Braithwaite in his work *An Empiricist's View*. Cf. the differentiation of the conceptions of truth, rightness, legitimacy in: Reininger, *Metaphysik der Wirklichkeit* I, p. 218.

344) Braithwaite, *An Empiricist's View*, p. 161.

345) Ibid,, p. 161 f.

346) Ibid, p. 163.

347) Ibid, p. 161.

348) Ibid.

349) Ulmer, *Lebenswelt*, p. 157.

350) Cf. Ferré, *Language*, p. 161.

351) Ibid, p. 164.

352) Ulmer, *Lebenswelt*, p. 158.

353) In this way, Demos, for example, in his discussion contribution by the symposium "Are Religious Dogmas Meaningful?" (*Journal of Philosophy* LI, 1954, p. 172) proceeds from the fact that the analogical principle is the mediating factor on the basis of which religious statements can also be allocated cognition. It mediates between different types of knowledge: "I agree... that religious belief, in that it is existential. And here let me make use of my notion of analogy. Religious knowing, scientific knowing, artistic knowing (or, better reasoning) are indeed not the same *genus* of reasoning. The differences are vital and they should not be hushed up. Yet it is valid to speak of them all as cases of reasoning, in the sense that reason here is used as an analogical term" (p. 172).
Cf. the problematic of the term "analogous" as discussed by Demos in the contribution of S. Hook in the same symposium (p. 165 f).

354) MacIntyre, John. "Analogy", p. 20.

355) This is not true without exception. Therefore it is, for example, not the case for Ross, "Analogy as a Rule of Meaning for Religious Language". Here Ross tries to formulate Thomas' doctrine of analogy in the terminology of modern semantics, and, also on the basis of this procedure, comes to the conclusion that "if one wishes to render philosophically plausible the claim of most orthodx Christians that their traditional descriptive statements about God are both literally meaningful and *true*, one must employ an analogy theory fundamentally similar to that of St.

Thomas, and, I might add, the existence of such a theory... renders quite plausible the belief of many Christians that their theological utterance are indeed literally meaningful" (p. 502).

Here Ross certainly overlooks that, in the sense of his theory, the Christian believer only comes to the conviction of the truth of his statements and, therefore to their meaning in a literal sense under the supposition of the axiom of creation upon which Thomas' doctrine of analogy failed.

356) Wittgenstein, *Tractatus*, p. 101.

357) Hepburn, *Christianity and Paradox*, p. 16.

358) Cf. Ramsey, "Paradox in Religion", p. 139 (p. 133f).

359) Cf. Schupp, *Auf dem Wege zu einer kritischen Theologie*, p. 20 ff.

360) Ramsey, "Paradox", p. 140 (p. 134)

361) Ibid, p. 141 (p. 136).

362) The extent to which the formation of analogy follows correctly here may remain outside of consideration here. However, in this context it should be pointed out that the presentation of mathematical parallels for religious paradoxes is no less questionable than the application of scientific parallels. So is - for example - Ramsey's reference to the mathematical paradox of a geometrical series, which possesses an endless sum although such a thing would never be directly produced by adding an endless line of numbers. The parallel between mathematical and religious paradoxes construed in reference to the conception eternal, experiences here its limitation in that mathematical infinitude - exactly speaking - is set as a definite finite dimension from the very beginning. Cf. Arnold, *Die Entelechie*, p. 40, as well as footnote 14, p. 244.

363) Ramsey, "Paradox", p. 144 (p. 139).

364) Evans-Pritchard, *Nuer Religion*, p. 128, quoted according to Ramsey, "Paradox", p. 144 f (p. 140).

365) Ibid, p. 145 f (p. 141).

366) Ibid, p. 144 (p. 140).

367) Ibid, p. 159 (p. 156).

368) Phillips, *The Concept of Prayer*, p. 50; cf. Hick, Faith, p. 120.

369) Wittgenstein, *Lectures*, p. 96; Phillips, "Religious Belief", p. 120.

370) Cf. MacIntyre, "The Logical Status of Religious Belief, p. 211.

371) Kant, *Prolegomena* 357.

372) Mascall, Existence and Analogy, p. 87.

373) It can be seen from the oppositional viewpoints of Blackstone and Hartshorne that for a religious language to be explained to be analogous, the question of the possiblity of language at all arises. In this manner, Blackstone writes in "Crombie's Defense of the Assertion-Status of Religious Claims": "A meaningful use of analogy is that taking some characteristic *found in our experience* and postulating a higher degree of that characteristic than is shown in our experience, for example, it is quite meaningful to speak of men attaining a higher degree of knowledge or a higher degree of moral goodness than they now have" (p. 227).

Hartshorne, "The Idea of God - Literal or Analogical?" Applying the argument Descartes presented in the IIIth Meditation, means that we can only see our limitations in comparison to an absolute being: "Concerning the 'analogy of faith' in which we compare the creatures to God, not God to creatures, there is an old argument: we know our defects only in so far as we know the divine standard; we do not first know our defects independently, and then, by denying these, conceive God. Who knows what human knowledge is, or human love? Think of the variety of theories! Self-knowledge and knowledge of God are apparently inseparably. Neither is clear unless both are somehow clear" (p. 136).

374) Cf. McPherson, "Assertion and Analogy", p. 197.

375) Ibid, p. 198.

376) Ramsey, "Religion and Science", p. 53 (p. 50).

377) Mascall, *Existence and Analogy*, p. 102.

378) Wagner, *Analogie*, p. 167.

379) Cf. Hayner, "Analogical Predication".

380) Hayner, "Analogical Predication", p. 860.

381) Hayner is thoroughly aware of this objection and he believes to have considered it sufficiently: "Another question which may be anticipated is whether in this view of analogical predication justice is done to what religious people sometimes refer to as the 'majesty' of God, i.e., His transcendence over all earthly categories and things. I believe such 'majesty', or transcendence, is preserved by the circumstance that the terms predicated of God signify a *combination* of properties which is unique and hence qualitatively different from those signified by the same terms when predicated of other things. The fact that God may be said to share some properties with His creatures does not, in itself, necessarily impugn His 'majesty' inasmuch as He may still be regarded as, in some sense, qualitatively 'above' His creatures" (p. 861). However, it is to be held in opposition to this claim that the notion of the majesty of God is only

comparatively definable. This becomes evident, especially, from the last sentence of this quotation.

382) Wittgenstein, *Philosophical Investigations*, § 2 and § 19.

383) Apel, *Idee der Sprache*, p. 33.

384) Rhees, "Wittgenstein's Builders", p. 262, quoted with: Phillips, *Religious Beliefs and Language Games*, p. 32.

385) Phillips, *Religious Beliefs and Language Games*, p. 33.

386) Schulz, *Wittgenstein*, p. 70.

387) Wittgenstein, *Philosophical Investigations*, § 22.

388) Braithwaite, *An Empiricist's View*.

389) Van Buren, *The Secular Meaning*, p. 15.

390) Apel, "Wittgenstein", p. 71.

391) Cf. Wagner, *Analogie*.

392) Ferré, *Language, Logic and God*, p. 76.

393) Ferré, *Language, Logic and God*, p. 76 f. Cf. the essay "Analogy in Theology", especially the section "Evaluation of the Way of Analogy" by the same author. Here Ferré, in the evaluation of analogy, comes to the same result as in the book which was just quoted:
"It remains possible even aside from these issues, however, that the fairly precise rules worked out for the application of theological analogies may serve a useful function within the theological enterprise at the systematic level that originally provoqued the need for an analogical way. Rather than looking to these analogies for the stablishment of meaningful connections between theological systems and general knowledge, philosophers might consider investigating their functions in maintaining syntactical connections and embodying standards for the construction of well-formed formulae within such systems. This approach might reveal much about how doctrines of analogy have actually functioned as statemental rules, and much about the logic of theological thinking in general. With respect to the latter, the study of analogy with attention to the internal systematic rwquirements that demand analogy lays bare a basic epistemological dynamic in Judeo-Christian thought: The constant tension between affirmation and negation, anthropomorphism and agnosticism, the provision of vivid images and their abrupt withdrawal" (p. 96).

Chapter V

394) Phillips, *The Concept of Prayer*, p. 22 f.

395) Cf. Phillips, "Religious Belief", p. 119 (p. 253).

396) As far as that goes, Hick, in his attempt to descriptively analize of the verb "to believe", writes that religious belief is a "form of cognition by acquaintance... is *more like* sense perception than like propositional belief" ("Religious Faith as Experiencing - As", p. 22).

397) Phillips, "Religious Belief", p. 119 (p. 253).

398) Ferré, *Language, Logic and God*, p. 48. Ferré definitely recognizes the function which is allotted to the proofs of God. However, he doubts that these are able to do justice to the expectations. "One feature shared by all theological arguments of this sort is the tendency to try to accomplish the (a priori unpromising) task of leaping the gulf between finite and infinite." ("The Use and Abuse of Theological Arguments", p. 188). According to Ferré, prooves of God actually are confined "to provide a means of reviewing incompatible disciplined thought" (p. 191).

399) Ferré, *Language*, p. 60.

400) Ibid, p. 61.

401) Martin, C.B., "A religious Way of Knowing".

402) Ferré, *Language*, p. 114 f.

403) Collingwood, *Essay on Philosophical Method*, p. 124 f. Cf. the assessment of the cosmological and teleological proof of God in the analytical philosophy of religion in:
1. Hepburn, "Cosmological Argument for the Existence of God",
2. Alston, "Teleological Argument for the Existence of God".

404) Cf. Durfee, "The Reformulation of the Question as to the Existence of God".

405) Harris, "Mr. Ryle and the Ontological Argument", p. 266.

406) Anselm, *Proslogion*, Chapters 2 and 3.

407) Russell, "General Propositions and Existence", p. 220.

408) Ibid.

409) Ibid, p. 222.

410) Hick, "The Ontological Argument (Introductory Notes)", p. 466.

411) Moore, "Is Existence a Predicate?".

412) Ibid, p. 82 f.

413) F. Sontag, "The Meaning of Argument in Anselm's Ontological 'Proof', indeed agrees with Malcolm and Hartshorne in regard to the first and second form of proof. However, he claims at the same time that, to be precise, in the second form it no longer has to do with a proof. Rather the transition is nothing other than "a shift from considering the implications of a concept held in the understanding to a direct discussion of the nature of

God and of what is peculiarly true of such a being" (p. 483). Sontag's argument attempts to show that Anselm did not want to offer a proof of the existence of God as much a mediation of a conception of the difficulties which reflection upon the nature of God brings itself. One must conclude, due to the dispute of the character of proof of Anselm's argumentation, that a nature, a necessary existence, does not necessarily belong to this.

414) Anselm, Proslogion, p. 174 f.

415) Plantinga, "Kant's Objection to the Ontological Argument", is less content with Kant's argument. Plantinga understands Anselm's argumentation as reductio ad absurdum (p. 537), and believes that Kant's attempt at refutation is not to be applied to Anselm's form of proof. Yet, as opposed to this, Coburn, "Animadversions of Plantinga's Kant", objects that such an attempt at refutation, as Plantinga attributed to Kant, cannot be found in his work. Consequently Plantinga's conclusion"... Kant's objection shows neither that there are no necessary existential propositions nor that the proposition *God exists* is not necessary - any more than it shows that *there is a prime between 50 and 55* is a contingent proposition" (Plantinga, p. 546) is false (p. 548). G.I. Mavrodes, "Properties, Predicates and the Ontological Argument", as opposed to this. He claims that if Plantinga's interpretation of Kant is correct, Anselm's argument is not logical (p. 549). Mavrodes proceeds from Plantinga's differentiation between "first order property" and "second order property". In connection with Frege, Mavrodes characterized existence as "second order property". He writes in his interpretion of Frege that existence is a characteristic of conceptions and not of objects. Here Mavrodes argues that a "second order predicate" of an object can have no constitutive character because this object as object is a "first order" concept which is exclusively defined constitutively by "first order" predicates. He deduces from this differentiation that Anselm's formulation rests on a false conception of that which can possibly be perceived "because there is no such thing as *conceiving* to exist... no second order property can be attached to a concept merely by conceiving it as attached" (p. 550).

416) Anselm, *Proslogion*, p. 118.

417) Malcolm, "Anselm's Ontological Argument", p. 143.

418) Descartes, *Meditationes*, p. 542.

419) Ibid, p. 79 f.

420) Henrich, *Der ontologische Gottesbeweis*, p. 11.

421) Descartes, *Meditationes*, p. 79.

422) Henle, "Uses of the Ontological Argument".

423) Malcolm, "Anselm's Ontological Argument", p. 146.

424) Henle, "Uses of the Ontological Argument", p. 173.

425) Descartes, *Meditationes*, p. 152.

426) Cf. Findlay, "Can God's Existence be Disproved?", p. 120.

427) Ibid, p. 117.

428) Ibid.

429) Ibid, p. 119.

430) Heintel, *Labyrinthe*, p. 43.

431) For instance, Baumer, "Ontological Arguments still Fail", argues in this manner. His criticism is formulated against Harthorne in connection with Kant. However, it remains on the logical level and basically passes by the decisive question of how the relationship between language and reality is to be defined. His seeing the question, however, means that this is exclusively of relevance for the ontological argument: "But if nonimpossibility cannot, without invalidating equivocation, be established at the merely conceptual level, it must be established at the level of the concept to object relation. Moreover, because it must go beyond the concepts involved, must show not just that the concept to object relation is not impossible on the side of the concepts but that this is not impossible through and through, establishment of this nonimpossibility is *ipso facto* establishment that God or perfection exists. To put this another way, either we appeal to thought and reality, or we appeal to reality. But the first appeal lands in the variation of the ontological argument already criticized, and the other two presuppose what is to be proved" (p. 140).

432) Findlay, "Can God's Existence be Disproved?"

433) Cf. Findlay, ibid, p. 118 f. and Malcolm, "Anselm's Ontological Argument", p. 151.

434) Ibid, p. 152 f.

435) Ibid, p. 155. To this also compare Schelling's criticism of Descartes' arguments, Schelling, *Werke* V, p. 87.

436) If Brown, "Professor Malcolm on 'Anselm's Ontological Arguments'" means that Malcolm should rather have said, "if God does not exist, then His existence is eternally *precluded* (because He is by definition eternal)" (p. 14), then this only shows that he did not understand Malcolm's line of argumentation.

437) Ryle, *The Nature of Metaphysics, Final Discussion*, p. 50, cf. Malcolm, "Anselm's Ontological Argument", p. 150.

438) Smart, "The Existence of God", p. 34.

439) Cf. Wittgenstein, *Philosophical Investigations*, § 657.

440) Malcolm, "Anselm's Ontological Argument", p. 153.

441) In regard to the definition of the relationship between language and reality, those questions are also of interest which Sontag brings up in: "The Meaning of Argument in Anselm's Ontological 'Proof'" and his analysis of the ontological proof of God in: "How does reason function for Anselm, and what status do words have?" (p. 459). A question which he expounds upon is as follows: "How is the mind related to its objects, and is there really a 'third thing' namely words, which shares a mode of existence on a par with that of the mind and its objects?" (p. 460). He answers that that which brings thought into the picture is not language or its words but rather the "things themselves". Words are nothing other than signs: "Words function as signs for the mind, they are not its real object" (p. 468).

442) Malcolm, "Anselm's Ontological Argument", p. 151.

443) Therefore, Hartshorne also complains that Malcolm did not succeed in decisively refuting Findlay's objections, in that he actually proved that the expression "ens necessarium" only deals with a conceptual definition in which it is attempted to derive the concrete from the abstract ("The Logic of the Ontological Argument", p. 472).

444) Findlay, *Language, Mind and Value* (Introduction). Plantinga quotes this passage in connection with Findlay's essay "Can God's Existence be Disproved?" in: *The Ontological Argument*.

445) Cf. Hick, "A Critique of the Second Argument", p. 344.

446) Ibid, p. 344 f. The same reflections are found in Hick's essay "God as Necessary Being". Here it is also pointed out that in reference to the difference between logically necessary and factually necessary the authors of the Bible as well as the significant theologians of the West made use of a notion of God which presupposed God to be factually and necessarily existent. (Cf. p. 725 f.)

447) Cf. Geach, *Three Philosophers*, p. 114 f.

448) Hick, "A Critique", p. 345.

449) Kant, *Kritik der reinen Vernunft*, p. 279. To Kant see Heintel, *Die Bedeutung der Kritik der aesthetischen Urteilskraft für die transzendentale Systematik*.

450) Henrich, Der ontologische Gottesbeweis, p. 166.

451) Liebrucks, *Sprache und Bewußtsein*, III, p. 123. Certainly, the basic question raised by Durfee concerning the suppositions of philosophical reflection comes to such a conclusion. The dialectic of its thought is still not answered by this: "What are the presuppositions of philosophical reflection

itself which allow it to so incarnate the dialectic of existence? It is not enough to know that philosophy is open for communication as distinct from all types of dogmatic assertion. We need to know what it is about either being or our 'existenz' which brings dialectic forth as the essential character of the reflective process." ("Karl Jaspers as the Metaphysician of Tolerance", p. 210).

452) Liebrucks, *Sprache und Bewußtsein*, IV, p. 123.

453) Cf. Hick's essay "God as a Necessary Being". By implementing the modes of application of the conception of God in the philosophical and theological tradition of the characteristics of God, an attempt is made to develop the categories of eternity, indestructibility, bodylessness. Here, Hick explains "that the concept of God as eternal, and as not dependent on any other reality, but on the contrary, as the creator of everything other than himself... is a concept concerning which the factual question can properly by raised: Is there a being or a reality, to which this concept applies?" (p. 734). Hick may be asked to what extent his differentiations of logical from ontological and logical from factual are not only verbal but intend exactly that which Malcolm means when he speaks of ontological or factual necessity. For in reality this corresponds to the developed notion that this is only possible under the presupposition that the notion of God is not ontologically conceived. Cf. p. 222 f.

454) Hartshorne, "The Irreducibly Modal Structure of the Argument", p. 337 f. However, the conception that the notion of God deals with a formal logical term was dismissed by Hartshorne again and again. This was also the case when criticizing Alstons, "The Ontological Argument Revisited". He writes: "It is almost comical to see so many able minds, living and dead, striving to treat 'deity' as simply one more predicate term, or God as simply one more being whose existence is entirely in the same logical class with all other cases of existence. In such attempts it is not God but an idol, a fetish of some kind, whose existence is really being discussed. 'God is conceptually, not just factually unique'". ("Is the Denial of Existence ever contradictory?", p. 92).

455) Hick, "A Critique", p. 352.

456) Stegmüller, *Wahrheitsproblem*, p. 305.

457) Hartshorne's suggestion that one should conceive God as simultaneously incidental and necessary, which he expresses in this relation seems to be of much greater interest. This is also expressed in the short essay "The Logic of the Ontological Argument". There we read: "That God is both necessary and contingent, hence both abstract and concrete, or that He has an essential but abstract character which is bound in any possible state of

affairs to be actualized or concretized *somehow*, the how being always contingent" (p. 472).

458) Hick, "A Critique", p. 356. Werner, "The Ontological Argument for the Existence of God", comes to a similar conclusion: "We can at the very least, I should suggest, regard it [the ontological proof] as a living philosophical problem" (p. 279). Werner does not attempt to solve this philosophical problem, but rather is satisfied with listing the various standpoints in this question.

459) In a theory of eschatological verification Crombie sees only a possibility of proving the assertive status of religious statements. The doctrine of analogy is seen as a further one.

460) The principle ability of religious statements to be verified, as is advocated by Hick, is contradicted by Sontag by the reference that such an undertaking presupposes, that the same logical rules can be applied for perceiving God as are applied to all other statements. He argues that the variation of the conception of God varies according to the question of its verification: "We cannot, then, decide about verification, until we have specified which conception of God we are talking about, nor until we have considered, whether any special exceptions apply to reasoning about such special object." ("The Meaning of Argument...", p. 486). In this sense Sontag advocates the claim that Anselm is not interested in a proof but rather in the adequacy of the notion of God.

461) Cf. Hick, *Faith and Knowledge*, p. 134.

462) Cf. Hick, "Theology and Verification", p. 152.

463) Ibid, p. 153.

464) Ibid, p. 152.

465) Ibid.

466) Hick, *Faith and Knowledge*, p. 132.

467) Flew, "Can a Man Witness His Own Funeral?"

468) Cf. Schlick, "Meaning and Verification", p. 160. Passmore, "Christianity and Positivism", believes it to be a contradiction to speak of a "greater unterstanding after my death", because death means the disintegration of the "I" (p. 135). Duff-Forbes "Theology and Falsification Again", emphasizes that the thesis of a life after death must be dealt with as a religious statement and as a result "the statement that such a test can be applied to religious utterances, enabling us to say they are factual statements, is itself expresses as one of the religious utterances in question" (p. 152).

469) Cf. Hick, "Theology and Verficiation", p. 155.

470) Ibid.

471) Hick, *Faith and Knowledge*, p. 129.

472) Ibid, p. 128 f.

473) Hick, "Theology and Verification", p. 158.

474) Ibid, p. 156.

475) Smart, R. N., "The Concept of Heaven", who compares the various notions of heaven and comes to the conclusion, "however, the possibility of consistent: notion of heaven as the place of God does not guarantee the possibility of a consistent idea of the disembodied existence of the soul in the next world" (p. 235).

476) Wittgenstein, *Tractatus*, 6.4311. Cf. the article by Edwards, "My Death". Without making reference to Wittgenstein, Edwards disputes Freud's claim that it is not possible to imagine one's own death and says of Goethe that it is impossible for a thinking being to conceive of its own non-existence. Here, he comes to the conclusion that both thinkers are wrong on this point. They confused the content of a thought with the time of its appearance. Edwards' attempt at refutation shows the difficulty of his understanding because this is based on the idea that 'my death' plays the same role for 'my existence' as a planned visit to the London zoo. Thereby, Edwards proceeds from the wrong supposition that another person could very well conceive of 'my death'. He concludes that if another person could, then I must be able to also. However, in contrast to Edwards, at least Wittgenstein's proposition distinguishes between observing death and my own death. One can find similar arguments in Lazerowitz' work: *The Structure of Metaphysics*.

477) Hick, "Theology and Verification", p. 161 f.

478) Ibid, p. 163. In this way, McTaggart, the self-declared atheist, believes in immortality. Cf. Edwards, "Atheism", p. 188. For the exposition of the question of death: Wiplinger, *Der personal verstandene Tod*.

479) Cf. Hick, "Theology and Verification", p. 163.

480) At this point Nielsen, "Eschatological Verification", critiques Hick: "What we cannot do is have faith in a proposition we do not understand, for in such a situation we literally cannot know *what* it is we are supposed to have faith in. If we cannot conceive of there being a state of affairs that would make "God exists" true or false, we cannot understand, conceivable state of affairs, we are being asked to accept on faith. We can, by an act of faith, accept as true an antecedently understood proposition" (p. 281).

EPILOGUE

481) Hick, "Theology and Verfication", p. 163 f.

482) Lazerowitz, *The Structure of Metaphysics*, p. 79.

483) Chomsky, *Sprache und Geist*, p. 106.

484) Kant, Kr. d. r. V., Bd. 84. Cf. Hofmeister, "The Problem of Truth in the 'Critique of Pure Reason'".

LIST OF ABBREVIATIONS

AARJ	American Academy of Religion Journal
AJP	Australian Journal Philosophy
APQ	American Philosophical Quarterly
CC	Christian Century
CJT	Canadian Journal of Theology
CQR	Church Quarterly Review
CRT	Current Religious Thought
CS	Christian Scholar
DR	Downside Review
EOP	The Encyclopedia of Philosophy, 8 Vol., ed. by Paul Edwards, New York, London 1967
HJ	Hibbert Journal
HTR	Harvard Theological Review
IJPR	International Journal for Philosophy and Religion
IPQ	International Philosophical Quarterly
JP	Journal of Philosophy
JR	Journal of Religion
JRT	Journal of Religious Thought
JSSR	Journal of the Scientific Study of Religion
JTS	Journal of Theological Studies
NZSThR	Neue Zeitschrift für systematische Theologie und Religionsphilosophie
PAS	Proceedings of the Aristotelian Society
PAS,SV	Proceedings of the Aristotelian Society, Supplementary Volume
PhJ	Philosophisches Jahrbuch
PPR	Philosophy and Phenomenological Research
PQ	Philosophical Quarterly
PR	Philosophical Review
PS	Philosophical Studies
RGG	Die Religion in Geschichte und Gegenwart, 6+1 Vol., ed. by Kurt Golling, Tübingen 1957-1965
RL	Religion in Life
RM	Review of Metaphysics
RS	Religion Studies
SJP	Southern Journal of Philosophy
SJT	Scottish Journal of Theology

TS	Theological Studies
TT	Theology Today
WJPh	Wiener Jahrbuch für Philosophie
ZPhF	Zeitschrift für Philosophische Forschung
ZThK	Zeitschrift für Theologie und Kirche

BIBLIOGRAPHY

Abelson, Raziel, "Not Necessarily"; PR, LXX (1961), 67-84.

Abernethy, George L., and Thomas A. Langford, eds., *Philosophy of Religion*, London 1968.

Abraham, W.E., "Is the Concept of Necessary Existence Self-Contradictory?", Inquiry, V (1962), 143-157.

Adams, Marilyn McCord, "Is the Existence of God a 'Hard' Fact?", PR, LXXVI (1967), 492-503.

Adams, R.M,, "Must God Create the Best?", PR, LXXXI (1972), 317-332.

Albert, Hans, *Traktat über kritische Vernunft*, Tübingen 1969.

Albert, Hans, *Theologische Holzwege*, Tübingen 1973.

Aldrich, Virgil C., "Messrs. Schlick and Ayer on Immortality", PR, XLVII (1938), 209-213.

Aldrich, Virgil C., "Tinkling Symbols", in Hick, ed., *Faith and the Philosophers* (1964), 38-52.

Aldwinckle, R.F., "Karl Barth and Religious Language", CJT, XI (1965), 164-173.

Allen, Diogenes, *The Reasonableness of Faith*, Washington 1969.

Allen, R.E., "The Ontological Argument"; PR, LXX (1961), 56-66.

Allison, Henry E., "Faith and Falsifiability", RM, XXII (1969), 499-522.

Alston, William P., "Are Positivists Metaphysicians?", PR, LXIII (1954), 43-57.

Alston, William P., ed., *Religious Beliefs and Philosophical Thought*, New York 1963.

Alston, William P., "The Ontological Argument Revisited", PR, LXIX (1960), 452-475. Printed in Plantinga, ed., *The Ontological Argument* (1965), 86-110.

Alston, William P., "Psychoanalytic Theory and Theistic Belief", in Hick, ed., *Faith and the Philosophers* (1964), 63-102.

Alston, William P., "Emotive Meaning", EOP (1967), II, 486-493.

Alston, William P., "Religious Language", EOP (1967), VII, 168-174.

Alston, William P., "Teleological Argument for the Existence of God", EOP (1967), VIII, 84-88.

Alston, William P., *Philosophy of Language*, Englewood Cliffs 1964.

Anderson, Albert, "Anselm and the Logic of Religious Belief, HTR (1968), 149-173.

Anscombe, G.E.M., "Misinformation: What Wittgenstein Really Said", *The Tablet*, CCIII (1954), 373.

Anscombe, G.E.M., and Peter T. Geach, *Three Philosophers: Aristotle, Aquinas, Frege*, Oxford 1961.

Anselm von Canterbury, *St. Anselm's Proslogion*, Oxford 1965. Latin and English: *St. Anselm's Proslogion with a Reply on Behalf of the Fool by Gaunilo and the Authors Reply to Gaunilo*. Translated by M.J. Charlesworth, Oxford 1965.

Apel, Karl-Otto, "Die Entfaltung der 'sprachanalytischen' Philosophie und das Problem der 'Geisteswissenschaften'", PhJ, LXXII (1965), 239-289.

Apel, Karl-Otto, "Wittgenstein und das Problem des hermeneutischen Verstehens", ZThK, LXIII (1966), 49-87.

Apel, Karl-Otto, *Die Idee der Sprache in der Tradition des Humanismus von Dante bis Vico*, Bonn 1963.

Arnold, Uwe, *Die Entelechie, Systematik bei Platon und Aristoteles*, Wien, München o.J.

Ashe, Geoffrey, "Meaning and Analogy", HJ, XLIX (1950/51), 388-393.

Atkins, Anselm, "Religious Assertions and Doctrinal Development", TS, XXVII (1966), 523-552.

Austin, William H., Relgious Commitment and the Logical Status of Doctrines, RS, IX (1973), 39-48.

Ayer, Alfred Jules, "The Genesis of Metaphysics", *Analysis*, I (1933/34), 55-58.

Ayer, Alfred Jules, "Demonstration of the Impossibility of Metaphysics", *Mind*, XLIII (1934), 335-345. Printed in Edwards and Pap, eds., *A Modern Introduction to Philosophy* (1965), 684-693.

Ayer, Alfred Jules, *Language, Truth and Logic*, New York 1952.

Ayer, Alfred Jules, and F.C. Copleston, "Logical Positivism - A Debate", in Edwards and Pap, eds., *A Modern Introduction to Philosophy* (1965), 726-756.

Baier, Kurt E.M., "Existence", PAS, LXI (1960/61), 19-40.

Baillie, John, *The Sense of the Presence of God*, London 1962.

Bambrough, Renford, *Reason, Truth and God*, London 1969.

Barr, James, *The Semantics of Biblical Language*, Oxford 1961; German: *Bibelexegese und moderne Semantik*, München 1965.

Barth, Karl, "Das Wort Gottes als Aufgabe der Theologie", in Barth, ed., *Das Wort Gottes und die Theologie* (1924).

Barth, Karl, ed., *Das Wort Gottes und die Theologie*, 1924.

Bartley, William W., III. *The Retreat to Commitment*, London 1964; German: *Flucht ins Engagement*, München 1962.

Baumer, William H., Anselm. Truth and Necessary Being", *Philosophy*, XXXVII (1962), 257-258.

Baumer, William H., "Ontological Arguments still Fail", Monist, L (1966), 130-144.

Baur, Uwe, and Dietmar Goltschnigg, ed., *Vom "Törless" zum "Mann ohne Eigenschaften"*, München, Salzburg 1973.

Bayer, Oswald, *Was ist das: Theologie?*, Stuttgart 1973.

Bell, Richard H., "Wittgenstein and Descriptive Theology", RS, V (1969), 1-18.

Bendall, Kent, and Frederick Ferré, *Exploring the Logic of Faith*, New York 1962.

Benedikt, Michael, *Wissen und Glauben*, Wien 1975.

Berg, Jan, "An Examination of the Ontological Proof", Theoria, XXVII (1961), 99-106.

Binkley, Luther J., "What Characterizes Religious Language?", JSSR, II (1962), 18-22.

Binkley, Luther J., "Reply", JSSR, II (1962), 228-230.

Biser, Eugen, *Theologische Sprachtheorie und Hermeneutik*, München 1970.

Blackstone, R.M., "Is Philosophy of Religion Possible?", IJPR, III (1972), 176-184.

Blackstone, William T., "Crombie's Defense of the Assertion-Status of Religious Claims", Personalist, XLIV (1963), 220-230.

Blackstone, William T., "The Status of God-Talk", JSSR, V (1965/66), 357-365.

Blackstone, William T., *The Problem of Religious Knowledge: The Impact of Philosophical Analysis on the Question of Religious Knowledge*, Prentice-Hall 1963.

Blackstone, William T., *Meaning and Existence*, New York 1971.

222

Bochenski, J.M., "On Analogy", *Thomist*, XI (1948), 424-447.

Braithwaite, R.B., *An Empiricist's View of the Nature of Religious Belief*, Cambridge 1955. Partly in Hick, ed., *Classical and Contemporary Reading in the Philosophy of Religion*, Prentice Hall 1964, 429-439.

Brandt, Richard, "Critique of MacIntyre's Starting Point", in Hick, ed., *Faith and the Philosophers* (1964), 150-153.

Bridgman, Percy, *Reflections of a Physicist*, New York 1955.

Britton, Karl, "The Truth of Religious Propositions", *Analysis*, III (1935/36), 21-27.

Broiles, R. David, "Is There a God?", *Sophia* IV, No. 3 (1965), 3-9.

Broiles, R. David, "Logic and Religious Language", *Sophia* V, No. 2 (1966), 10-14.

Brown, Patterson, and Alan G. Nasser, "Hartshorne's Epistemic Proof", AJP, XLVII (1968), 61-64.

Brown, Stuart C., *Do Religious Claims Make Sense?*, New York 1969.

Brown, T.P., "Professor Malcolm on 'Anselm's Ontological Arguments'", Analysis, XXII (1961), 12-14.

Burbidge, John W., "The Language of Christian Faith", CJT, XII (1966), 21-26.

Burkle, Howard R., "Counting Against and Counting Decisively Against", JR, XLIV (1964), 223-229.

Burrell, David, "Religious Language and the Logic of Analogy: Apropos of McInerny's Book and Ross' Review", IPQ, II (1962), 643-658.

Burrell, David, "Aquinas on Naming God", TS, XXIV (1963), 183-212.

Burrell, David, "Religious Life and Understanding", RM, XXII (1969), 676-699.

Burtt, E.A., "What is Metaphysics?", PR, LIV (1945), 533-557.

Burtt, E.A., "Descriptive Metaphysics", Ind, LXXII (1963), 18-39.

Cameron, J.H., "Religious Discourse and Theological Discourse", AJP, XXXIV (1956), 203-207.

Campbell, James I., *The Language of Religion*, New York, London 1971.

Carmichael, Peter A., "Limits of Religious Knowledge, PPR, X (1949/50), 53-64.

Carnap, Rudolf, and Hans Reichenbach, *Erkenntnis I-III*, Leipzig 1930-1932.

Carnap, Rudolf, *Logische Syntax der Sprache*, Wien 1934.

Carnap, Rudolf, *Testability and Meaning, Philosophy of Science*, Vol. III 1936, Vol. IV 1937, Reprint: New Haven 1950.

Carnap, Rudolf, *Introduction to Semantics*, Cambridge/Mass. 1942.

Carnap, Rudolf, *Einführung in die symbolische Logik*, Wien 1954. English: *Introduction to Symbolic Logic and its Applications*. Translated by W.H. Meyer and J. Wilkenson. New York 1958.

Carnap, Rudolf, *Scheinprobleme in der Philosophie*, Frankfurt a.M. 1966.

Chapman, Raymond, "Language and Religious Experience", CQR, CLXII (1961), 323-330.

Charlesworth, M.J., "Linguistic Analysis and Language About God", IPQ, I (1961), 139-167.

Charlesworth, M.J., "St. Anselm's Argument", *Sophia*, I, No. 2 (1962), 26-36.

Charlesworth, M.J., *Philosophy and Lingustic Analysis*, Pittsburgh 1961.

Chomsky, Noam, *Sprache und Geist*, Frankfurt a.M. 1970.

Christian, William A., "A Definition of Religion", *Review of Religion*, V (1941), 412-429.

Christian, William A., "Some Varieties of Religious Belief", RM, IV (1951), 595-616,

Christian, William A., "Three Kinds of Philosophy of Religion", JR, XXXVII (1957), 31-36.

Christian, William A., "Philosophical Analysis and Philosophy of Religion", JR, XXXIX (1959), 77-87.

Christian, William A., "Truth-Claims in Religion", JR, XLII (1962), 52-62.

Christian, William A., *Meaning and Truth in Religion*, Princeton 1964.

Clarke, Bowman L., "Linguistic Analysis and the Philosophy of Religion", *Monist*, XLVII (1962/63), 365-386. Printed in Blackstone, ed., *Meaning and Existence* (1971), 168-181.

Clarke, Bowman L., "Philosophical Arguments for God", *Sophia*, III, No. 3 (1964), 3-14.

Clarke, Bowman L., "How do We Talk about God?", *Modern Schoolman*, XLV (1968), 91-104.

Clarke, Bowman L., "Theology and Philosophy", AARJ, XXXVIII (1970), 276-288.

Clarke, J.J., "John Hick's Resurrection", Sophia, X, No. 3 (1971), 18-22.

Clarke, W. Norris, "Some Criteria Offered", in Hick, ed., *Faith and the Philosophers* (1964), 58-60.

224

Clarke, W. Norris, "It is Compatible!", in Hick, ed., *Faith and the Philosophers* (1964), 134-147.

Clarke, W. Norris, "A Further Critique of MacIntyre's Thesis", in Hick, ed., *Faith and the Philosophers* (1964), 147-150.

Clifford, Paul R., "Omnipotence and the Problem of Evil", JR, XLI (1961), 118-128.

Clifford, Paul R., "The Factual Reference of Theological Assertions", RS, III (1967/68), 339-346.

Coates, J.B., "God and the Positivists", HJ, L (1952), 22-231.

Coburn, Robert C., "A Neglected Use of Theological Language", Mind, LXXII (1963), 369-385. Printed in High, ed., *New Essays on Religious Language* (1969), 215-235.

Coburn, Robert C., "Professor Malcolm on God", AJP, XLI (1963), 143-162.

Coburn, Robert C., "The Concept of God", RS, II (1966), 61-74.

Coburn, Robert C., "Animadversions on Plantinga's Kant", JP, LXIII (1966), 546-548.

Collingwood, R.G., *An Essay on Philosophical Method*, Oxford 1933.

Coreth, Emerich, *Metaphysik*, Innsbruck, Wien, München 1964.

Crombie, I.M., "Theology and Falsification", *Socratic Digest*, V. Reprinted in Flew and MacIntyre, eds., *New Essays in Philosophical Theology* (1955), 109-130.

Crombie, I.M., "The Possibility of Theological Statements", in Mitchel, ed., *Faith and Logic* (1957), 31-83.

Dalferth, Ingolf U., ed., *Sprachlogik des Glaubens, Texte analytischer Religionsphilosophie und Theologie zur religiösen Sprache*, München 1974.

Dantine, Wilhelm, *Der heilige und der unheilige Geist*, Über eine Erneuerung der Urteilsfähigkeit, Stuttgart 1973.

Dantine, Wilhelm, *Jesus von Nazareth in der gegenwärtigen Diskussion*, Gütersloh 1974.

Demos, Raphael, "Are Religious Dogmas Cognitive and Meaningful?", JP, LI (1954), 170-172.

Demos, Raphael, "The Meaningfulness of Religious Language", PPR, XVIII (1957/58), 96-106.

Descartes, René, *Meditationes de prima philosophia, Oeuvres*, Vol. VII, Paris 1964.

Descartes, René, *Meditationen über die Grundlagen der Philosophie*, Lepizig 1915.

Diamond, Malcolm, "Contemporary Analysis: The Metaphysical Target and the Theological Victim", JR, SLVII (1967), 210-232.

Dilley, Frank B., *Metaphysics and Religious Language*, New York 1964.

Downing, F. Gerald, "God and the Problem of Evil", *Sophia*, VII, No. 1 (1968), 12-18.

Downing, F. Gerald, "Games, Families, The Public, and Religion", *Philosophy*, XLVII (1972), 38-54.

Ducasse, C.J., "Verification, Verifiability, and Meaningfulness", JP, XXXIII (1936), 230-236.

Duff-Forbes, D.R., "Theology and Falsification Again", AJP, XXXIX (1961), 143-154.

Duff-Forbes, D.R., "Reply to Professor Flew", AJP, XL (1962), 324-327.

Durfee, Harold A., "The Reformulation of the Question as to the Existence of God", PPR, XXVIII (1968), 385-391.

Durfee, Harold A., "Karl Jaspers as the Metaphysician of Tolerance", IJPR, I (1970), 201-210.

Durrant, Michael, "'Religion as the Inexpressible' - Some Logical Difficulties", *Sophia*, IV, No. 1 (1965), 14-21; No. 2 (1965), 3-9.

Durrant, Michael, "God and Analogy", *Sophia*, VIII, No. 3 (1969), 11-24.

Ebeling, Gerhard, "Theologie", RGG (1962), VI, 754-769.

Ebeling, Gerhard, *Einführung in theologische Sprachlehre*, Tübingen 1971.

Ebeling, Gerhard, *Kritischer Rationalismus?* Zu Hans Alberts "Traktat über kritische Vernunft", Tübingen 1973.

Edwards, Paul, and Arthur Pap, eds., *A Modern Introduction to Philosophy*, New York 1965.

Edwards, Paul, "The Existence of God: Introduction", in Edwards and Pap, eds., *A Modern Introduction to Philosophy* (1965), 374-389.

Edwards, Paul, "Atheism", EOP (1967), I, 174-189.

Edwards, Paul, "Atheismusstreit", EOP (1967), I, 189-192.

Edwards, Paul, "Common Consent Arguments for the Existence of God", EOP (1967), II, 147-155.

Edwards, Paul, "My Death", EOP (1967), V, 416-419.

Edwards, Rem B., "An Emotivist Analysis of the Ontological Argument", *Personalist*, XLVIII (1967), 25-31.

Edwards, Rem B., "Existential Experience and Limited Questions and Answers", IJPR, IV (1973), 65-79.

Eklund, Harald, "Reflections on the Religious Use of the Word 'Believe'", *Bulletin de la Société Royale des Lettres de Lund*, II (1955/56), 27-34.

Eklund, Harald, "On the Logic of Creeds", *Theoria*, XXII (1956), 75-84.

Elton, William, "On Hartshorne's Formulation of the Ontological Argument: A Criticism", PR, LIV (1945), 63.

Emmet, Dorothy, *The Nature of Metaphysical Thinking*, London 1946.

Etges, Peter J., *Kritik der analytischen Theologie*, Hamburg 1973.

Evans, Donald D., *The Logic of Self-Involvment*, London 1963.

Evans - Pritchard, E.E., *Nuer Religion*, Oxford 1956.

Ewing, A.C., "Meaningless", *Mind*, LVI (1937), 347-364.

Ewing, A.C., "Is Metaphysics Possible?", *Analysis*, VIII (1947/48), 33-38.

Ewing, A.C., "Religious Assertions in the Light of Contemporary Philosophy", *Philosophy*, XXXII (1957), 206-218.

Ewing, A.C., "Two 'Proofs' of God's Existence", RS, I (1965), 29-45.

Ewing, A.C., "Further Thoughts on the Ontological Argument", RS, V (1969), 41-48.

Ewing, Wayne A., "Linguistic Analysis and the Theological Enterprise", The South East Asia Journal of Theology, IX (1967), 60-73.

Fahrenbach, Helmut, "Sprachanalyse und Ethik", in Gadamer, ed., *Das Problem der Sprache* (1967), 369-385.

Fahrenbach, Helmut, ed., *Wirklichkeit und Reflexion, Walter Schulz zum 60. Geburtstag*, Pfullingen 1973.

Fairfax, Warwick, "Are Statements of Religion Worth Discussing: A Reply to Jan Srzednicki", *Sophia*, II, No. 2 (1962), 17-20.

Farrell, P.M., "Evil and Omnipotence", *Mind*, LVII (1958), 399-403.

Farrer, Austin, "A Starting-Point for the Philosophical Examination of Theological Belief", in Mitchell, ed., *Faith and Logic* (1957), 9-30.

Farrer, Austin, Finite and Infinite: *A Philosophical Essay*, Westminster 1943.

Farrer, Austin, Love Almighty and Ills Unlimited: *An Essay on Providence and Evil*, Garden City 1961.

Farrer, Austin, *God is not Dead*, New York 1966.

Farrer, Austin, *Faith and Speculation: An Essay in Philosophical Theology*, New York 1967.

Feigl, Hans, and Wilfrid Sellars, eds., *Readings in Philosophical Analysis*, New York 1949.

Feigl, Herbert, "Empiricism versus Theology", in Edwards and Pap, eds., *A Modern Introduction to Philosophy* (1957), 533-538.

Ferré, Frederick, "Is Language about God Fraudulent?", SJT, XII (1959), 337-360.

Ferré, Frederick, "The Use and Abuse of Theological Arguments", JR; XLI (1961), 182-193.

Ferré, Frederick, "Verification, Faith, and Credulity", RL, XXXII (1962/63), 46-57.

Ferré, Frederick, "Mapping the Logic of Models in Science and Theology", CS, XLVI (1963), 9-39. Printed in High, ed., *New Essays on Religious Language* (1969), 54-96.

Ferré, Frederick, "Analogy in Theology", EOP (1967), I, 94-97.

Ferré, Frederick, "Metaphors, Models, and Religion", *Soundings*, LI (1968), 327-345.

Ferré, Frederick, "The Definition of Religion", AARJ, XXXVIII (1970), 3-16.

Ferré, Frederick, *Language, Logic and God*, New York 1961.

Ferré, Frederick, and Kent Bendall, *Exploring the Logic of Faith*, New York 1962.

Ferré, Frederick, *Basic Modern Philosophy of Religion*, New York 1967.

Findlay, John N., "Can God's Existence be Disproved?", *Mind*, LVII (1948), 176-183. Printed in Flew and MacIntyre, eds., *New Essays in Philosophical Theology* (1955), 47-55, 71-75; Language, Mind, and Value, by J.N. Findlay, London 1963, 96-104; Plantinga, ed., *The Ontological Argument* (1965), 111-122.

Fischer, Helmut, *Glaubensaussage und Sprachstruktur*, Hamburg 1972.

Fitzer, Gottfried, *Was Luther wirklich sagte*, Wien, München, Zürich 1968.

Flew, Antony G.N., "Theology and Falsification", *University* (1950/51). Printed in Hick, ed., *Classical and Contemporary Readings in the Philosophy of Religion* (1964), 440-442, 446-448; Flew and MacIntyre, eds., *New Essays in Philosophical Theology* (1955), 96-99, 106-108.

Flew, Antony G.N., "Death", *University* (1951/52). Printed in Flew and MacIntyre, eds., *New Essays in Philosophical Theology* (1955), 267-272.

Flew, Antony G.N., "Divine Omnipotence and Human Freedom", in Flew and MacIntyre, eds., *New Essays in Philosophical Theology* (1955), 144-169.

Flew, Antony G.N., "Can a Man Witness his Own Funeral?", HJ, LIV (1956), 243-250.

Flew, Antony G.N., "Falsification and Hypothesis in Theology", AJP, XL (1962), 318-323.

Flew, Antony G.N., "Reflections on 'The Reality of God'", JR, XLVIII (1968), 150-161.

Flew, Antony G.N., *A New Approach to Psychical Research*, Londn 1953.

Flew, Antony G.N., and Alasdair MacIntyre, eds., *New Essays in Philosophical Theology*, New York 1955.

Flew, Antony G.N., *Hume's Philosophy of Belief*, London 1961.

Flew, Antony G.N., *God and Philosophy*, London 166.

Fontana, V.V., "Linguistic Analysis and Inference about God", *Thomist*, XXXII (1968), 201-212.

Foster, Michael B., "The Christian Doctrine of Creation and the Rise of Modern Natural Science", *Mind*, XLIII (1934), 446-468.

Foster, Michael B., "We' in Modern Philosophy", in Mitchell, ed., *Faith and Logic* (1957), 194-220.

Franklin, R.L., "Necessary Being", AJP, XXXV (1957), 97-110.

Gadamer, Hans-Georg, *Wahrheit und Methode*, Tübingen 1965. English: *Truth and Method*. Eds. Garrett Barden and John Cumming. New York 1975.

Gadamer, Hans-Georg, ed., *Das Problem der Sprache*, München 1967.

Gatzemeier, Matthias, *Theologie als Wissenschaft?*, Vol. I, Stuttgart 1974.

Geach, Peter T., "Nominalism", *Sophia*, III, No. 2 (1964), 3-14.

Geach, Peter T., "God's Relation to the World", *Sophia*, VIII, No. 2 (1969), 1-9.

Geach, Peter T., *God and the Soul*, New York 1969.

Geach, Peter T., and G.E.M. Anscombe, *Three Philosophers: Aristotle, Aquinas, Frege*, Oxford 1969.

Gellner, Ernest, "Analysis and Ontology", PQ, I (1950/51), 408-415.

Gellner, Ernest, "Is Belief Really Necessary?", HJ; LVI (1957), 31-41.

Gellner, Ernest, *Words and Things*, Harmondsworth 1968.

Gibson, A. Boyce, "Empirical Evidence and Religious Faith", JR, XXXVI (1956), 24-35.

Gilkey, Langdon, *Naming the Whirlwind: The Renewal of God-Language*, Indianapolis 1969.

Gill, Jerry H., "Wittgenstein and Religious Language", TT, XXI (1964), 59-72.

Gill, Jerry H., "A Case of Mistaken Identity: Paul van Buren as Linguistic Analyst", CS, XLIX (1966), 147-151.

Gill, Jerry H., "Wittgenstein's Concept of Truth", IPQ, VI (1966), 71-80.

Gill, Jerry H., "The Tacit Structure of Religious Knowing", IPQ, IX (1969), 533-559.

Gill, Jerry H., "J.L. Austin and the Religious Use of Language", *Sophia*, VIII, No. 2 (1969), 29-37.

Gill, Jerry H., ed., *Philosophy and Religion: Some Contemporary Perspectives*, Minneapolis 1968.

Glasgow, W.D., "Knowledge of God", *Philosophy*, XXXII (1957), 229-240.

Glenn, A.A., "Criteria for Theological Models", SJT, XXV (1972), 296-303.

Gollwitzer, Helmut, and Wilhelm Weischedel, *Denken und Glauben, ein Streitgespräch*, Stuttgart, Berlin, Köln, Mainz 1965.

Gowen, J., "Religion, Reason and Ninian Smart", RS, IX (1973), 219-227.

Grabner-Haider, Anton, *Semiotik und Theologie*, München 1973.

Gunderson, Keith, "Are there Criteria for 'Encountering God'?", in Hick, ed., *Faith and the Philosophers* (1964), 57-58.

Hardin, C.L., "An Empricial Refutation of the Ontological Argument", *Analysis*, XXII (1962), 90-91.

Hardwick, Charley D., *Faith and Objectivity*, The Hague 1972.

Hare, R.M., "Theology and Falsification", *University* (1950/51). Printed in Hick, ed., *Classical and Contemporary Readings in the Philosophy of Religion* (1964), 442-445; Flew and MacIntyre, eds., *New Essays in Philosophical Theology* (1955), 99-102.

Hare, R.M., "Religion and Morals", in Mitchell, ed., *Faith and Logic* (1957), 176-193.

Hare, R.M., *The Language of Morals*, Oxford 1952; German: *Die Sprache der Moral*, Frankfurt 1972.

Hare, R.M., *Freedom and Reason*, Oxford 1963.

Harris, E.E., "Mr. Ryle and the Ontological Argument", *Mind*, XLV (1936), 474-480. Printed in Hick and McGill, eds., The Many-Faced Argument (1967), 261-268.

Harrison, Jonathan, "Can I have a Duty to Believe in God?", *Philosophy*, XXXII (1957), 241-252.

Hartshorne, Charles, "The Formal Validity and Real Significance of the Ontological Argument", PR, LIII (1944), 225-245.

Hartshorne, Charles, "On Hartshorne's Formulation of the Ontological Argument: A Rejoinder", PR, LIV (1945), 63-65.

Hartshorne, Charles, "The Idea of God - Literal or Analogical?", CS, XXXIX (1956), 131-136.

Hartshorne, Charles, "The Structure of Metaphysics: A Criticism of Lazerowitz's Theory", PPR, XIX (1958/59), 226-240.

Hartshorne, Charles, "The Logic of the Ontological Argument", JP, LVIII (1961), 471-473.

Hartshorne, Charles, "Is God's Existence a State of Affairs?", in Hick, ed., *Faith and the Philosophers* (1964), 26-32.

Hartshorne, Charles, "Is the Denial of Existence ever Contradictory?", JP, LXIII (1966), 85-93.

Hartshorne, Charles, "What did Anselm Discover?". Printed in Hick and McGill, eds., *The Many-Faced Argument* (1967), 321-333.

Hartshorne, Charles, "The Irreducible Modal Structure of the Argument", in Hick, ed., *The Many-Faced Argument* (1967), 334-340.

Hartshorne, Charles, *Man's Vision of God and the Logic of Theism*, Chicago 1941.

Hartshorne, Charles, *Anselm's Discovery: A Re-Examination of the Ontological Proof for God's Existence*, La Salle 1965.

Hayner, David C., "Metaphysical Statements and Religious Belief", SJP, II (1964), 63-69.

Hayner Paul C., "Analogical Predication", JP, LV (1958), 855-862.

Heimbeck, Raeburne S., *Theology and Meaning: A Critique of Metatheological Scepticism*, Stanford 1969.

Heintel, Erich, "Der Begriff des Menschen und der 'spekulative Satz'", *Hegel-Studien*, I (1961), 201-227.

Heintel, Erich, "Sokratisches Wissen und praktischer Primat", in Kaulbach and Ritter, eds., *Kritik und Metaphysik* (1966), 212-223.

Heintel, Erich, "Gottes Transzendenz", NZSThR, XIV (1972), 277-293.

Heintel, Erich, "Humor and Agape", WJPh, VII (1972), 166-199.

Heintel, Erich, "Glaube in Zweideutigkeit. R. Musils 'Tonka'", in Baur and Golschnigg, eds., *Vom "Törless" zum "Mann ohne Eigenschaften"* (1973), 47-88.

Heintel, Erich, "Transzendenz und Analogie - Ein Beitrag zur bestimmten Negation bei Thomas von Aquin", in Fahrenbach, ed., *Wirklichkeit und Reflexion* (1973), 267-290.

Heintel, Erich, *Hegel und die Analogia entis*, Bonn 1958.

Heintel, Erich, *Die beiden Labyrinthe der Philosophie, Systemtheoretische Betrachtungen zur Fundamental-philosophie des abendländischen Denkens*, Wien, München 1968.

Heintel, Erich, *Einführung in die Sprachphilosophie*, Darmstadt 1972.

Heintel, *Die Bedeutung der Kritik der ästhetischen Urteilskraft für die transzendentale Systematik*, Bonn 1970.

Henle, Paul, "Uses of the Ontological Argument", PR, LXX (1961), 102-109. Printed in Plantinga, ed., *The Ontological Argument* (1965), 171-180.

Henrich, Dieter, *Der ontologische Gottesbeweis. Sein Problem und seine Geschichte in der Neuzeit*, Tübingen 1967.

Henry, D.P., "The Proslogion Proofs", PQ, V (1955), 147-151.

Henze, Donald F., "Language Games and the Ontological Argument", RS, IV (1968), 147-152.

Hepburn, Ronald W., "Demythologizing and the Problem of Validity". Printed in Flew and MacIntyre, eds., *New Essays in Philosophical Theology* (1955), 227-242.

Hepburn, Ronald W., "Cosmological Argument for the Existence of God", EOP (1967), II, 232-237.

Hepburn, Ronald W., "Religious Experience, Argument for the Existence of God", EOP (1967), VII, 163-168.

Hepburn, Ronald W., *Christianity and Paradox: Critical Studies in Twentieth-Century Theology*, London 1958.

Hesse, Mary, "Talk of God", *Philosophy*, XLIV (1969), 343-349.

Hick, John, "God as Necessary Being", JP, LVII (1960), 725-734.

Hick, John, "Theology and Verification", TT, XVII (1960), 12-31. Printed in Blackstone, ed., *Meaning and Existence* (1971), 152-167.

Hick, John, "Comment", JSR, II (1962), 22-24.

Hick, John, "A Comment on Professor Binkley's Reply", JSSR, II (1962), 231-232.

Hick, John, "Introductory Notes and Bibliographies", in Hick, ed., *Classical and Contemporary Readings* (1964), 465-485.

Hick, John, "Sceptics and Believers", in Hick, ed., *Faith and the Philosophers* (1964), 235-250.

Hick, John, "A Critique of the 'Second Argument'", in Hick and McGill, eds., *The Many-Faced Argument* (1967), 341-356.

Hick, John, "Faith", EOP (1967), III, 165-169.

Hick, John, "Ontological Argument for the Existence of God", EOP (1967), V, 538-542.

Hick, John, "The Justification of Religious Belief", *Theology*, LXXI (1968), 100-107. Printed (German) in Dalferth, ed., *Sprachlogik des Glaubens* (1974), 229-237.

Hick, John, "Religious Faith as Experiencing-As", in *Talk of God* (1969), 20-35.

Hick, John, *Philosophy of Religion*, Englewood Cliffs 1953.

Hick, John, ed., *Faith and the Philosophers*, London 1964.

Hick, John, ed., *Classical and Contemporary Readings in the Philosophy of Religion*, Englewood Cliffs 1964.

Hick, John, ed., *The Existence of God*, New York 1964.

Hick, John, *Evil and the God of Love*, New York 1966.

Hick, John, *Faith and Knowledge*, Ithaca 1966.

Hick, John, and Arthur C. McGill, eds., *The Many-Faced Argument: Recent Studies in the Ontological Argument for the Existence of God*, New York 1967.

High, Dallas M., *Language, Persons and Belief: Studies in Wittgenstein's Philosophical Investigations and Religious Uses of Language*, New York 1967.

High, Dalls M., ed., *New Essays on Religious Language*, New York 1969; German: Sprachanalyse und religiöses Sprechen, Düsseldorf 1972.

Hodges, H.A., *Languages, Standpoints and Attitudes*, London 1953.

Hofmeister, Heimo, "Synthesis and Judgment", WJPH, IV (1971), 127-136.

Hofmeister, Heimo, "The Problem of Truth in the 'Critique of Pure Reason'", *Proceedings of the Third International Kant Congress* (1972), 316-321.

Hofmeister, Heimo, "The Ethical Problem of the Lie in Kant", *Kant-Studien*, LXIII (1972), 353-368.

Hofmeister, Heimo, "Truth and Truthfulness", *Ethics*, LXXXII (1972), 262-267.

Hofmeister, Heimo, "Semantische oder transzendentale Sprachkritik?", in Klein and Oeser, eds., *Geschichte und System* (1972), 25-51.

Holcomb, Harmon R., "Comment", JSSR, I (1961), 55-60.

Holmer, Paul, "The Nature of Theology", JRT, IX (1951/52), 137-145.

Holmer, Paul, "Scientific Language and the Language of Religion", JSSR, I (1961), 42-55.

Holmer, Paul, "Language and Theology; Some Critical Notes", HTR, LVIII (1965), 241-261.

Holmer, Paul, "Metaphysics and Theology: The Foundations of Theology", *The Lutheran Quarterly*, XVII (1965), 291-315.

Hook, Sidney, "Are Religious Dogmas Cognitive and Meaningful?", JP, LI (1954), 165-168.

Hordern, William, *Speaking of God: The Nature and Purpose of Theological Language*, New York 1964.

Horsburgh, H.J.N., "Mr. Hare on Theology and Falsification", PQ, VI (1956), 256-259.

Howe, Leroy T., "Existence as Perfection; A Reconsideration of the Ontological Argument, RS, IV (1968), 78-102.

Hudson, W. Donald, "An Attempt to Defend Theism", Philosophy, XXXIX (1964), 18-28.

Hudson, W. Donald, "The Philosophical Discussion of Religious Discourse", *Theology*, LXXI (1968), 98-100.

Hudson, W. Donald, *Ludwig Wittgenstein. The Bearing of his Philosophy upon Religious Belief*. Richmond 1968.

Hughes, G.E., "Has God's Existence been Disproved? A Reply to Professor J.N. Findlay", *Mind*, LVIII (1949), 67-74. Printed in Flew and MacIntyre, eds., *New Essays in Philosophical Theology* (1955) 56-66.

Hume, David, *A Treatise of Human Nature*, Oxford 1968.

Hutchings, Patrick A.E., "Necessary Being", AJP, XXXV (1957), 201-206.

Hutchings, Patrick A.E., "God and Existence, *Sophia*, II, No. 1 (1963), 1-10.

Hutchings, Patrick A.E., "Do we Talk that Nonsense?", *Sophia*, II, No. 2 (1963), 6-13.

Hutchison, John A., "The Religious Use of Language", CS, XXXVIII (1955), 182-188.

Hutchison, John A., "The Uses of Natural Theology: An Essay in Redefinition", JP. LV (1958), 936-944.

Hutchison, John A., "Language Analysis and Theology: Present and Future", AARJ, XXXV (1967), 323-336.

Hutchison, John A., *Language and Faith*, Philadelphia 1963.

Jeans, James, *Physics and Philosophy*, New York 1943.

Jüngel, Eberhard, "Metaphorische Wahrheit", in *Evangelische Theologie*, Sonderheft 1, München 1974.

Just, Wolf-Dieter, *Religiöse Sprache und analytische Philosophie, Sinn und Unsinn religiöser Aussagen*, Stuttgart, Berlin, Köln, Mainz 1975.

Kant, Immanuel, *Werke, Akad. Ausgabe*, Berlin 1968.

Kaufmann, Gordon D., "Philosophy of Religion: Subjective or Objective?", JPR, LV (1958), 57-70.

Kaufmann, Gordon D., "On the Meaning of 'God': Transcendence Without Mythology", HTR, LIX (1966), 105-132.

Kaulbach, Friedrich, "Stand der Sprache, praktische Vernunft und Handeln, ZPhF, XXVI (1972), 493-519.

Kaulbach, Friedrich, and Joachim Ritter, eds., *Kritik und Metaphysik, Festschrift für Heinz Heimsoeth*, Berlin 1966.

Kellenberger, J., "The Falsification Challenge", RS, V (1969), 69-76.

Kellenberger, J., "We no Longer Have Need of that Hypothesis", *Sophia*, VIII, No. 3 (1969), 25-32.

Kennick, W.E., "The Language of Religion", PR, XLV (1956), 56-71.

Kenny, Anthony, "Aquinas and Wittgenstein", DR, LXXVII (1958), 217-235.

Kenny, Anthony, "Necessary Being", *Sophia*, I, No. 3 (1962), 1-8.

Kenny, Anthony, *The Five Ways: St. Thomas Aquina's Proofs of God's Existence*, New York 1969.

Kerényi, Karl, "Die griechischen Götter", in Schaefer, ed., *Der Gottesgedanke im Abendland* (1964), 13-20.

King-Farlow, John, "Justifications of Religious Belief", PQ, XII (1962), 261-263.

King-Farlow, John, "Religion, Reality, and Ordinary Language", *Pacific Philosophy Forum*, V (Feb. 1967), 3-55.

Kiteley, Murray, "Existence and the Ontological Argument", PPR, SVIII (1957/58), 533-535.

Kitzinger, Uwe, "Logical Analysis and Christian Faith", JRT, IX (1951/52), 48-54.

Klein, Hans-Dieter, *Vernunft und Wirklichkeit, Bd. 1: Untersuchungen zur Kritik der Vernunft*, Wien, München 1975.

Klein, Hans-Dieter, and Erhard Oeser, eds., *Geschichte und System, Festschrift für Erich Heintel*, Wien, München 1972.

Klemke, E.D., "Are Religious Statements Meaningful?", JR, XL (1960), 27-39.

Kolar, Heinz, *Das Methodenproblem in der Religionsphilosophie Paul Tillichs*, phil. Diss., Wien 1967.

Kraft, Victor, *Erkenntnislehre*, Wien 1960.

Kraft, Victor, *Der Wiener Kreis, Der Ursprung des Neopositi-vismus. Ein Kapitel der jüngsten Philosophiegeschichte*. Wien, New York 1968.

Kutschera, Franz von, *Sprachphilosophie*, München 1971.

Ladrière, Jean, *Rede der Wissenschaft - Wort des Glaubens*, München 1972.

Lang, Martin, *Wittgensteins philosophische Grammatik, Entstehung und Perspektiven der Strategie eines radikalen Aufklärers*, Den Haag 1971.

Lauer, R.Z., "St. Thomas and Modern Semiotic", *Sophia*, XI (1972), 13-20.

Lazerowitz, Morris, *The Structure of Metaphysics*, London 1955.

Leon, Philip, "The Meaning of Religious Propositions", HJ, LIII (1954/55), 151-156.

Lewis, H.D., "What is Theology?", *Philosophy*, XXVII (1952), 345-358.

Lewis, H.D., "The Cognitive Factor in Religious Experience", PAS, XXIX (1955), 61-92.

Lewis, H.D., "Contemporary Empiricism and the Philosophy of Religion", *Philosophy*, XXXII (2957), 193-205.

Liebrucks, Bruno, *Sprache und Bewußtsein, Bd. 3: Wege zum Bewußtsein*, Frankfurt a.M. 1966; Bd. 4: *Die erste Revolution der Denkungsart*, Kant: *Kritik der reinen Vernunft*, Frankfurt a.M. 1968.

Litzenburg, Thomas V., Jr., "'Faith-in' and 'In-faith' - Reply to Professor H.H. Price", RS, II (1967), 247-254.

Llewelyn, J.E., "Three Conceptions of Faith", JP, LXI (2964), 237-244.

Londey, David, "Causality and Creation", *Sophia*, I, No. 3 (1962), 22-27.

Londey, David, "God is the (a) Necessary Being", *Sophia*, II, No. 2 (1963), 15-16.

Losee, John, "Two Proposed Demarcations for Theological Statements", Monist, XLVII (1962/63), 455-465.

Lübbe, Hermann, "Wittgenstein - ein Existentialist?", in Lübbe, ed., *Bewußtsein in Geschichten* (1972), 115-131.

Lübbe, Hermann, *Bewußtsein in Geschichten, Studien zur Phänomenologie der Subjektivität*, Mach, Husserl, Schapp und Wittgenstein, Freiburg 1972.

Lucas, J.R., "The Soul", in Mitchell, ed., *Faith and Logic* (1957), 132-148.

Luther, Martin, Weimarer Ausgabe, Weimar 1883ff.

Lüthi, Karl, *Theologie als Dialog mit der Welt von heute*, Freiburg, Basel, Wien 1971.

MacGregor, Geddes, "The Nature of Religious Utterance", CS, XXXVIII (1955), 173-181.

MacIntyre, Alasdair C., "Visions", in Flew and MacIntyre, eds., *New Essays in Philosophical Theology* (1955), 254-260.

MacIntyre, Alasdair C., "The Logical Status of Religious Belief", in MacIntyre, ed., *Metaphysical Beliefs* (1957), 167-211.

MacIntyre, Alasdair C., "Freudian and Christian Dogmas as Equally Unverifiable", in Hick, ed., *Faith and the Philosophers* (1964), 110-111.

MacIntyre, Alasdair C., "Is Understanding Religion Compatible with Believing?", in Hick, ed., *Faith and the Philosophers* (1964), 115-133.

MacIntyre, Alasdair C., "Essence and Existence", EOP (1967), III, 59-61.

MacIntyre, Alasdair C., "Myth", EOP (1967), V, 434-437.

MacIntyre, Alasdair C., "Ontology", EOP (1967), V, 542-543.

MacIntyre, Alasdair C., *Marxism and Christianity*, New York 1968.

MacIntyre, Alasdair C., ed., *Metaphysical Beliefs: Three Essays*, London 1957.

MacIntyre, John, "Analogy", SJT, XII (1959), 1-20.

MacKay, D.M., "Language, Meaning and God", *Philosophy*, XLVII (1972), 1-17.

Mackinnon, Donald M., "Death", *University* (1951/52), printed in Flew and MacIntyre, eds., *New Essays in Philosophical Theology* (1955), 261-266.

Mackinnon, Donald M., "Metaphysical and Religious Language", PAS, LIV (1953/54), 207-221.

Mackinnon, Edward M., "Theism and Scientific Explanation", *Continum*, V (1967), 70-88.

Macquarrie, John, *God-Talk: An Examination of the Language and Logic of Theology*, New York 1967.

Mader, Johann, *Die logische Struktur des personalen Denkens*, Wien 1965.

Mader, Johann, *Zwischen Hegel und Marx*, Wien, München 1975.

Malcolm, Norman, "Anselm's Ontological Arguments", PR, LXIX (1960), 41-62. Printed in Hick and McGill, eds., *The Many-Faced Argument* (1967), 301-320; Plantinga, ed., *The Ontological Argument* (1965), 136-159.

Malcolm, Norman, "Is it a Religious Belief that 'God Exists'?", in Hick, ed., *Faith and the Philosophers* (1964), 103-109.

Malcolm, Norman, *Ludwig Wittgenstein: A Memoir*, London 1958.

Mann, Ulrich, *Einführung in die Religionsphilosophie*, Darmstadt 1970.

Marshall, G.W., "Faith and Assent", *Sophia*, V, No. 1 (1966), 24-34.

Martin, C.B., "A Religios Way of Knowing", *Mind*, LXI (1952), 497-512. Printed in Flew and MacIntyre, eds., *New Essays in Philosophical Theology* (1955), 76-95.

Martin, C.B., "The Perfect Good", AJP, XXXIII (1955), 20-31. Printed in Flew and MacIntyre, eds., *New Essays in Philosophical Theology* (1955), 212-226.

Martin, C.B., *Religious Belief*, Ithaca 1959.

Martin, James A., *The New Dialogue between Philosophy and Theology*, New York, 1966; German: *Philosophische Sprachprüfung der Theologie*, München 1974.

Mascall, E.L., "Theological Reductionism", Sophia, VI, No. 2 (1967), 3-5.

Mascall, E.L., *Existence and Analogy*, London 1949.

Masterman, Margaret, "The Philosophy of Language, or the Study of Framework", Theology, LIV (1951), 51-58.

Matson, Wallace I., *The Existence of God*, Ithaca 1965.

Matthews, Gareth B., "On Conceivability in Anselm and Malcolm", PR, LXX (1961), 110-111.

Mavrodes, George I., "God and Verification", CJT, X (1964), 187-191.

Mavrodes, George I., "Properties, Predicates and the Ontological Argument", JP, LXIII (1966), 549-550.

McCloskey, H.J., "Kant's Refutation of the Proofs of God's Existence", *The Rationalist Annual* (1963), 78-90.

McCloskey, H.J., "Would Any Being Merit Worship?", SJP, II (1964), 157-164.

McCloskey, H.J., "On Being an Atheist", *Question*, I (1968), 62-69.

McGlynn, James V., "Philosophy and Analysis", DR, LXXVIII (1959/60), 25-35, 93-107.

McKinnon, Alastair, "Unfalsifiability and the Uses of Religious Language", APQ, II (1965), 229-237.

McKinnon, Alastair, "Religious Language' and the Assumptions of Religious Belief", CS, XLIX (1966), 50-59.

McKinnon, Alastair, "Unfalsifiability and Religious Belief", CJT, XII (1966), 118-125.

McKinnon, Alastair, "Miracle' and 'Paradox'", APQ, IV (1967), 308-314.

McLain, F. Michael, "On Theological Models", HTR, LXII (1969), 155-187.

McPherson, Thomas, "The Existence of God", Mind, LIX (1950), 545-550.

McPherson, Thomas, "Positivism and Religion", PPR, XIV (1953/54), 319-330. Printed as "Religion as the Inexpressible" in Flew and MacIntyre, eds., *New Essays in Philosophical Theology* (1955), 131-143.

McPherson, Thomas, "Philosophy and Language", CQR, CLVI (1955), 158-169.

McPherson, Thomas, "Finite and Infinite", *Mind*, LXVI (1957), 379-384.

McPherson, Thomas, "Assertion and Analogy", PAS, LX (1959/60), 155-170. Printed in High, ed., *New Essays on Religious Language* (1969), 198-214.

McPherson, Thomas, "Religion and Rationality", CQR, CLXI (1960), 200-212.

McPherson, Thomas, "The Falsification Challenge: A Comment", RS, V (1969), 81-84.

McPherson, Thomas, *The Philosophy of Religion*, New York 1965.

Michalson, Carl, "The Ghost of Logical Positivism", CS, XLIII (1960), 223-230.

Miles, T.R., "A Note on Existence", Mind, LX (1951), 399-402.

Milford, T.R., "The Necessity of and the Limits of Analytical Reasoning", *Theology*, LXI (1958), 267-273.

Miller, Barry, "God-Talk and Creature-Talk", *Sophia*, VIII, No. 1 (1969), 25-35.

Miller, Barry, "The No-Evidence Defence", IJPR, III (1972), 44-50.

Mitchell, Basil, "Theology and Falsification", *University* (1950/51). Printed in Hick, ed., *Classical and Contemporary Readings in the Philosophy of Religion* (1964), 445-446; Flew and MacIntyre, eds., *New Essays in Philosophical Theology* (1955), 103-105.

Mitchell, Basil, "The Grace of God", in Mitchell, ed., *Faith and Logic* (1957), 149-175.

Mitchell, Basil, "The Justification of Religious Belief", PQ, XI (1961), 213-226. Printed in High, ed., *New Essays on Religious Language* (1969), 178-197.

Mitchell, Basil, ed., *Faith and Logic*, London, Boston 1957.

Moore, John M., "Analytical Philosophy and its Bearing upon Theology", JRT, XVII (1960), 87-100.

Moore, George Edward, "Is Existence a Predicate?", PAS, SV XV (1936). Printed in Plantinga, ed., *The Ontological Argument* (1965), 71-85.

Moore, Georg Edward, *Principia Ethica*, Cambridge 1966.

Morris, Ch.W., *Signs, Language and Behaviour*, New Yoprk 1946.

Morris, John S., "Religion and Theological Language", HJ, LXVI (1967/68), 15-20.

Munz, Peter, *Problems of Religious Knowledge*, London 1959.

Myers, Gerald E., "Metaphysics and Extended Meaning", AJP, XLII (1964), 211-215.

Myers, Gerald E., "Justifying Belief-Assertions", JP, LXIV (1967), 210-214.

Nagel, Ernest, "Philosophical Concepts of Atheism", in Edwards and Pap, eds., *A Modern Introduction to Philosophy* (1965), 460-472.

Nelson, John O., "Model Logic and the Ontological Proof of God's Existence", RM, XVII (1963/64), 235-242.

Niederwimmer, Kurt, *Der Begriff der Freiheit im Neuen Testament*, Berlin 1966.

Nielsen, Harry A., "Language as Existent", *Notre Dame Journal of Formal Logic*, II (1961), 244-250.

Nielsen, Harry A., "Analytical Philosophy of Religion", *New Scholasticism*, XL (1966), 62-79.

Nielsen, Kai, "The Functions of Moral Discourse", PQ, VII (1957), 236-248.

Nielsen, Kai, "On Talk about God", JP, LV (1958), 888-890.

Nielsen, Kai, "On Speaking of God", Theoria, XXVIII (1962), 110-137.

Nielsen, Kai, "Eschatological Verification", CJT, IX (1963), 271-281.

Nielsen, Kai, "Can Faith Validate God-Talk?", TT, XX (1963/64), 158-173.

Nielsen, Kai, " Sceptic's Reply", in Hick, ed., *Faith and the Philosophers* (1964), 229-232.

Nielsen, Kai, "God-Talk", *Sophia*, III, No. 3 (1964), 15-19.

Nielsen, Kai, "On Being Moral", PS, XVI (1965), 1-3.

Nielsen, Kai, "Religious Perplexity and Faith", *The Crain Review*, VII (1965).

Nielsen, Kai, "On Believing that God Exists", SJP, V (1967), 167-172.

Nielsen, Kai, "Wittgensteinian Fideism", *Philosophy*, XLII (1967), 191-209.

Nielsen, Kai, "Language and the Concept of God", *Question*, 2 (1969), 39-52.

Nowell-Smith, Patrick, "Miracles - The Philosophical Approach", HJ, XLVIII (1949/50), 354-360. Printed in Flew and MacIntyre, eds., *New Essays in Philosophical Theology* (1955), 243-253.

O'Brian, Dennis, "On the Limitations of Reason", in Hick, ed., *Faith and the Philosophers* (1964), 232-234.

O'Connor, M.J.A., "New Aspects of Omnipotence and Necessity in Anselm", RS, IV (1968), 133-146.

240

O'Donovan, Leo J., "Methodology in Some Recent Studies of Analogy", PS. XVI (1967), 63-81.

Oeser, Erhard, *Begriff und Systematik der Abstraktion*, Wien, München 1969.

Ogden, Schubert M., "God and Philosophy: A Discussion with Antony Flew", JR, XLVIII (1968), 161-181.

Otto, Rudolf, *Das Heilige. Über das Irrationale in der Idee des Göttlichen und sein Verhältnis zum Rationalen*, München 1947.

Pailin, David A., "Some Comments on Hartshorne's Presentation of the Ontological Argument", RS, IV (1968/69), 103-122.

Palmer, Humphrey, "Affirmation and Assertion, *Philosophy*, XXXIX (1964), 120-136.

Palmer, Humphrey, "Understanding First", *Theology*, LXXI (1968), 107-114. Printed (German) in Dalferth, ed., *Sprachlogik des Glaubens* (1974), 237-247.

Pannenberg, Wolfhart, *Wissenschaftstheorie und Theologie*, Frankfurt a.M., 1973. English: *Theology and Philosophy of Science*. Translated by Francis McDonagh. Philadelphia 1976.

Passmore, J.A., "Christianity and Positivism", AJP, XXXV (1957), 125-136.

Paton, H.J., "Faith and Logic", *Philosophy*, XXXIII (1958), 357-360.

Paton, H.J., *The Modern Predicament*, New York 1955.

Pearl, Leon, "Religious and Secular Beliefs", *Mind*, LXIX (1960), 408-412.

Pears, D.F., ed., *The Nature of Metaphysics*, New York 1957.

Penelhum, Terence, "Logic and Theology", CJT, IV (1958), 255-265.

Penelhum, Terence, "On the Second Ontological Argument", PR, LXX (1961), 85-92.

Perkins, R.L., "Mr. Blackstone and 'The Status of God Talk'", JSSR, VII (1968), 110-111.

Peukert, Helmut, "Zur Einführung: Bemerkungen zum Verhältnis von Sprachanalyse und Theologie", in High, ed., *Sprachanalyse und religiöses Sprechen* (1972), IX-XXIV.

Phillips, Dewi Z., "Philosophy, Theology and the Reality of God", PQ, XIII (1963), 344-350.

Phillips, Dewi Z., "Religion and Epistemology: Some Contemporary Confusions", AJP, XLIV (1966), 316-330.

Phillips, Dewi Z., "Faith and Philosophy", *The University Quarterly*, XXI (1966/67), 233-242.

Phillips, Dewi Z., "Religious Beliefs and Philosophical Enquiry", *Theology*, LXXI (1968), 114-122. Printed in Dalferth, ed., *Sprachlogik des Glaubens* 82974), 247-257.

Phillips, Dewi Z., "Religious Beliefs and Language Games", *Ratio*, XII (1970), 26-46; German edition, 21-39. Printed (German) in Dalferth, ed., *Sprachlogik des Glaubens* (1974), 258-282.

Phillips, Dewi Z., *The Concept of Prayer*, London 1965.

Plantinga, Alvin, "A Valid Ontological Argument?", PR, LXX (1961), 93-101. Printed in Plantinga, ed., *The Ontological Argument* (1965), 160-171.

Plantinga, Alvin, "The Sceptics Strategy", in Hick, ed., *Faith and the Philosophers* (1964), 226-227.

Plantinga, Alvin, "Kant's Objection to the Ontological Argument, JP, LXIII (1966), 537-546.

Plantinga, Alvin, "Malcolm, Norman", EOP (1967), V, 139-140.

Plantinga, Alvin, ed., *The Ontological Argument, from Anselm to Contemporary Philosophers*, Garden City 1965.

Popper, Karl, *Conjectures and Refutations*, London 1965.

Popper, Karl, *Logik der Forschung*, Tübingen 1966. English: *The Logic of Scientific Discovery*. 2nd Ed. London 1959.

Poteat, William H., "Faith and Existence", HJ, LII (1953/54).

Poteat, William H., "The Absence of God", HJ, LV (1957), 115-123.

Poteat, William H., "On the Meaning of Grace", HJ, LVII (1958/59), 156-160.

Poteat, William H., "God and the 'Private-I'", PPR, XX (1959/60), 400-416. Printed in High, ed., *New Essays on Religious Language* (1969), 127-137.

Power, W.L., "Descriptive Language and the Term 'God'", IJPR, III (1972), 223-239.

Presa, Kevin, "Assent, Belief and Faith", *Sophia*, VII, No. 3 (1968), 20-25.

Price, H.H., "Logical Positivism and Theology", *Philosophy*, X (1935), 313-331.

Price, H.H., "Faith and Belief", in Hick, ed., *Faith and the Philosophers* (1964), 3-25.

Price, H.H., "Response to Aldrich", in Hick, *Faith and the Philosophers* (1964), 53-57.

Price, H.H. "Response to Hartshorne", in Hick, ed., *Faith and the Philosophers* (1964), 33-37.

Price, H.H., "Belief 'In' and Belief 'That'", RS, I (1966),, 5-27.

Prior, A.N., "Can Religion be Discussed?", AJP, XX (1942), 141-151. Printed in Flew and MacIntyre, eds., *New Essays in Philosophical Theology* (1955), 1-11.

Radcliff, Peter, "Beliefs, Attitudes and Actions", Dialogue, IV (1966), 456-464.

Rahner, Karl. *Mysterium salutis II*, Einsiedeln 1967.

Rainer, A.C.A., "Necessity and God: A Reply to Professor Findlay", Mind, LVIII (1949), 75-77. Printed in Flew and MacIntyre, eds., *New Essays in Philosophical Theology* (1955), 67-70.

Ramm, Bernard, "Karl Barth and Analytic Philosophy", CC, LXXIX (1962), 453-455.

Ramsey, Ian T., "The Challenge of Contemporary Philosophy to Christianity", *Modern Churchman*, XLII (1952).

Ramsey, Ian T., "Persons and Funerals: What do Person Words Mean?", HJ, LIV (1955/56), 330-338.

Ramsey, Ian T., "Religion and Empiricism", *Cambridge Review* (1956).

Ramsey, Ian T., "The Logical Character of Resurrection Belief", *Theology*, LX (1957), 186-192.

Ramsey, Ian T., "Paradox in Religion", PAS, SV, XXXIII (1959), 195-218. Printed in High, ed., *New Essays on Religious Language* (1969), 138-161.

Ramsey, Ian T., "Religion and Science: A Philosopher's Approach", CQR, CIXII (1961), 77-91. Printed in High, ed., *New Essays on Religious Language* (1969), 36-53.

Ramsey, Ian T., *Religious Language*, London 1957.

Ramsey, Ian T., *Models and Mystery*, London 1964.

Reininger, Robert, *Metaphysik der Wirklichkeit*, München, Basel 1970.

Rescher, N., "The Ontological Proof Revisited", AJP, XXXVII (1959), 138-148.

Resnick, L., "God and the Best Possible World", APQ, X (1973), 313-317.

Rhees, Rush, "Unanswerable Questions", PAS, SV, XL (1966), 173-186.

Rice, Vernon, "Necessary Being", *Sophia*, III, No. 3 (1964), 28-31.

Richardson, C.C., "The Sceptics' Myth", in Hick, ed., *Faith and the Philosophers* (1964), 228-229.

Richmond, James, *Theology and Metaphysics*, New York 1971.

Rickman, H.P., "Metaphysics as the Creation of Meaning", HJ, LII (1953/54), 166-174.

Riser, John, "Toward the Philosophical Analysis of Theological Statements", *Monist*, XLVII (1962/63), 387-400.

Robinson, N.H.G., "Karl Barth's Empiricism", HJ, XLIX (1951), 362-367.

Robinson, N.H.G., "Faith and Truth", SJT, XLX (1966), 144-159.

Robinson, N.H.G., "The Logic of Religious Language", in *Talk of God* (1969), 1-19; printed (German) in Dalferth, ed., *Sprachlogik des Glaubens* (1974), 190-207.

Robinson, N.H.G., "Mystery and Logic", CJT, XV (1969), 30-44.

Rokita, Gottfried, *Ist Theologie notwendig?*, theol. Diss., Wien 1970.

Ross, James F., "Analogy as a Rule of Meaning of Religious Language", IPQ, I (1961), 468-502.

Ross, James F., "Logically Necessary Existential Statements", JP, LVIII (1961), 253-262.

Ross, James F., "Does 'X Ys Possible' Ever Yield 'X Exists'?", *Theoria*, XXVIII (1962), 173-195.

Routley, Richard, and Keith Gunderson, "Mr. Rescher's Reformulation of the Ontological Proof", AJP, XXXVIII (1960), 246-252.

Russell, Bertrand, and Frederick C. Coplestone, "A Debate on the Existence of God", *Humanitas*. Printed in Edwards and Pap, eds., *A Modern Introduction to Philosophy* (1965), 473-490.

Russell, Bertrand, "General Propositions and Existence" in Hick and McGill, eds., *The Many-Faced Argument* (1967), 219-225.

Russell, Bertrand, *Why I am not a Christian*, New York 1927.

Russell, L.J., "The Justification of Beliefs", *Philosophy*, XXXIII (1958), 121-131.

Ryle, Gilbert, "Mr. Collingwood and the Ontological Argument", *Mind*, XLIV (1935), 137-151. Printed in Hick and McGill, eds., *The Many-Faced Argument* (1967), 246-260.

Ryle, Gilbert, "Back to the Ontological Argument", *Mind*, XLVI (1937), 53-57. Printed in Hick and McGill, eds., *The Many-Faced Argument* (1967), 269-274.

Ryle, Gilbert, *The Nature of Metaphysics, Final Discussion*, in Pears, ed., The Nature of Metaphysics (1957), 142-164.

Sauter, Gerhard, *Theologie als Wissenschaft*, München 1971.

Sauter, Gerhard, ed., *Wissenschaftstheoretische Kritik der Theologie; Die Theologie und die neuere wissenschaftstheoretische Diskussion. Materialien, Analysen, Entwürfe*, München 1973.

Savigny, Eike v., Analytische Philosophie, Freiburg, München 1970.

Schäfer, Lothar, "Über die Diskrepanz zwischen Methodologie und Metaphysik bei Popper", *Studium Generale*, XXIII (1970).

Schaefer, Albert, ed., *Der Gottesgedanke im Abendland*, Stuttgart 1964.

Schaeffler, Richard, *Religion und kritisches Bewußtsein*, Freiburg, München 1973.

Schelling, Friedrich Wilhelm Josef, *Werke I, V u. VI*, München 1965.

Schlick, Moritz, "Meaning and Verification", PR XXXV (1936). Printed in Feigl and Sellars, eds., *Readings in Philosophical Analysis* (1949).

Schmidt, Paul F., "Is There Religious Knowledge?", JP, LV (1958), 529-538.

Schmidt, Paul F., *Religious Knowledge*, Illinois 1961.

Schulz, Walter, *Wittgenstein, Die Negation der Philosophie*, Pfullingen 1967.

Schulz, Walter, *Philosophie in der veränderten Welt*, Pfullingen 1972.

Schupp, Franz, *Auf dem Weg zu einer kritischen Theologie*, Freiburg, Basel, Wien 1974.

Schwarz, Gerhard, *Was Jesus wirklich sagte*, Wien, München, Zürich 1971.

Seiffert, Helmut, *Einführung in die Wissenschaftstheorie, Bd. 1*, München 1971.

Shaffer, Jerome, "Existence, Predication and the Ontological Argument", *Mind*, LXXI (1962), 305-325. Printed in Hick and MacGill, eds., *The Many-Faced Argument* (1967), 226-245.

Simon, Josef, *Sprache und Raum. Philosophische Untersuchungen zum Verhältnis zwischen Wahrheit und Bestimmtheit von Sätzen*, Berlin 1969.

Simon, Josef, *Philosophie und linguistische Theorie*, Berlin, New York 1971.

Simons, Eberhard, "Das Dilemma der Theologie", PhJ, LXXIX, 335-360.

Slater, Peter, "Parables, Analogies and Symbols", RS, IV (1968), 25-35.

Sleeper, Ralph W., "Linguistic Philosophy and Religious Belief", *Cross Currents*, XIV (1964), 335-359.

Smart, J.J.C., "The Existence of God", CQR, CLVI (1955), 178-194. Printed in Flew and MacIntyre, eds., *New Essays in Philosophical Theology* (1955), 28-46.

Smart, J.J.C., "Metaphysics, Logic and Theology", in Flew and MacIntyre, eds., *New Essays in Philosophical Theology* (1955), 12-27.

Smart, J.J.C., "Philosophy and Religion", AJP, XXXVI (1958), 56-58.

Smart, J.J.C., "Religion and Science", EOP (1967), VII, 158-163.

Smart, R. Ninian, "Paradox in Religion", PAS, SV, XXXIII (1959), 219-232.

Smart, R. Ninian, "The Concept of Heaven", in *Talk of God* (1969), 226-238.

Smart, R. Ninian, *Reasons and Faith*, London 1958.

Smith, C.I., "Knowledge of God", *Philosophy*, XXXIII (1958), 56.

Smith, John E., "Three Types and Two Dogmas of Empiricism", CS, XLIII (1960), 199-212.

Smith, J. Macdonald, "How do We Prove that God Exists?", DR, LXXIX (1960/61), 217-231.

Smith, J. Macdonald, "Philosophy and God", CQR, CLXVIII (1967), 75-83.

Smith, J. Macdonald, and James Williams McClendon, Jr., "Religious Language after J.L. Austin", RS, VIII (1972), 55-63.

Sontag, Frederick, "The Platonist's Concept of Language", JP, LI (1954), 823-830.

Sontag, Frederick, "The Meaning of Argument in Anselm's Ontological 'Proof'", JP, LXIV (1967), 459-486.

Srzednicki, Jan., "Are Statements of Religion Really Worth Discussing?", *Sophia*, II, No. 1 (1963), 26-30.

Srzednicki, Jan., "A Reply to my Critics", *Sophia*, II, No. 2 (1963), 21-27.

Srzednicki, Jan., "The Ontological Proof and the Concept of 'Absolute'", *Sophia*, IV, No. 3 (1965), 28-32.

Stace, W.T., "Metaphysics and Meaning", *Mind*, XLIV (1935), 417-438. Printed in Edwards and Pap, eds., *A Modern Introduction to Philosophy* (1965), 694-704.

Stace, W.T., "The Problem of Unreasoned Beliefs", *Mind*, LIV (1945), 26-49.

Stace, W.T., *Religion and the Modern Mind*, Philadelphia 1952.

Stead, G.C., "How Theologians Reason", in Mitchell, ed., *Faith and Logic* (1957), 108-131.

Stegmüller, Wolfgang, *Das Wahrheitsproblem und die Idee der Semantik. Eine Einführung in die Theorien von A. Tarski und R. Carnap*, Wien, New York 1968.

Stegmüller, Wolfgang, *Hauptströmungen der Gegenwarts-philosophie*, Stuttgart 1969.

Stenius, Erik, *Wittgensteins Traktat. Eine kritische Darlegung seiner Hauptgedanken*, Frankfurt a.M. 1969.

Stevenson, C.L. *Ethics and Language*, New Haven, London 1965.

Swenson, D.F., "Logical Analysis and Metaphysics", JP, XXXII (1935), 293-294.

Tayler, W.S., "Analogical Thinking in Theology", SJT, XVII (1964), 279-288.

Thomas Aquinas, *Summa Theologica*.

Thompson, Samuel, "Philosophy and Theology: A Reply to Professor W.F. Zuurdeeg", JR, XL (1960), 9-17.

Tillich, Paul, *Systematische Theologie*, Vol. 1, Stuttgart 1956. English: *Systematic Theology*. Vol. 1. Chicago 1951.

Tillich, Paul, *Wesen und Wandel des Glaubens*, Frankfurt a.M. 1961. English: *Dynamics of Faith*, New York 1957.

Tillich, Paul, *Gesammelte Werke V*, Stuttgart 1964.

Toulmin, Stephen, "Contemporary Scientific Mythology", in MacIntyre, ed., *Metaphysical Beliefs* (1957), 13-81.

Toulmin, Stephen, *The Philosophy of Science*, London 1953; German: *Einführung in die Philosophie der Wissenschaft*, Göttingen 1953.

Trethowan, Illtyd, "Do we Infer God's Existence?", CQR, CL (1950), 100-110.

Trethowan, Illtyd, "Dr. Hick and the Problem of Evil", JTS, XVIII (1967), 407-416.

Trillhaas, Wolfgang, *Religionsphilosophie*, Berlin, New York 1972.

Ulmer, Karl, *Von der Sache der Philosophie*, Freiburg, München 1959.

Ulmer, Karl, *Philosophie der modernen Lebenswelt*, Tübingen 1972.

Van Buren, Paul M., "The Dissolution of the Absolute", RL, XXXIV (1964/65), 334-342.

Van Buren, Paul, "On Doing Theology", in *Talk of God* (1969), 52-71.

Van Buren, Paul, *The Secular Meaning of the Gospel*, New York 1963; German: *Reden von Gott - in der Sprache der Welt*, Zürich, Stuttgart 1965.

Veatch, Henry, "The Truths of Metaphysics", RM, XVII (1963/64), 372-395.

Vesey, G.N.A., ed., *Talk of God, Royal Institute of Philosophy Lectures II 1967/68*, London 1970.

Wagner, Hans, *Existenz, Analogie und Dialektik. Religio pura seu transcendentalis*, München, Basel 1953.

Walsh, W.H., *Metaphysics*, London 1963.

Warnach, V., "Was ist exegetische Aussage?", *Catholica*, XVI (1962).

Weizsäcker, Carl F. v., *Die Einheit der Natur*, München 1971.

Wellmer, A., *Methodologie als Erkenntnistheorie. Zur Wissenschaftstheorie Karl Poppers*, 1967.

Werner, Charles G., "The Ontological Argument for the Existence of God", *Personalist*, XLVI (1965), 269-283.

Whorf, Benjamin Lee, *Sprache, Denken, Wirklichkeit. Beiträge zur Metalinguistik und Sprachphilosophie*, Reinbek bei Hamburg 1963.

Wicker, B., *God and Modern Philosophy*, London 1964.

Williams, Bernard, "Tertullian's Paradox", in Flew and MacIntyre, eds., New Essays in *Philosophical Theology* (1955), 187-211.

Williams, L., "God and Logical Analysis", DR, LXXIV (1956).

Wilson, John B., "Religious Assertions", HJ, LVI (1958), 148-160.

Wilson, John B., *Language and Christian Belief*, London 1958.

Wilson, John B., *The Truth of Religion*, London 1958.

Wilson, Martin, "The Meaningfulness of Religious Statements", *Sophia*, II, No. 2 (1963), 13-15.

Wilson, Martin, "The Meaningfulness of Religious Statements", *Sophia*, II, No. 3 (1963), 25-30.

Wilson, Martin, "The Meaningfulness of Religious Statements", *Sophia*, III, No. 2 (1964), 25-27.

Winch, Peter, *The Idea of a Social Science*, London 1958.

Wiplinger, Fridolin, *Der personal verstandene Tod. Todeserfahrung als Selbsterfahrung*, Freiburg, München 1970.

Wisdom, John, "Gods", PAS (1944). Printed in Hick, ed., *Classical and Contemporary Readings in the Philosophy of Religion* (1964), 413-528.

Wisdom, John, *Other Minds*, Oxford 1952.

Wisdom, John, *Paradox and Discovery*, New York 1965.

Wittgenstein, Ludwig, *The Blue and Brown Books*, Oxford 1960.

Wittgenstein, Ludwig, *Lectures and Conversations on Aestetics, Psychology and Religious Belief*, ed. Barrett, Oxford 1966; German: *Vorlesungen und Gespräche über Ästhetik, Psychologie und Religion*, Göttingen 1971.

Wittgenstein, Ludwig, *Tractatus Logico-Philosophicus*, Schriften 1, Frankfurt a.M. 1969. English: *Tractatus Logico-Philosophicus*. 5th Ed. Introduction by Bertrand Russell. London 1951.

Wittgenstein, Ludwig, *Philosophische Untersuchungen*, Schriften 1, Frankfurt a.M. 1969. English and German: *Philosophische Untersuchungen/Philosophical Investigations*. Translated by G.E.M. Anscombe. Oxford 1953.

Wittgenstein, Ludwig, *Tagebücher*, Schriften 1, Frankfurt a.M. 1969.

Wittgenstein, Ludwig, *Letters to C.K. Ogden, with Comments on the English Translation of the Tractatus Logio-Philosophicus*; G.H. von Wright, ed., Oxford, London, Boston, o.J.

Wood, F., Jr., "The Relation of the Ontological Argument to Metaphysics", IJPR, IV (1973), 92-104.

Wood, Richard James, "Conceptual Frameworks and 'Necessary Existence'", JR, XLVI (1966), 477-490.

Woods, G.F., "The Use of Analogy in Christian Theology, JTS, VII (1956), 226-238.

Yolton, John W., "Professor Malcolm on St. Anselm, Belief and Existence", *Philosophy*, XXXVI (1961), 367-370.

Young, R., "The Resurrection of the Body", *Sophia*, IX, No. 2 (1970), 1-15.

Young, R., "Professor Penelhum on the Resurrection of the Body", RS, IX (1973), 181-187.

Zuurdeeg, Willem F., "The Nature of Theological Language", JR, XL (1960), 1-8.

Zuurdeeg, Willem F., "The Implications of Analytical Philosophy for Theology", *Journal of Bible and Religion*, XXIX (1961), 204-210.

Zuurdeeg, Willem F., *An Analytical Philosophy of Religion*, New York 1958.

INDEX

STUDIES IN PHILOSOPHY AND RELIGION

1. E.-R. FREUND: *Franz Rosenzweig's Philosophy of Existence*. An Analysis of 'The Star of Redemption'. (Translation from the German revised edition) 1979
ISBN 90-247-2091-5

2. A. M. OLSON: *Transcendence and Hermeneutics*. An Interpretation of the Philosophy of Karl Jaspers. 1979　　　　ISBN 90-247-2092-3

3. A. VERDU: *The Philosophy of Buddhism*. A 'Totalistic' Synthesis. 1981
ISBN 90-247-2224-1

4. H. H. OLIVER: *A Relational Metaphysic*. 1981　　　ISBN 90-247-2457-0

5. J. G. ARAPURA: *Gnosis and the Question of Thought in Vedānta*. Dialogue with the Foundations. 1986　　　　ISBN 90-247-3061-9

6. W. HOROSZ and T. CLEMENTS (eds.): *Religion and Human Purpose*. A Cross Disciplinary Approach. 1987　　　　ISBN 90-247-3000-7

7. S. SIA: *God in Process Thought*. A Study in Charles Hartshorne's Concept of God. 1985　　　　ISBN 90-247-3103-8

8. J. F. KOBLER: *Vatican II and Phenomenology*. Reflections on the Life-World of the Church. 1985　　　　ISBN 90-247-3193-3

9. J. J. GODFREY: *A Philosophy of Human Hope*. 1987
ISBN Hb 90-247-3353-7; Pb 90-247-3354-5

10. R. W. PERRETT: *Death and Immortality*. 1987　　　ISBN 90-247-3440-1

11. R. S. GALL: *Beyond Theism and Atheism*. Heidegger's Significance for Religious Thinking. 1987　　　　ISBN 90-247-3623-4

12. S. SIA (ed.): *Charles Hartshorne's Concept of God*. Philosophical and Theological Responses. 1990　　　　ISBN 0-7923-0290-7

13. R. W. PERRETT (ed.): *Indian Philosophy of Religion*. 1989　ISBN 0-7923-0437-3

14. H. E. M. HOFMEISTER: *Truth and Belief*. Interpretation and Critique of the Analytical Theory of Religion. 1990　　　　ISBN 0-7923-0976-6

KLUWER ACADEMIC PUBLISHERS – DORDRECHT / BOSTON / LONDON

American University Publications in Philosophy

1. *Explanation.* New Directions in Philosophy. Edited by the Faculty of Philosophy at the American University. 1973   ISBN 90-247-1517-2

2. H. A. Durfee (ed.): *Analytical Philosophy and Phenomenology.* 1976
    ISBN 90-247-1880-5

3. D. Dutton and M. Krausz (eds.): *The Concept of Creativity in Science and Art.* 1981   ISBN 90-247-2418-X
   Also published as Volume 6 in the Martinus Nijhoff Philosophy Library.

4. H. A. Durfee: *Foundational Reflections.* Studies in Contemporary Philosophy. 1987   ISBN 90-247-3504-1
   Also published as Volume 29 in the Martinus Nijhoff Philosophy Library.

5. H. A. Durfee and D. F. T. Rodier (eds.): *Phenomenology and Beyond.* The Self and Its Language. 1989   ISBN 0-7923-0511-6
   Also published as Volume 3 in Contributions to Phenomenology.

6. H. E. M. Hofmeister: *Truth and Belief.* Interpretation and Critique of Analytical Theory of Religion. 1990   ISBN 0-7923-0976-6
   Also published as Volume 14 in Studies in Philosophy and Religion.

KLUWER ACADEMIC PUBLISHERS – DORDRECHT / BOSTON / LONDON